MACCLESFIELD TOWN
FOOTBALL CLUB
THE LEAGUE STORY SO FAR
MACCLESFIELD TOWN
SINCE 1874

MACCLESFIELD TOWN FOOTBALL CLUB

THE LEAGUE STORY SO FAR

Geoffrey Knights

breedon books
PUBLISHING

First published in Great Britain in 2009 by
The Breedon Books Publishing Company Limited
Breedon House, 3 The Parker Centre,
Derby, DE21 4SZ.

This book is dedicated to
Sammy McIlroy MBE, Gil Prescott
and the 1997 Conference Championship-winning squad of players.

'Football is an alternative universe, as serious and as stressful as work, with the same worries and hopes and disappointments and occasional elations.'

Fever Pitch by Nick Hornby

ISBN 978-1-85983-713-9
Printed and bound by MKT Print, Slovenia

CONTENTS

Acknowledgements 6

Foreword 7

Chapter One 1997–1998 Immediate Success 8

Chapter Two 1998–1999 A Bridge Too Far 19

Chapter Three 1999–2000 The End of an Era 36

Chapter Four 2000–2001 Davy and Gil in Charge 51

Chapter Five 2001–2002 A New Manager and the Reserve Team Triumph 64

Chapter Six 2002–2003 Welcome to Amar and Bashar 81

Chapter Seven 2003–2004 It Takes Three Managers 96

Chapter Eight 2004–2005 The Year of 'The Beast' 109

Chapter Nine 2005–2006 Back Down to Earth 123

Chapter Ten 2006–2007 The Great Escape 138

Chapter Eleven 2007–2008 Here We Go Again! 161

Chapter Twelve 2008–2009 Frustration and Inconsistency 180

Epilogue 201

Appendix One Stadium Development 202

Appendix Two Players 211

Appendix Three Playing Squad Season by Season 236

Appendix Four Match Results 240

Roll of Honour 254

ACKNOWLEDGEMENTS

Firstly, my thanks to Michael Hughes for his 'first' reading and recommendations.

To Mike Rance, chairman, and Patrick Nelson, chief executive, for their pertinent comments, additions and for officially signing off the content. Also to Alan Cash for his clarification of issues during his tenure as chairman.

My thanks go to everyone who has helped in the provision of photographs, of which a significant number are the work of John Rooney, who was the official club photographer for many years. David Lafferty (editor) and Mike Glendinning (sports editor), of the *Macclesfield Express* have provided photographs for the more recent seasons and have kindly allowed me the free use of content in published articles and match reports.

Other photographs have been made available by Cathie Rance, Geoff Findlow, Mike Moss, the current official club photographer, P.A. Photos, fellow League Two clubs and the author.

And finally, thanks to my wife Shirley for her assistance and support.

FOREWORD

Macclesfield Town's promotion to the Coca Cola Football League elite in 1997 came as a surprise to many. Even today, more than a decade later, the club, affectionately known as the Silkmen to reflect the industrial heritage of their home town, still raises eyebrows when they get the better of more venerable members of that exclusive group, a feat they continue to achieve on a regular basis.

In the intervening years the club has been able to consolidate its position in the League at a time when many of the game's household names have fallen on hard times. Geoff Knights' book tells the story of this period of the club's history, marking the highs and lows and faithfully recording the events as the Silkmen strived to build on the legacy created by Sammy McIlroy and his superb squad in the mid-1990s.

For the real aficionados this book will form a framework on which to hang their own memories of an important decade in the club's history. So whether your favourite moments include the trip to Maine Road, last-gasp survival at Bristol Rovers's Memorial Stadium or heroics in Hull, they will come flooding back in glorious Technicolor.

For the more detached reader this is the story of a club surviving and sometimes prospering with limited resources and 'Against all Odds', to borrow the phrase from Efe Sodje's bandana. It provides ample evidence of the fact that there is vibrant life in the game outside the Premiership.

Mike Rance
Chairman
Macclesfield Town FC
July 2009

CHAPTER ONE: 1997–1998

IMMEDIATE SUCCESS

Pre-season

Having been crowned Vauxhall Conference Champions for the second time in May 1997 and with the Moss Rose stadium conforming to League standards, Macclesfield Town's transformation into a Football League side began in earnest. The directors made plans to visit former Conference colleagues at Barnet, Wycombe Wanderers and Scarborough for advice and guidance on how to make a successful adjustment to life in the Nationwide League and subsequently were involved in a significant amount of work to ensure a smooth transition from non-League to League status.

Manager Sammy McIlroy signed a two-year extension to his contract, having received assurances that he could bring players into the side, and told the *Macclesfield Express* 'I love the place and the people, and we've had a great time here. It's going to be a brand new ball game from now on and we'll be taking things step by step.' However, the good news about Sammy was tempered by the dynamic Chris Byrne signing for Sunderland, for whom the club would eventually receive a transfer fee of £20,000. Gil Prescott continued as Sammy's assistant, with Peter Davenport appointed as player-coach.

The biggest change involved the playing staff moving from part-time to full-time employment, but not without a considerable amount of deliberation. As an example, following several years' study, including a two-year degree course, Darren Tinson had combined his non-League football career with that of a full-time operating department practitioner at Arrow Park Hospital on the Wirral. At the age of 27 it was a big decision to sign a full-time football contract, but Darren recognised that all-round fitness and stamina would be more important and, in any case, he was able to continue his career through an agency on a part-time basis with the blessing of the club. Steve Wood made the transition at the age of 34, with John Askey and Cec Edey, both 32 years of age, signing part-time contracts for the first season.

Sammy and Gil always maintained that a team's strength relied on a solid defence, so it was no surprise when Sammy's first League signing was full-back Steve Hitchen from Blackburn Rovers. The tall Nigerian centre-back Efetobore Sodje was signed from Stevenage Borough who, initially, wanted a fee of £250,000. As Macclesfield only had a figure in the region of £10,000 in mind the decision was left to the Transfer Tribunal. At the Tribunal, Stevenage opened their argument suggesting a fee of £100,000, and then Macclesfield made their case, trusting the Tribunal to back their factual presentation. Much to the relief of the directors of the club, the Tribunal's decision came in October 1997 when it was decided that an immediate payment of £12,500 should be made, with a further sum of £12,500 in January 1998 and a final sum of £5,000 to be paid when Sodje had completed 30 appearances. The total of £30,000 was, at that time, a club record transfer fee. Other signings were forwards Richard Landon from Stockport County, and Andy Mason, a former Bolton Wanderers trainee, from Chesterfield, and midfielders Colin Rose from Witton Albion and Stuart Whittaker from Bolton Wanderers.

In July Macclesfield's Conference Trophy took pride of place at a Lord's Taveners dinner alongside other trophies as part of a tribute to the success of north-west sporting teams.

Friendly Matches

It was notable that generally the opposition for friendlies were from higher Leagues, Dundee being the first visitors to the Moss Rose. They left with a 3–0 victory. A Manchester City side including Richard Edghill, who would much later move to the Moss Rose, Nicky Summerbee, Uwe Rosler, Chris Greenacre, Paul Dickov, Danny Tiatto and a young Rae Ingram won their match 1–0 with a bullet header by Rosler, although the Silkmen played gallantly. A Kevin Phillips goal gave Sunderland a 1–0 victory, and former Silkman Chris Byrne looked fully at home in the centre of midfield. The final pre-season match was against Gary Megson's Stockport County in front of a crowd of 1,732. County cruised into a 2–0 lead until Macclesfield made a triple substitution in the second half, the players coming on including Andy Mason, who scored with his first touch and then scored the equaliser 20 minutes later. It was then left to Brett Angel to clinch the match for Stockport in the 89th minute. After the match Sammy said 'I wanted a hard pre-season match against quality opposition and we've had that, and I now know the team I will pick for our first-ever League game.'

And so the scene was set for Macclesfield's first foray in the Football League – or was it? Only a week before kick-off the club were served with a High Court writ for £524,572.40 from the liquidators of Crossland Metals International Ltd, the late chairman Arthur Jones's company. Arthur Jones had vowed that if the club won the Conference for a second time the ground at the Moss Rose would be up to League standard, and he loaned funds to the club to ensure that this objective was achieved. At the time it was not known that these funds belonged to his company and were not his own monies. Following the service of the writ, the directors stated that they believed the figure due was far lower, but nevertheless it took over 12 months of negotiations before the matter was fully resolved.

SEASON REVIEW

August

And so the day arrived for Macclesfield's first Nationwide League match, which the Football League fixtures computer had deemed to be against Torquay United at home. Saturday 9 August was warm and sunny, and understandably excitement was running high. On entering the ground the most noticeable difference was the impact of segregation, with each section of the ground now being a separate area and the gates between each section firmly closed and guarded by a steward. The immediate impact of this change was that supporters would no longer be able to change ends at half-time.

At 14.58pm the teams emerged, side by side in accordance with Football Association rules, headed by the match officials, all of whom had to pass through the massed ranks of the media. With the pre-match formalities completed, the Silkmen played towards the Star Lane End in the first half. Unlike the present day, this had no real significance as the away supporters were accommodated on the Estate Road side of the ground.

Early in the match Colin Rose sent a pinpoint corner into the box, allowing Neil Howarth to flick the ball on, with 'Against all Odds' bandana-wearing Efe Sodje rising head and shoulders above everyone in a crowded penalty area to

Efe Sodje scores Macclesfield's first-ever League goal.

head the ball home. The first League goal had come in only seven minutes. Understandably the fans were ecstatic, but just two minutes later Torquay's Charlie Oatway made a mazy run in to the box to set up Andy Gurney, who drove home past the Silkmen's 'keeper Ryan Price.

Despite Torquay coming back so quickly, everyone was really enjoying the experience. With Sammy McIlroy at the helm, animatedly directing proceedings from the edge of his technical area, assisted by Gil Prescott who was continually running up and down the steps of the Main Stand to give Sammy pearls of wisdom, plus a team who had an unbelievable work rate, team spirit and camaraderie, surely nothing could go wrong.

At half-time the score was still 1–1. The same team of Price, Tinson, Rose, Payne, Howarth, Sodje, Askey, Wood, Landon, Mason and Sorvel took to the field for the second half, and 11 minutes later Torquay's 'keeper Matthew Greg could not hold a Neil Sorvel drive, allowing Richard Landon to roll the ball home from close range. Torquay then had their chances, but Ryan Price was in fine form, making several superb saves, and the match finished with the score 2–1 in favour of the home side. There were jubilant celebrations as the Silkmen won their first-ever League encounter in front of a crowd of 3,379.

As the fans left the Moss Rose, little did they know of the success the team would enjoy in the coming months, with contrasting fortunes at home and away and a record that even Premiership sides could not match. To celebrate the Silkmen's first-ever Nationwide League match, a First Day postal cover was produced at a cost of £4.00.

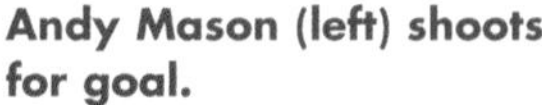

Andy Mason (left) shoots for goal.

Richard Landon (centre), scorer of Macclesfield's first away League goal.

The first away match was against Brighton & Hove Albion at Gillingham's Priestfield Stadium. This was Brighton's first 'home' match under a ground-sharing arrangement. For Macclesfield supporters this was rather galling as Brighton is some 75 miles away from Gillingham and the Silkmen had been refused permission to play their home matches at Chester when they had won the Conference in 1995. The Brighton supporters were voicing a protest against their board of directors throughout the match which ended in a 1–1 draw, Richard Landon scoring for the Silkmen in the first half, but Macclesfield almost won the match in the last minute when Steve Payne's header hit the crossbar.

A 3–0 home win against Doncaster with a goal from John Askey, a Richard Landon penalty and an own-goal saw the Silkmen momentarily top the League table. At this time Doncaster Rovers were going through a difficult time and, like the Brighton supporters the week before, throughout the match they were very vocal in getting their point of view across, which led to Neil Howarth posing the question 'Have all Third Division fans got axes to grind?' The next match was a dull and uneventful game at Hartlepool, which ended in a goalless draw and saw the Silkmen drop to fourth position.

September

Following consultations with the Police and the Safety Committee, to ensure easier crowd management a decision was taken to move the away fans from the Estate Road side to the Silkmen terrace behind the goal at the town end, allowing home fans to use the Estate Road side.

On the pitch, Rochdale secured a second-half 2–0 win at Spotland. The next match was brought forward by 24 hours to Friday evening as a mark of respect for Diana Princess of Wales, whose funeral took place the following day. Darlington took a first-half lead but the evergreen Phil Power firstly equalised and then in the 88th minute scored the winning goal. In this match Steve Wood suffered a fractured cheekbone and had to undergo an operation which sidelined him for four weeks.

A 3–0 home win against Swansea City put the Silkmen in second position until former non-League rivals Scarborough ran out 2–1 winners at the McCain Stadium. In this match Steve Hitchen, who was only making his second appearance for the Silkmen, had to be substituted with a hamstring problem, an injury which kept him out for the remainder of the season.

The month ended at home with a 1–1 draw against Peterborough United, Richard Landon equalising from the penalty spot in the 88th minute to leave the Silkmen in sixth position. In this match Neil Sorvel made his 300th appearance for the Silkmen and Ryan Price his 100th appearance.

October

Phil Power (right) in action at Chester City.

Striker Richard Irving (centre) causing problems for the Chester defence.

Worryingly, off the pitch there were rumours that manager Sammy McIlroy could be taking the Northern Ireland manager's job, and speculation was rife for many weeks. At one time it was suggested that Sammy might undertake the Northern Ireland role on a part-time basis, enabling him to retain his role at Macclesfield, but to everyone's relief Laurie McMenemy was eventually appointed.

The month commenced with a rather abrasive affair at Leyton Orient in which both sides lost players early in the match through injury. The home side took a first-half lead but Richard Landon scored the equaliser deep into time added on. At Notts County the Silkmen went behind again to a first-half goal and it was left to veteran midfielder Steve Wood to score a second-half equaliser.

Good home form continued when on-loan Mark Cooper scored the only goal of the home match against Mansfield Town. The next home match saw a stirring second-half performance against Exeter City who had taken a two-goal lead into the interval, but strikes from Mark Cooper and Stuart Whittaker levelled the score and the Silkmen almost won the match in the 94th minute when John Askey hit the post.

But the Silkmen could not find winning form away from home, and the month ended with a 1-1 draw at Chester City with the side slipping two places in the table to eighth position.

November

A loss at Rotherham by a single goal was followed by a goalless draw at the Moss Rose against Colchester, but there was a convincing 3–1 home win against Cambridge United with a Mark Gardiner goal and two from Phil Power.

At Shrewsbury there was a seven-goal thriller. Macclesfield took the lead, lost it and then drew level, but it was the Shrews' star man Devon White's hat-trick which won the match for the home side. His third goal became the winner after the officials adjudged that it had crossed the line, the ball having first hit the underside of the crossbar.

A 2–0 home win against Hull City, with goals from Nathan Peel and substitute Richard Landon, was followed by a 1–1 draw at Lincoln City. There was controversy in this match when Lincoln manager John Beck encouraged the ball boys to throw the ball in the mud when it went out of play for a Macclesfield throw-in, yet he shouted to them to wipe the ball with a towel at the time of a Lincoln throw. His actions resulted in Lincoln being warned about their behaviour by the FA. Unfortunately, Steve Wood fractured his other cheekbone in this match.

Colin Rose in action at Hull City.

Towards the end of the month a break from competitive football saw a Macclesfield XI invited to New Mills for a friendly match to celebrate the switching-on of their new floodlights, with Sammy McIlroy playing and Peter Davenport's former Nottingham Forest teammate and Northern Ireland international David Campbell also making an appearance for the Silkmen.

December

December saw the return of midfielder Martin McDonald, who was signed from Doncaster Rovers for a fee of £20,000 having originally left the Silkmen for Southport in November 1995 for a similar fee.

Macclesfield became Barnet's 50th League opponent since their elevation to the Football League in 1993, and Barnet celebrated with a 3–1 win. In this match Steve Wood bravely returned wearing a plastic protective mask and Lee Howarth, brother of Macclesfield's Neil, played for Barnet, the first time that the brothers had ever shared the same pitch in a competitive match.

The club's excellent home form continued with a 1–0 win against Cardiff City, in which Steve Wood scored a late second-half goal, but on Boxing Day at Darlington the home side stretched their unbeaten run to 11 League games with a comprehensive 4–2 win. Neil Howarth's penalty secured all three points when Rochdale were the visitors for the last match of the year, but by then the Silkmen had slipped down the table to 12th position.

Steve Wood wearing his protective mask at Barnet.

Brothers Lee and Neil (right) Howarth, captains on opposing sides at Barnet.

January

The New Year started with the postponement of two home games and then continued with the only defeat of the month at Torquay by a 2–0 scoreline.

When Hartlepool were the visitors, the game came to life in the second half with two goals in 60 seconds, the first by Macclesfield's Leroy Chambers and the second by Jon Cullen for Hartlepool, but it was a stunning 25-yard strike by Steve Wood which won the match for the Silkmen. Macclesfield won the next home match against Scunthorpe United with two first-half goals.

Then came the first away victory of the campaign on 24 January 1998 at Doncaster by a 3–0 scoreline, with a goal from midfielder Neil Sorvel and two from the influential Steve Wood giving the Silkmen their first-ever Football League double.

The programme editor for Doncaster at that time was Bernard Jordan, who became Macclesfield's programme editor a few years later.

John Askey beats a Cardiff City player to the ball.

The month ended with a 1–1 draw at Swansea City which exploded into life when Neil Howarth scored for the Silkmen in the eighth minute and Julian Alsop equalised two minutes later.

An extremely successful month saw the Silkmen move into fifth position, and Sammy McIlroy was named as Nationwide Division Three Manager of the Month, the team having amassed 13 points. The presentation was made to Sammy, the last of the Busby Babes, appropriately on the 40th anniversary of the Manchester United Munich Disaster.

Midfielder Neil Sorvel on his way to scoring the first goal at Doncaster.

Sammy McIlroy, Manager of the Month for January.

February

This was another successful month, in which the Silkmen only lost one match. An incident-packed first half at the Moss Rose against Scarborough saw Macclesfield take a three-goal lead into the break with goals from John Askey, Steve Wood and Neil Howarth, who netted a 30-yard drive. A late penalty for the visitors turned out to be merely a consolation goal. In the next match 'keeper Ryan Price came straight from hospital, where his wife had given birth to their first child, to give a match-winning performance in the promotion battle against Leyton Orient at the Moss Rose, in which Martin McDonald's 14th-minute goal gave the Silkmen victory.

The second away win of the campaign was recorded at Peterborough through a John Askey goal, but the next away match at Mansfield resulted in a 1–0 defeat.

In front of a crowd of 5,122 the League leaders Notts County came to the Moss Rose, but it was the home side who were victorious with goals from John Askey and Steve Wood ending Notts County's 16-match unbeaten run. Ryan Price put the icing on the cake when he saved Ian Barraclough's 89th-minute penalty, and with this victory Macclesfield finished the month in third position, an automatic promotion place.

March

The Silkmen could probably consider themselves fortunate to have remained in third position by the end of March as they only won one match throughout the month. In a swirling wind it was a battle of two defences at Cambridge with the match ending in a goalless draw. A heavy and waterlogged Moss Rose pitch made playing conditions difficult but even though Rotherham United, the visitors, were reduced to 10 men on the hour, Macclesfield could not press home their advantage and the match ended in another goalless draw.

A humiliating 5–1 defeat at Colchester was followed by a 2–1 home victory against Shrewsbury Town, but not before the visitors had taken the lead two minutes into the second half. Leroy Chambers scored the equaliser but up popped Steve Wood again to score a late winner, chipping the 'keeper from 15 yards.

During the month Sammy McIlroy expressed his frustration in the local press and, at the same time, expressed his delight that the supporters had flooded back to the Moss Rose. He commented: 'I want to bring in quality signings, but it's a constant struggle as I have only had a budget of £50,000 all season.' At this time the board were engaged in raising funds to settle the High Court writ served on the club the previous August by the liquidators of Crossland Metals International Ltd.

The board responded and worked hard to raise funds to help Sammy. Three important signings were subsequently made with Rae Ingram, a defender, signing on loan from Manchester City, Kieron Durkan, a midfielder, signing for a fee of £15,000 from Stockport County and Ben Sedgemore, another midfielder, signing for a fee of £25,000 from Mansfield Town. All three of these players made an excellent contribution in their time at the Moss Rose.

April

An 88th-minute goal by Steve Wood gave the Silkmen victory against Lincoln City at home, but unfortunately this match will probably be remembered for a brawl that took place after an hour's play rather than the important victory. After a coming together between Lincoln 'keeper Barry Richardson and Macclesfield's Martin McDonald, Richardson started kicking McDonald while Martin was still on the ground, which resulted in almost all of the players and members of the dug-outs getting involved. After the referee had gained control and consulted his assistants, Richardson and recently signed Sedgemore (who had only been protecting McDonald) were dismissed. Earlier in the match coins had been thrown at the Macclesfield 'keeper Ryan Price, and at half-time the club mascot, Roary the Lion, was escorted from the ground after allegedly inciting the Lincoln fans by waving his tail between his legs.

Having lost 1–0 at Scunthorpe, Macclesfield were fortunate to retain third position, but a thoroughly professional display at home against Barnet with goals from Efe Sodje and Phil Power saw them then move up to second position. A visit to Cardiff City saw Efe Sodje on the score sheet again, and together with a Neil Sorvel goal the Silkmen claimed a 2–1 victory, only their third away win of the season, to retain second position to runaway leaders Notts County.

	Played	Points
Notts County	44	96
Macclesfield Town	**44**	**76**
Torquay United	44	71
Colchester United	44	70
Scarborough	44	70
Barnet	44	70

Macclesfield still had to win at least one of their final two matches to ensure automatic promotion without relying on the results of the teams below them, even though they had a superior goal difference, hence the importance of their penultimate match at home to Chester City. There was significant interest in the town and supporters flocked to the Moss Rose, forming queues around the outside of the stadium and forcing the gates to be locked some 30 minutes before kick-off, which left many Macclesfield fans locked out and disappointed. The crowd of 5,982 was the highest gate since the crowd of 5,800 for the second-round FA Cup tie against Stockport County in the 1992–93 season.

Steve Wood opened the scoring for the Silkmen when he converted a Stuart Whittaker corner in the 14th minute, with Neil Sorvel extending the lead in the 49th minute after scoring from Martin McDonald's cross. Spencer Whelan then pulled one back for Chester, but Phil Power scored Macclesfield's third goal in the 59th minute. With the Silkmen leading 3–1, the penultimate match at Halifax the previous season was very much in mind, when Macclesfield had been again leading 3–1 and had drawn 3–3 in the end, failing to secure the Conference Championship until the following week. Does lightning strike twice? Certainly when Rod Thomas scored Chester's second goal in the 79th minute doubts arose, but the Silkmen gallantly hung on and the 3–2 victory ensured that they retained second position in the League to achieve automatic promotion.

May

The following week the Silkmen celebrated their achievement with a 3–1 victory at Exeter City with goals from Steve Wood, Peter Davenport and Tony Philliskirk, and Stuart Whittaker had a hand in all three strikes. It was Tony Philliskirk's first and last goal for the Silkmen and Peter Davenport's strike was his 100th career League goal. Another milestone saw 'keeper Ryan Price

League Managers

Sammy McIlroy 1997–2000
Peter Davenport 2000
Gil Prescott 2001
Kevin Keen (acting) 2001
David Moss 2001–03
John Askey 2003–04
Brian Horton 2004–06
Paul Ince 2006–07
Ian Brightwell 2007–08
Keith Alexander 2008–

become the only member of the squad to appear in all 51 competitive matches during the season. At the conclusion of the match many of the Exeter supporters formed a line on the pitch and came to the away end to give their best wishes for the future to all the Macclesfield fans, a gesture which was most appreciated by all the travelling supporters.

In true McIlroy style the back line of Neil Howarth, Steve Payne, Efe Sodje and Darren Tinson held firm, only conceding 11 goals at home and 33 on the road. There were significant contributions from midfielders Phil Power, Neil Sorvel, Stuart Whittaker and striker/winger John Askey, but it was veteran midfielder Steve Wood who had been the most influential player on the pitch. He completed the season as top scorer with 15 goals in all competitions and thoroughly deserved to win the Player of the Year award.

The town celebrates promotion.

And so, Macclesfield completed an exciting and most enjoyable season in second position with 82 points, gaining automatic promotion at the first attempt with an undefeated home League record of 19 wins and four draws, a record no other English professional club could match.

Post Season

For the fourth consecutive year (after two Conference Championships, an FA Trophy win and now promotion to Division Two) the players and officials toured the town in an open-top bus to celebrate, prior to a Civic Reception at the Town Hall.

An excellent limited edition book titled *Against All Odds* by Paul Atherton, with a written account by Neil Howarth and David Lafferty, was published. It is a great photographic record of the Silkmen's first year as members of the Football League and was launched with an exhibition of prints in the library, an official launch at Bar Cuba and a book-signing event at Waterstone's, where Sammy McIlroy was presented with book number one.

Cup Competitions

Hull City were the opponents in the first round of the **League Cup** sponsored by Coca-Cola, with the first leg at the Moss Rose ending in a 0–0 draw. Two weeks later at Hull, the home side took an early lead but Andy Mason equalised just before half-time and so the score remained level at the end of 90 minutes, Macclesfield having been denied by the Hull 'keeper, the woodwork and the offside flag. However, Hull found additional strength in extra-time and won the match in the 117th minute.

The **JC Thomson Shield**, competed for each season between the Conference Champions and the winners of the FA Trophy, saw a 3–1 victory to the Silkmen against Woking with two goals from Richard Landon and one from Mark Cooper, thereby winning the Trophy for the third time to equal the record previously achieved by Wycombe Wanderers.

In the first round of the **FA Cup** the Silkmen visited Hartlepool United, who were reduced to 10 men in the first half following a brawl, but the tie came alive after the break to become a pulsating match with first Macclesfield taking the lead through a Steve Wood goal and then Hartlepool scoring twice in 10 minutes to take the lead. In the 71st minute Stuart Whittaker headed the equaliser and 10 minutes later Steve Wood scrambled the ball home to re-take the lead. It was a well-taken solo goal in the 88th minute by Stuart Whittaker which gave the Silkmen a well deserved 4–2 victory. Walsall demolished the Silkmen 7–0 in the second round at the Moss Rose, giving them their biggest away win in the previous 50 years and ending the Silkmen's run of 29 consecutive home matches in all competitions without a defeat.

In the **Auto Windscreens Shield** Macclesfield were given a bye in the first round and drew Preston North End at home in the second round. The visitors won by a single goal scored in the second half.

A 19th win in the **Cheshire Senior Cup** came courtesy of a Stuart Whittaker goal against Runcorn at Northwich Victoria. With Martin MacDonald injured in the match, despite this competition having given the supporters a lot of interest over the years, Sammy McIlroy questioned the need for a Football League side to be involved. It was a condition that all Premier/Football League clubs had to play in their respective County Cup competitions to maintain the right to play in the FA Cup, but there was the option to pay an exemption fee for those clubs who did not want to participate.

CHAPTER TWO: 1998–1999

A BRIDGE TOO FAR

Pre-season

With promotion to the third tier of English football, it was no surprise that the sale of season tickets was successful, quickly selling three times those sold the previous season with supporters eagerly anticipating the visits of well established clubs such as Manchester City, Fulham, Preston North End and Burnley. To eliminate any possible problems with queues on matchdays it was decided that all home matches would be all-ticket, and for those supporters who did not wish to purchase a season ticket they were encouraged to join a membership scheme at a cost of £12 which entitled them to priority purchase of home match tickets.

Also, to ensure that the Moss Rose ground provided enhanced facilities for the supporters and additional revenue for the club, a modular stand was erected on the Estate Road side as a temporary measure pending the building of a permanent stand which, according to the initial announcement, would have a capacity of 1,728 seats.

This was a time of expansion for the club, the ever popular Gil Prescott being appointed director of football on a four-year contract but, unlike many directors of football who move 'upstairs', Gil's workload increased instead. He retained his role as Sammy McIlroy's assistant and was also given responsibility to oversee the newly formed reserve side, which was managed by Jeff Lutley, the formation of a centre of excellence and development of the club's youth programme. At the same time Paul O'Neill (centre-back), Phil Cain (right-back), Chris Leonard (left-midfield) and Matthew Buckley (wide left-midfield) became the club's very first players to be signed under the youth training scheme.

In the meantime, Sammy McIlroy was looking at ways he could strengthen his squad for the forthcoming demanding season. In all, he made five signings – Phil Morgan, a goalkeeper from Stoke City, Graeme Tomlinson, the former Manchester United striker, Dominic Barclay, a striker from Bristol City, Rae Ingram, who had made an excellent impression while on loan from Manchester City the previous season, and Steve Brown, a former striker at Lincoln City. While none of these players had any extensive Football League experience, Sammy's hands were tied financially and he managed to sign all five players on free transfers.

Leaving the club were veteran Cec Edey, who moved to Hyde United, and Phil Power, who had been offered a three-month contract at the Moss Rose, but as he wanted more security he accepted a two-year deal at Altrincham together with a five-figure signing-on fee. Sammy was disappointed at losing Phil, who had given sterling service to the Silkmen, and said that he was one of his best-ever signings. This was also a loss for the fans, who had affectionately named him the Maltese Falcon.

Friendly Matches

This season's friendly matches provided something of a mixed bag of opposition. The Silkmen were guests at non-League sides Leek Town, Winsford United and Congleton Town, but Scottish club Hibernian provided the first

League opposition of the season at the Moss Rose. The match somehow ended in a goalless draw after both sides had many opportunities, with Hibernian kept at bay by the Macclesfield 'keeper Ryan Price, who was on top form.

A Manchester United XI secured a 2–1 victory at the Moss Rose, with goals from Erik Nevland and David Healy for United and Neil Sorvel for the Silkmen. The former Lille striker Ghendouz Jawel, on trial at the Moss Rose, played in this match and looked a class act, but before Sammy McIlroy could sign him, his agent John Beck, a former Lincoln City manager, recommended him to Lincoln.

Greek opposition in the form of Aris Salonika came next. They had taken part in various European competitions against opposition including Benfica, Juventus, Hibernian, Chelsea and Rapid Wien. Sammy McIlroy was disappointed with the Silkmen's performance as they created few chances and could not break down the visitors' strong opposition, with the match ending in a goaless draw. The Silkmen visited Gresty Road for the final pre-season game which saw the Silkmen take the lead through Steve Wood, but Crewe scored two second-half goals to win the match. However, the Silkmen had matched their higher League opponents throughout and only lost to a late goal, and the overall feeling was that they had set themselves up nicely for the challenging season ahead.

SEASON REVIEW

August

The first League match was at home against Kevin Keegan's Fulham. Sammy McIlroy kept faith with his players from the previous season with a starting line up of Price, Tinson, Ingram, Payne, McDonald, Sodje, Askey, Wood, Landon, Sedgemore and Whittaker, although new signing Dominc Barclay made his debut for the Silkmen in the second half and Neil Howarth was a late substitute. But the Silkmen immediately found themselves in a different world, with the Macclesfield matchday squad costing less than £100,000 in direct contrast to the visitors who included Maik Taylor, who came with a transfer fee of £800,000, Rufus Brevit (£375,000), Wayne Collins (£400,000) and Chris Coleman (£2.5 million), and there was even talent totalling £875,000 on their bench including on-loan Peter Beardsley. Unfortunately there was no fairytale ending to the match, although the Silkmen were not overawed by this expensive opposition and had their chances in front of a crowd of 3,933. It was the former England international John Salako whose 19th-minute goal gave the visitors victory when they were awarded a free-kick. Paul Bracewell touched the ball to Salako who drove the ball around a nine-man wall. And so, the Silkmen's 19-month unbeaten home League run came to an end. Kevin Keegan was impressed by the Silkmen but he did rather put the 'kiss of death' on them when he predicted that the side would not be relegated.

Next came three successive matches against Stoke City, two legs in the Worthington Cup followed by the first away League match in the higher Division, which Stoke won 2–0 having applied pressure from the start. This was Macclesfield's first experience of a large modern stadium with refreshment facilities on the concourse below the stand and television screens on which the match was shown live. Lincoln City, also newly promoted, were the next visitors to the Moss Rose, the match ending in a 0–0 draw with Lincoln's long-ball approach dominant.

And then to Millwall for the Silkmen's 50th League match. There was a large police presence including mounted police inside the stadium, which was approached through a high metal gate and surrounding fence. Allocated to the upper tier of the North Stand, there was an exceptional view of the pitch for the travelling fans. The match ended in a 0–0 draw but players and supporters alike were frustrated as Graeme Tomlinson hit the woodwork on three occasions and Neil Howarth almost stole the points in the last minute, but he too hit the crossbar.

The final match in August was at home against newly promoted, and the previous year's champions, Notts County, who won 1–0 from a free-kick, leaving the Silkmen in 23rd position with two points and no goals.

September

The month began with a trip to Wales on a warm and sunny afternoon. The supporters were a little despondent when Wrexham took the lead in the fifth minute, however the Silkmen hung on and early in the second half veteran Steve Wood scored the Silkmen's first League goal of the season. But the celebrations were short lived as Wrexham took the lead six minutes later and ran out winners.

Macclesfield were off to Boundary Park the following Tuesday on a cool and windy evening, where yet again the hosts took the lead and were well on top in the opening period. But never-say-die Macclesfield equalised in the 55th minute through Dominic Barclay, and then minutes later Oldham's Toddy Orlygsson fouled John Askey in the penalty area, for which Orlygsson was dismissed. Up stepped Steve Wood, who was born in Oldham and was delighted to be playing in front of family and friends, to take the penalty in front of the

Manchester City scorer Shaun Goater (left) with Rae Ingram, a former City player.

travelling supporters only to see his shot blocked by the 'keeper, much to the dismay of the Silkmen fans, but Steve was the quickest to react and right-footed the ball home from six yards to secure the Silkmen's first League win of the season.

And then came the match which everyone was waiting for, especially as three years earlier Manchester City were playing in the Premiership and Macclesfield were still members of the Conference. But on Saturday 12 September 1998 Manchester City met Macclesfield Town as equals at the Moss Rose in an all-ticket match.

The Moss Rose was packed to the rafters and the attendance of 6,381 remains a Moss Rose League record to this day. Corporate facilities were laid on in a marquee on adjacent land to the club owned by director Harry Armstrong, which is now the Audi Car Showroom, and secure car parking was also provided. Over 200 supporters, many of them Manchester City fans, dined in relative luxury and then walked down to the Moss Rose to enjoy the

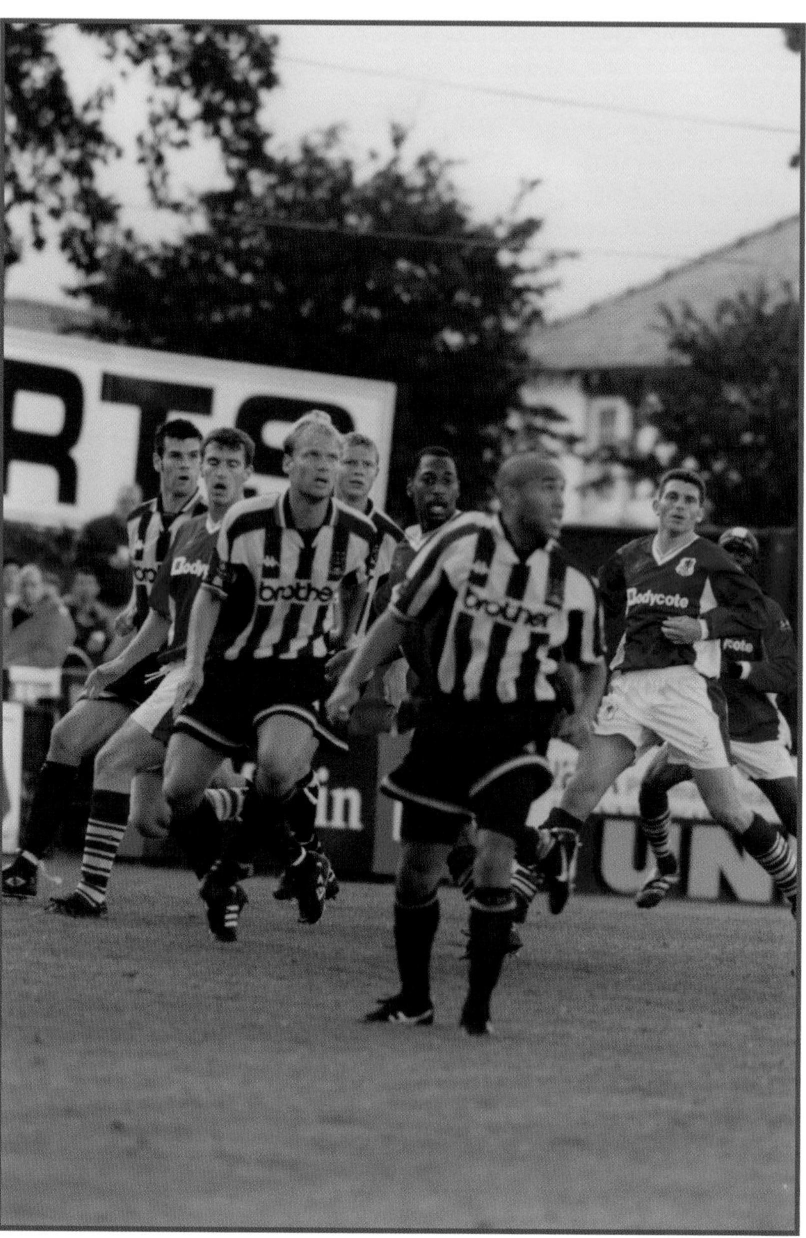

Future Silkman Richard Edghill defending for Manchester City at the Moss Rose.

Steve Payne and Efe Sodje defending against Manchester City.

match from the modular stand on the Estate Road side of the ground, returning to the marquee at the end of the match.

The Silkmen battled hard and both sides had their chances, but just as it seemed that the match would end in a draw Jim Whitley's cross caught out the Macclesfield defence and allowed Shaun Goater to steal a match-winning goal. Neil Howarth made his 250th appearance for the Silkmen in this match and Ryan Price his 150th appearance.

Another 'big' club followed in the shape of Dave Whelan's Wigan Athletic, who had been regular opponents of the Silkmen in the Northern Premier League. This match took place at their old Springfield Stadium, although their new JJB Stadium was well under construction. In desperation Sammy paired forward Dominic Barclay with centre-back Neil Howarth as the strike force, an experiment which only lasted 45 minutes. The Silkmen were undone by two errors to give Wigan a 2–0 win.

Sammy McIlroy was doing his best with the resources at his disposal and for the home match against Reading made several changes. He took the difficult decision to replace the ever-dependable Steve Payne with the ever-popular team captain Neil Howarth, and three teenagers were also brought into the side. Peter Smith, on a month's loan from Crewe, together with Michael Holt on loan from Preston North End, formed the strike force, and reserve-team player Peter Griffiths operated on the wing. And it worked, with Michael Holt scoring on his debut in the 25th minute. Reading equalised from the penalty spot in the second half but the double substitution of John Askey for Steve Wood and Stuart Whittaker for Peter Smith was inspirational, as only four minutes later Stuart Whittaker made a pinpoint cross which found John Askey, who headed home allowing Macclesfield to chalk up their second victory of the campaign. Although this had been a much more productive month, the Silkmen remained in the relegation zone in 21st position.

However, there was good news off the pitch. Chairman Alan Cash announced that an out of court settlement had been reached with the liquidators of the former chairman's company, Crossland Metals International Ltd, who had served a writ on the club in August 1997 for £524,572. A figure of £227,553 had been acknowledged as having been paid into the club by Arthur Jones but the settlement involved the payment of only £150,000. £100,000 had been paid in August 1998 with the balance due to be paid by 28 May 1999, although if the Silkmen remained in the Second Division a further sum of £50,000 would have to be paid. From a financial perspective this was a difficult time for the club which, because of the writ, was on the verge of closure towards the end of the previous year. Mr Cash explained that funds had been in short supply to strengthen the team due to the settlement of the writ but that a sum of £180,000 had already been spent on new players. He emphasised that the club's financial position was now more secure and the board wanted to support the management in consolidating the team's position in Division Two.

October

On a bitterly cold day the Silkmen visited Gillingham's Priestfield Stadium for the first match of the month, and the home side were made to chase the game when the Silkmen took the lead twice through superb goals by Martin McDonald. With Gillingham reduced to 10 men following the dismissal of Carl Asaba and with the Silkmen leading 2–1 it looked as though victory was on the way until John Hodge scored the equaliser in time added on.

Another frustrating match took place at the Moss Rose against AFC Bournemouth where the Silkmen again were leading 2–1 in the second half through goals by Peter Smith and Stuart Whittaker, only to see Mark Stein equalise for the visitors following a needlessly given away free-kick. It has been said that Stuart Whittaker's goal was one of the finest scored at the Moss Rose during the club's Football League years. Stuart made a glorious 30-yard run, checked and then struck a stunning 15-yard curling drive into the top corner of the net. The cost of children's tickets were reduced for this match to mark the centenary of the Football League – for each adult, two children gained admission for £1 each with additional children's tickets costing £3.50, and Junior Blue members only paid £1.

The next fixture was at Wycombe Wanderers, who dominated the match from start to finish and won 3–0. Deepdale was another magnificent stadium and the Silkmen were not overawed in front of a crowd in excess of 10,000, taking a two-goal lead in the first 13 minutes courtesy of Efe Sodje and Peter Smith, a lead which they held to the interval. The second half was a different matter as the Silkmen conceeded too many corners and often lost possession, which led to Preston scoring two goals with the equaliser, yet again, coming in the final minutes of the match.

On a day when it rained continuously throughout the match, leaving a muddy and water-logged pitch, it was the Silkmen who adapted to the conditions far better than the visitors from Burnley. The men in claret and blue went behind to a Ben Sedgemore 25-yard strike in the first half but their best player by far, Glen Little, equalised in the 71st minute.

Efe Sodje and Burnley's Andy Cooke at the Moss Rose.

Silkmen goalkeeper Ryan Price keeps his eye on the ball against Burnley.

Not to be outdone, Peter Smith scored a stunning 20-yard right-foot drive in the 84th minute to win the match for the Silkmen.

The month ended with a defeat at Northampton Town, who won by a single first-half goal, but the Silkmen's cause was not helped by the dismissal of midfielder Martin McDonald. This result put the Silkmen back in the relegation zone in 21st position.

November

In the first match of the month, a 30-yard shot by Peter Griffiths, his very first League goal, gave the Silkmen a first-half lead at Colchester, but after the interval Colchester dominated the match with David Greene scoring the equaliser in the 75th minute.

A welcome victory at York City saw first-half goals come from midfielders Ben Sedgemore and Neil Sorvel, but the home side made the Silkmen defend well in the second half. However, the match was marred by the dismissal of Martin McDonald for violent conduct, his second dismissal in quick succession for which he eventually received a seven-match ban.

High-flying Walsall were the next visitors to the Moss Rose for an entertaining match full of quality football by both sides. Just on the stroke of half-time a short corner by Neil Sorvel went straight to Walsall's Darren Wrack, who sprinted 70 yards up the pitch to pass to debutant Argentinian Walter Otta, who slotted past Ryan Price. Price made a string of fine saves throughout the match, earning him the Man of the Match award, and Graeme Tomlinson scored the equaliser only four minutes after his introduction from the substitutes' bench to give the Silkmen a precious point.

The final League match of the month was lost at Chesterfield 2–0, and while the Silkmen pushed the home side and showed plenty of fight they could not find a telling finish. Nevertheless, Macclesfield completed the month one place higher than the previous month, in 20th position.

Ryan Price received the 'Matchman of the Month' award from *Match* magazine in recognition of a string of impressive performances during the month.

December

After protracted negotiations, the former Spanish Under-21 front-man Pedro Miguel Manuel Matias was signed from Longrones having previously been on the books of Real Madrid and Almeria. Simon Davies was also signed from Luton Town, having started his career at Manchester United where he had progressed through the youth team to the first team and made Premiership and European appearances.

With the second round of the FA Cup taking place on the first Saturday of the month, the first home match did not take place until 12 December when Luton Town were the visitors. Luton took a third-minute lead but Neil Sorvel equalised in the first half, and then early in the second half Graeme Tomlinson gave the home side a 2–1 lead. But it was the same old story again as Luton equalised in time added on.

The visit to Bristol Rovers on a cold and damp Tuesday evening saw the debut of new signings Pedro Matias and Simon Davies. It was, however, an instantly forgettable match, with only two attempts on goal, which ended goalless. Macclesfield Town became the 100th League opponent for Bristol Rovers.

Worse was to come when bottom side Lincoln City were the victors by a single goal at Sincel Bank in atrocious conditions, and then Blackpool won by a single goal in the last match of the year on a heavy Moss Rose pitch which cut up badly. After a month of disappointing results the Silkmen completed the year in 23rd position with just 21 points, with only Lincoln City below them who had accumulated 17 points.

January

In an attempt to provide more competition for places two loan signings were made. Anthony Williams, a Welsh Under-21 'keeper, came from Blackburn Rovers and Alan Bailey, a promising young striker, signed from Manchester City. Alan was a local lad who had attended Fallibroome High School.

There were only three League matches during the month due to the postponement of matches against Stoke City and Notts County. The first took place at Craven Cottage where the home side won by the same margin of a single goal as they had on the first day of the season at the Moss Rose; however, Fulham could consider themselves fortunate as it was a speculative shot by Steve Hayward which was deflected by Geoff Horsfield to deceive Anthony Williams in the Macclesfield goal. Defeats against Blackpool and Millwall followed.

A 2–0 defeat by Millwall at home was followed by a visit to Blackpool, who recorded their first home win for four months with a 2–1 victory over the Silkmen, who had taken a first-half lead with a goal from Efe Sodje.

With no points earned in the month and the Silkmen remaining in bottom place the situation was beginning to look a little bleak. The team's form was giving concern to such an extent that there were several letters in the *Macclesfield Express* from supporters frustrated by recent results and the lack of any announcement from the directors about the introduction of further funding for Sammy McIlroy. In response Sammy said that he was a little disappointed by the reactions of some of the fans and that he was doing his best to turn things around but recognised that the club were at a level far away from the Conference. However, he promised that he and the players would keep battling.

On a brighter note, to support the club's financial position the former chairman, Alan Brocklehurst, announced that he would undertake a sponsored bike ride from Macclesfield to his home in Ibiza, a distance of 900 land miles. Also, a supporter, Doctor Michael Hughes, who was later to become the club's doctor, opened a 'Silk Purse' asking fans to donate a regular monthly amount. His initiative was featured on Radio 5 Live, North West Tonight and Local Radio. In the end they raised a significant amount with donations coming from fans as far away as Norway and Germany.

February

The month started badly with a 2–0 home defeat by Wrexham, who got off to a good start by scoring in the sixth minute. The Silkmen battled hard but could not find an equaliser, and the Welshmen sealed victory with a second goal in the 90th minute. The Welsh fans were in fine voice, singing to the Welsh tune *Cwm Rhondda* towards the end of the match.

There was a big sigh of relief when the final whistle blew in the next match when the first and only double of the season was completed against Oldham

Simon Davies (left) in excellent form at Maine Road.

Spaniard Pedro Matias shoots for goal at Maine Road.

Athletic. A single 84th-minute headed goal by Efe Sodje gave the Silkmen their first win since November.

It was then off to Maine Road, where Simon Davies had possibly his best performance in a Silkmen shirt when he relished the chance to perform on the bigger stage once again.

Macclesfield played some attractive football, but they were no match for promotion chasing City who won by two clear goals. The attendance of 31,086 (some 1,500 higher than the total of our home League attendances for the whole of our final season in the Conference) was the highest crowd which the Silkmen had ever performed in front of at that time; the previous highest had been at the FA Trophy Final at the old Wembley Stadium on 2 May 1970 when the attendance was 28,000.

The final match of the month was at home and resulted in another defeat, this time at the hands of Wigan Athletic who basically won the match with a sixth-minute goal scored by David Lee whose speculative cross, aided by the wind, looped over Ryan Price. The Silkmen remained in bottom place.

Disappointingly, Neil Howarth moved to Cheltenham Town for a fee of £7,500 at the end of the month as he wanted regular first-team football. Since Macclesfield had been promoted to the Football League Neil had been playing out of position at left-back and for much of the current season had been on the substitutes' bench. He made his debut for the Silkmen in September 1993 against Dagenham & Redbridge at the Moss Rose and had been particularly successful at non-League level, including representing England at semi-professional level. He was a worthy team captain and his weekly column in the *Macclesfield Express* was always full of amusing comment on events behind the scenes. On leaving the club he said 'The times I've had at Macc have been the best of my career and I doubt I'll ever experience anything like it in the future.' Steve Payne was appointed team captain in place of Neil.

Wigan's then Under-21 Northern Ireland international goalkeeper Roy Carroll thwarts another Silkmen attack.

Steve Wood makes a determined attack on the ball against Wigan Athletic in front of the modular stand at the Moss Rose.

Off the field the club's financial position was again giving concern. It was reported at the Annual General Meeting that a loss of £80,000 had been incurred the previous year and that a loss of £250,000 was predicted for the current year. Four new directors were appointed to bolster the board: Andrew White, Mike Rance, Jeremy Turner and Eddie Furlong, two of whom were to become chairmen of the club in years to come.

March

The playing surface was giving even more concern and following the postponement of the match against Stoke City, and after Sammy McIlroy expressed his own concerns, Colin Garlick (director) stated that action had already been taken by the board, who had brought in specialists. In addition, he stated that work would be carried out to the playing surface over the forthcoming summer months.

The first match of the month gave no indication of the good things to come. Reading's Madejski Stadium is another modern and comfortable facility which was opened in 1998 with an all-seater capacity of 24,200, although on the day of the Silkmen's visit there was only a crowd of 8,085. A single goal by the home side saw Macclesfield lose again.

Gillingham visited the Moss Rose the following Tuesday with the match in doubt until 19.00pm following heavy rain. But as the visitors had only lost twice in their last 27 outings it looked as though there would be an impossible mountain to climb. Up stepped Richard Landon, who had been out of favour in recent weeks, to head home a Pedro Matias pinpoint cross in the first half, which was followed by a pulsating second half in which Sammy McIlroy's men defended stoutly to send Gillingham home empty handed.

The following Saturday, Colchester United were the guests at the Moss Rose and the match came to life in the second half. Despite the state of the pitch

Macclesfield played some attractive passing football and Richard Landon's header just crept over the line, with the assistant referee awarding the goal. In the 90th minute, on-loan Alan Bailey raced onto a Kieron Durkan through ball, held off two defenders and lobbed the 'keeper from 20 yards. Back-to-back wins lifted the Silkmen off the bottom and gave the supporters some hope. Even better was to come with an away win at Northampton Town, when two second-half goals by midfielders Steve Wood and Neil Sorvel secured another three precious points and a third straight win.

And then to Burnley, another 'big' club whose stadium, Turf Moor, had been significantly improved over the years and where the team were regularly attracting five-figure attendances. This was another pulsating match from start to finish and Kieron Durkan enjoyed one of his best performances in a Macclesfield shirt.

Kieron Durkan and John Askey gave the Silkmen a two-goal lead in the first 14 minutes but the home side pulled a goal back three minutes later. Tom Cowan equalised for the Clarets in the second half but Macclesfield came back again, Kieron Durkan's volley from eight yards giving them the lead for a second time. But Burnley were not finished. Andy Payton's goal saw the Clarets equalise for a second time to set the match up for a grandstand finish. But it ended in heartbreak for the Silkmen, when an unmarked Steve Davies headed home in the 89th minute to give Burnley a 4–3 victory to leave the Silkmen in 23rd position.

During the month Martin McDonald left Macclesfield for the second time, moving to non-League Altrincham. Since his seven-match ban he had played very few matches and had gone 'missing' for a period of time. Steve Soley was signed on loan from Portsmouth who had paid Leek Town a fee of £30,000 in the summer of 1998.

John Askey celebrates his goal against Burnley.

Kieron Durkan celebrates one of his two goals at Burnley.

An ambitious overhead kick by Richard Landon at Turf Moor.

April

This was a busy month with seven League matches, starting off at the Moss Rose against Wycombe Wanderers, fellow relegation strugglers. The visitors won 3–1, and Efe Sodje made life difficult for the Silkmen when he was dismissed for a second bookable offence. This match was preceded by a minute's silence for John Cleaver, who had died recently. At the time John was as knowledgeable as any one about the recent history of the club and contributed a 'Look Back' article in the matchday programme in the Conference days. There was a second defeat away at Bournemouth when Mark Stein scored the only goal of the match in the 84th minute.

The next two matches brought consecutive wins. The first at home came against Preston North End, who took the lead in the first half, but a frenetic second half with goals from John Askey, Kieron Durkan and Steve Wood gave the Silkmen a 3–1 lead. However, a minute after Steve Wood's goal Steve Basham scored his second of the match to make the score 3–2, but the Macclesfield defence held out resolutely.

Darren Tinson and Kieron Durkan defend against Preston North End.

In the second home match of the month Steve Payne scored his first-ever League goal with a 25-yard volley and then a second with a simple tap-in against Chesterfield, who had two players dismissed in the second half.

Unfortunately, normal service was then resumed with three consecutive defeats. Walsall, chasing automatic promotion, proved too strong a side, winning at the Bescott Stadium 2–0, and that game was followed by a home defeat of 1–2 against York City and then the re-arranged match from January against Stoke City, who ran out 2–1 winners at the Moss Rose.

Earlier in the month Peter Davenport was appointed assistant manager, a promotion from his previous role of player-coach. This change was made so that Gil Prescott could concentrate mainly on youth development and the Football in the Community programme, but it brought to an end a six-year partnership with Sammy McIlroy which had started at Northwich Victoria.

Steve Wood celebrates scoring the winning goal against Preston North End with John Askey.

For some time Rae Ingram had been performing well below his best and in the end the club announced that he was suffering from the chronic fatigue syndrome ME, which had been kept a closely guarded secret for many weeks. Over the ensuing months, following rest and a careful diet, Rae made a full recovery and returned to become one of the most consistent players at the club.

May

And so to the final three matches of the season. A trip to Kenilworth Road on the first day in May saw Macclesfield take a two-goal lead into the interval with goals from Neil Sorvel and Simon Davies, who was making his first visit to Luton since his transfer to the Silkmen. There was a scare when Luton's Gary Doherty scored a late goal but the Silkmen held out to win 2–1.

On the following Tuesday there was another away fixture, this time at Notts County where the Silkmen needed to win to have any hope of avoiding relegation, but the match ended in a 1–1 draw. Unfortunately, the single point was insufficient to save the Silkmen from relegation.

The final match summed up the Silkmen's season when they again took an early lead against Bristol Rovers and at the interval were leading 2–1. Simon Davies extended the lead to 3–1 soon after the re-start but two goals in as many minutes saw the Pirates draw level. Efe Sodje then conspired to get himself dismissed for the third time in the season, following which Jamie Cureton completed his hat-trick in the 85th minute to secure victory for his side, leaving the Silkmen in 24th position with only 43 points.

Steve Hitchen won the Player of the Year award. Having missed most of the previous season, Steve made a remarkable comeback as a valuable member of the back four in what had been a trying season for the defence as a whole.

For the first time in their history Macclesfield were relegated, along with York City, Northampton Town and Lincoln City. It had been a difficult season, with few financial resources to call upon which meant that Sammy McIlroy had to manage with players on free transfers, often with little previous League experience, together with loan players. On his return to the Moss Rose many years later as manager of Morecambe he recalled, 'even the relegation season was not that bad, it was almost inevitable when we had the likes of Manchester City, Gillingham and Fulham in our League. There were lots of big clubs and we were effectively still a Conference side.' The financial position was not helped by the fact that attendances had only shown an average increase of 400 per match in comparison to the previous season, especially bearing in mind the calibre of players and teams who had visited the Moss Rose. From the supporters' point of view it had been a frustrating season but the visits to many different and splendid stadia was an added bonus. It had certainly proved to have been 'A bridge too far', but at least Sammy McIlroy remained as manager – but for how long?

Cup Competitions

Stoke City were the Silkmen's first-round opponents in the **Worthington Cup**, with the first leg taking place at the Moss Rose in the middle of August. It was a wonderful end-to-end encounter with a total of 42 attempts on goal between the two sides, but it was Macclesfield who ran out easy winners with an early goal by Steve Wood and two late goals by Stoke-born John Askey against a single goal from the visitors. The second leg at the Britannia Stadium was a much more dull affair, with Stoke scoring the only goal in the 78th minute after which the Silkmen put up the shutters and held on to go through to the next round 3–2 on aggregate.

In the second round Birmingham City were the opponents but the Silkmen were no match for a slick City side who triumphed 3–0 at the Moss Rose and 6–0 at St Andrews.

In the **Auto Windscreens Shield** Wrexham were the visitors in the first round. After an early penalty miss by Silkman Peter Smith, Wrexham took

Graeme Tomlinson (number 11), FA Cup hat-trick hero against Cambridge United.

charge and scored the one and only goal in the 48th minute, putting Macclesfield out of the competition at the first hurdle for the second consecutive season.

The **FA Cup** gave the Silkmen more success when they progressed to the third round. Drawn against former Conference rivals Slough Town in the first round, Slough gave the Silkmen a run for their money with an exciting match at the Moss Rose in which the visitors took a two-goal lead in the first half. Despite a glut of chances, the Silkmen could not convert them until the 72nd minute when Graeme Tomlinson pulled a goal back, and just as it looked as though the non-League side were going to be victorious Efe Sodje levelled the scores in the 87th minute. At the conclusion of the match Sammy McIlroy was so incensed by remarks from the Slough bench that, completely out of character, he punched Slough substitute Kenny Hughes. Sammy later admitted that he should not have reacted in this way and imposed a fine on himself, contributing the fine to the players' Christmas bash.

The replay at Slough was another action-packed match with Ben Sedgemore giving the Silkmen a seventh-minute lead only to see Kenny Hughes (of the first round incident) equalise some seven minutes later. Macclesfield were reduced to 10 men when Efe Sodje was dismissed, and to make matters worse the Slough 'keeper saved a Stuart Whittaker penalty. The score remained 1–1 after extra-time but the Silkmen won the penalty shoot-out 9–8, with Macclesfield 'keeper Ryan Price the hero scoring Macclesfield's 10th penalty (Graeme Tomlinson having missed the first penalty) and then returning to his place in goal to save Slough's 10th spot-kick.

In the second round the Silkmen were drawn at home again, with Cambridge United as the opposition. John Askey opened the scoring but his goal was cancelled out by Jamie Campbell in the 55th minute, after which there followed an 11-minute, match-winning hat-trick by Graeme Tomlinson to send the Silkmen through to the third round for only the third time in their history.

The Silkmen coming onto the pitch at Coventry City.

The Silkmen travelled to Premiership side Coventry City for the third round. The Coventry team was Hedman, Nilsson (Telfer), Shaw, Williams, Burrows (Shilton), Boateng, McAllister, Solvedt, Froggatt, Whelan (Aloisi) and Huckerby.

The Silkmen lined up with Price, Hitchen, Howarth, Payne, Wood (Lonergan), Sodje (Durkan), Askey, Sedgemore, Matias (Whittaker), Tomlinson and Davies.

Macclesfield matched the Premiership side until Steve Froggatt opened the scoring for Coventry in the 28th minute. By half-time the home side were winning 3–0 and they went on to score four more goals in the second half, with Darren Huckerby completing his hat-trick in the 90th minute. Steve Payne came the closest to scoring for the Silkmen near to the end of the match but his shot hit the crossbar.

Neil Howarth (centre) with Coventry hat-trick scorer Darren Huckerby.

CHAPTER THREE: 1999–2000

THE END OF AN ERA

Pre-season

During the summer substantial work was carried out to the pitch, which had given significant concerns in the 1998–1999 season when it had become waterlogged, muddy and cut up easily, making for extremely difficult playing conditions and forcing matches to be postponed. To fix this problem all the drains were replaced with bigger and better ones and the top inch of the pitch was cut off, leaving the old roots intact. The whole area was then covered with 200 tons of soil and sand and completely reseeded.

There were several key departures from the squad during the close season. After seven years of excellent service Neil Sorvel, a midfielder, returned to Crewe Alexandra and the ever-dependable defender Steve Payne left after five and a half years to join Chesterfield. Pedro Matias and Efe Sodje had been offered terms by Macclesfield but both had delayed in accepting new contracts and were eventually advised by the board that they could leave the club, at a time when the board were expressing concerns about the club's finances, especially as only 600 season tickets had been sold. Both players eventually moved to higher-division clubs; Matias to Tranmere Rovers and Sodje to Luton Town.

Joining the Silkmen were Simon Collins, a centre-back from Plymouth, forward Richie Barker from Brighton & Hove Albion, Gregor Rioch, a utility player and son of Bruce, from Hull City, Chris Priest, a central-midfielder from Chester City and 'keeper Lee Martin from Halifax Town. All signed on free transfers and all went on to make a significant contribution for the club. Just before the season commenced Damien Whitehead, a young striker, was signed for a nominal fee from Warrington Town where he had scored 58 goals in 43 starts. Sammy McIlroy announced that Gregor Rioch was to take on the responsibility of team captain.

There was one additional administrative task required to be completed before the start of the season – the introduction of squad numbers. The system of players wearing numbers 1 to 11, usually according to their positions on the field of play, with substitutes numbered 12, 13, 14, 15, was replaced with each player allocated a number for the whole of the season and, as a consequence of retaining the same shirt number, the player's surname was printed on the back of his shirt. The squad numbers for players who left during the season could be allocated to an incoming player, and on one occasion a single number was allocated to four different players during a single season.

Friendly Matches

A planned pre-season tour of Ireland had to be cancelled due to insufficient time for organisation, and a match against Stoke City was called off when the two teams were drawn against each other in the Worthington Cup. Nevertheless, there were plenty of other opportunities to prepare for the forthcoming season. A 4–0 win at Leek gave the Silkmen an excellent start, albeit against a side which had just been relegated from the Conference. All the new signings fitted in well and there were first-half goals from Richie Barker, Graeme Tomlinson and Simon Davies, with Tomlinson scoring again just after the break. Visits to non-League sides Winsford United, Congleton Town, Hyde United and St Helens followed.

The final three matches took place at the Moss Rose, with Stockport County the first of the visitors. Worryingly for Sammy McIlroy, prior to the match Richie Barker had to pull out and Rae Ingram, Paul Ware and Gregor Rioch all failed to finish. The match itself was a dull affair in the first half but came to life after the interval when Graeme Tomlinson narrowly missed an opportunity to open the scoring, but in the end it was Stockport's Tony Ellis who won the match for the visitors.

In the next match, Wigan's expensive signing Simon Howarth opened the scoring with an early goal, but Macclesfield battled back with veteran midfielder Steve Wood scoring the equaliser in the 70th minute. However, the Second Division side won the match just two minutes later when Andy Morris converted a Simon Howarth cross.

In the final pre-season match, against a full-strength Port Vale side, the Silkmen earned a thoroughly deserved victory through a Graeme Tomlinson goal in the second half.

After these two matches Sammy McIlroy was full of praise for Nigerian full-back George Abbey, who had given two fabulous performances including several accurate, long cross-field passes. George signed a two-year contract in the middle of August, moving to the Moss Rose from Sharks FC, Nigeria, for a fee of £10,000.

Steve Wood (right) in pre-season action against Port Vale.

SEASON REVIEW

August

There was an excellent start to the season with a 1–0 home win over Northampton Town, who were one of the promotion favourites. Price, Hitchen, Collins, Tinson, Rioch, Wood, Barker, Durkan, Davies, Askey and Priest formed the starting line up with Ingram and Sedgemore coming on from the substitutes' bench leaving Martin, Tomlinson and Whitehead as unused substitutes. All the debutants played well but Steve Hitchen was injured in the first half and was replaced by Rae Ingram, who only lasted some five minutes before being dismissed when he became the first Macclesfield player to fall foul of a new rule which stated that players must not swear at the referee. Richie Barker scored the winning goal on his debut when he chipped over the Northampton 'keeper following a defence-splitting pass from 36-year-old Steve Wood.

Richie Barker (left) scored on his debut against Northampton Town.

After the match it was diagnosed that Steve Hitchen had sustained damage to his cruciate ligaments, and it was an injury which kept him out of contention until the final month of the season. The club stood by him even though he had not signed a contract at the time of his injury and was playing on a week-to-week basis. His plight even hit the front page headlines of the *Macclesfield Express*.

The following Saturday the Silkmen travelled to Darlington where they lost 3–0, the home side scoring all their goals in the final eight minutes. A further defeat came at the Moss Rose when John Askey's 90th-minute goal was too little too late to stop Swansea City winning 2–1.

Gregor Rioch scoring a penalty for the Silkmen on his return to Hull City.

The penultimate match of the month saw the Silkmen pay a visit to Hull City for a heart-stopping encounter. Hull opened the scoring in the 13th minute but shortly afterwards their 'keeper, Lee Bracey, was sent off for a foul on Richie Barker in the penalty area, and Gregor Rioch, on his first return to his former employers, converted the resultant penalty.

John Schofield took over in goal for the spot-kick after which he was substituted for Matt Barker, who became their third 'keeper to feature in the match. Gregor Rioch scored a second goal for the Silkmen but Hull equalised nine minutes later. However, it was substitute Paul Ware who had the last word when he scored the goal of the season, converting a Darren Tinson cross with a right-foot bicycle-kick from just outside the area to win the match 3–2 for the Silkmen. There had been incidents taking place throughout the match. Ryan Price commented to the fans at the start of the second half 'It's absolutely mad at the other end'. Sammy McIlroy had water thrown over him by the Hull bench and Gregor Rioch had been booed throughout. The match ended in a brawl when Steve Wood and Gary Brabin were involved in a disagreement. Stewards and the police, as well as officials, were all involved in bringing the incident to a close.

Richie Barker scored a fourth-minute goal at home against Rotherham, who drew the match late in the second half with a goal from their tall striker Leo Fortune-West, and the result left the Silkmen in 14th place having accumulated seven points.

September

September was a disappointing month for results, starting with a 2–1 defeat at Barnet, although Richie Barker was on the score sheet again. A defeat by two goals to one by Southend United at the Moss Rose came about through errors by Silkmen players. The visitors' first goal came in the second minute from the

Central-defender Simon Collins (left) in action against Lincoln City.

penalty spot when on-loan Chris Byrne, who was recuperating from injury, handled the ball and in the 29th minute and later Rae Ingram headed past his own 'keeper.

In Macclesfield's 100th League match at Lincoln City, Richie Barker gave the Silkmen the lead, and with the Imps reduced to 10 men following the dismissal of full-back Terry Fleming it looked as though they were heading for their fifth consecutive defeat until they equalised with only eight minutes to go.

The only victory in the month came at Exeter City, with goals from Richie Barker, Gregor Rioch and Kieron Durkan. A decision 45 minutes before kick-off saw Kieron Durkan playing up-front for the first time to good effect, and Ryan Price was on form again, preserving a clean sheet which included a wonderful double save. Richie Barker created a new club record at that time, having scored in five consecutive League matches.

October

In October Sammy McIlroy had a change of mind on the captaincy of the team, appointing Darren Tinson in place of Gregor Rioch as he felt that it had been unfair on Gregor to throw him in at the deep end when he had to cope with a change of clubs and a move of house. In an attempt to boost attendances, season-ticket holders were given one free ticket each to pass on to a friend, with the tickets valid for any one of three specific matches.

On the playing side, the month started off badly with two home defeats. Torquay, with Neville Southall in goal, won 2–1 and then Halifax Town took all three points with a 2–0 win, although the Silkmen were unlucky in this match when both Richie Barker and Chris Priest hit the woodwork. Those two defeats left the Silkmen in 21st position

In recent matches 'keeper Ryan Price had suffered a dip in form, with the result that Lee Martin replaced him in goal for the next match at Chester City. Whether this change was the catalyst or not, the Silkmen then had a run of eight successive League matches undefeated to equal their League record set in January and February 1998. At the time there was a fairly settled starting line up of Martin, Ingram, Collins, Tinson, Rioch, Durkan, Priest, Wood, Davies, Barker and Askey. The substitutes' bench involved permutations using Sedgemore, Greg Brown, Whitehead, Tomlinson, Ware, Abbey and Whittaker.

A victory at Chester, owned and managed by American Terry Smith, by two goals to one could have been by a larger margin had so many chances not gone begging. On the following Tuesday a John Askey goal in the fifth minute gave the Silkmen victory at Rochdale when they put in a dedicated and hard-

Goalmouth action at Chester City.

working performance. An easy 1–0 win over Exeter through a Richie Barker goal at the Moss Rose in front of a crowd of only 1,893 saw Lee Martin having only one save to make deep into time added on. It was reported that some 19 scouts were present at this match, all watching the performance of striker Richie Barker. Those three consecutive wins lifted the side to 15th position.

November

For the first time since their promotion to the Football League, Macclesfield scored five goals in a game, winning 5–2 against Mansfield Town at the Moss Rose in front of a disappointingly low crowd of 1,541. One goal from Chris Priest and two from Richie Barker put the Silkmen 3–0 up in the first 17 minutes before the visitors clawed two goals back in the second half, but a powerful left-foot drive from 22 yards by Ben Sedgemore and a conversion of

Ben Sedgemore, scorer in the 5–2 win against Mansfield Town.

yet another Kieron Durkan cross by John Askey gave the home side a wonderful victory. This win shot the side up the table from 15th to eighth position.

In the next match at York, former Silkman Kevin Hulme was included in the home side. Kevin will be remembered for his solid approach as a Silkmen player but probably more for scoring the final goal in the 3–3 draw when he was on the playing staff of Halifax in the Silkmen's penultimate match in the Conference which denied them the Championship that evening. The Silkmen dominated the match at York and won 2–0. It was somewhat ironic that Kevin Hulme was dismissed for two bookable offences in this match.

John Askey celebrates scoring against Brighton & Hove Albion.

There then followed three drawn matches. The first was at home against Brighton & Hove Albion when John Askey put the Silkmen in front during the second half only to see the visitors score a late goal. The second was at Barry Fry's Peterborough, where Macclesfield were leading 2–1 at half-time thanks to goals from John Askey and Richie Barker, until three minutes into the second half the 'Posh' equalised.

In the third match at home against Hartlepool United, Darren Tinson became the first of the former Conference players to reach 100 League appearances. The local radio station Silk FM made a presentation to Darren before the match of a framed record of all his League appearances. Macclesfield dominated the early stages of the match and led 2–0 at the interval; however, as this was the last match as a Silkman for 'keeper Ryan Price and he was on 99 League appearances, he was substituted for Lee Martin at half-time. Hartlepool converted a penalty two minutes after the re-start and then John Askey gave the home side a 3–1 lead in the 67th minute. A misunderstanding between the defence and Ryan Price then allowed Hartlepool to score in the 84th and 90th minutes to take a share of the points, much to the disappointment of the supporters and the team. Nevertheless, after a successful month the team found themselves in a useful ninth place in the League. Ryan Price moved to Telford United for a fee of £10,000 having given good service to the club overall and winning the 'Matchman Player of the Month' award during his time as 'keeper.

December

There was an eventful start to the month. Lee Martin was unavailable for selection due to a back injury and with Ryan Price having just moved to non-League Telford United, Macclesfield found themselves with a goalkeeping crisis. They were fortunate to sign Richard Knight on loan from Derby County on the Friday as they were due to play at Northampton Town the next day. Richard had no time to train with the team before the match and was only introduced to the side at the pre-match meal. For Richard it was unfortunate that Northampton were in good form and never looked like losing, winning with a goal in each half. It was a bitterly cold day with rain and hail showers throughout the match making it an uncomfortable experience for the supporters, and the situation was exacerbated when the floodlights failed just before half-time. The players had to leave the pitch but play was resumed 20 minutes later when the final two and a half minutes of the first half were completed, followed by the full interval and then the second half. It was this defeat which ended the Silkmen's eight League match unbeaten run.

It was then off to Cheltenham, who included former Silkman Neil Howarth in their line-up. Kieron Durkan gave the Silkmen a second-half lead but a late goal by the experienced Neil Grayson saw the points shared. There was a better result against bottom club Leyton Orient when a Simon Davies goal was sufficient for victory.

A visit to Shrewsbury Town on Boxing Day caused problems for Macclesfield even before the kick-off when the referee declared that the strips for both teams were too alike. Macclesfield had only taken their gold-and-blue away strip so they had to play in Shrewsbury's 'Argentinian-in-appearance' away strip. Just before half-time Kieron Durkan profited from a lucky ricochet in the penalty box and scored with a low 15-yard shot which went under the 'keeper to give the Silkmen victory. Evidently this was not the first time that a visiting side had borrowed the Shrewsbury strip and won, leaving their manager, Kevin Ratcliffe, vowing that he was going to burn the strip!

The last match of the Millennium saw a late start at the Moss Rose when an accident on the M6 motorway delayed the Carlisle team coach. Kick-off was re-arranged for 15.15 but the game only came to life in the second half when Richard Tracey, who at a later date moved to the Moss Rose, scored for Carlisle. Macclesfield were then inspired by substitute John Askey, who was provider for Chris Priest's first goal in the 82nd minute. John was on hand again, well into time added on, when he passed to Chris Priest who scored a second from close range to win the match. Finishing well after all the other Football League matches, Chris's second goal was officially recognised as the last Football League goal scored in the 20th Century.

Three consecutive wins saw the side climb to a very creditable sixth position in the League.

January

The New Year started badly with a narrow 3–2 defeat at Plymouth Argyle, Macclesfield missing the consistently performing Chris Priest who was absent on compassionate leave after his baby had been rushed into hospital with breathing difficulties. But worse was to come.

For some time it had been known that Sammy McIlroy would probably become the next manager of the Northern Ireland team, and during the following week an official announcement was indeed made of his appointment. Sammy's last match in charge at Macclesfield took place on Saturday 8 January 2000. There was an above average attendance of 3,221 for the fixture, with many supporters there to say their farewells, and as Sammy walked onto the pitch for the last time the players formed a guard of honour and everyone in the stadium rose to their feet in acknowledgement. During his time at Macclesfield, Sammy had won every non-League competition available, including a trip to Wembley for the FA Trophy, the Conference Championship twice, promotion to the Football League and, in addition, promotion from Division Three to Division Two. Unfortunately, Macclesfield were undone that day by the visitors, Cheltenham Town, through their sheer physical approach which gave them the edge and saw them win 2–1.

And so this match signalled the end of Macclesfield's most successful time as a football club. It was truly the end of an era. Sammy was an inspiration to everyone and a thoroughly nice guy who always had the fans' interests at heart. In the *Macclesfield Express* he said 'I have loved my time here and Macclesfield will always be the first result I will look for in the future. Even though I have fulfilled my ambition it is still sad to leave Macclesfield Town after six and a half glorious years. It has been a great learning process as a manager.' He went on to say 'I would like to thank the fans for standing by me. They have been fantastic. It is easy when things are going well, but last season and the start of this one were difficult. The fans understood that, supporting me where many other sets of fans would not have done.'

The following week Peter Davenport was promoted from assistant manager to manager until the end of the season, and he appointed John Askey and Steve Wood as joint coaches. Peter Davenport's first League match in charge ended in victory when high-flying Darlington were beaten 2–1 in an exciting end-to-end encounter, John Askey scoring the winning goal. But the next two matches ended in defeat, by 1–0 at Swansea and 2–0 against Hull City at home, when

Newly appointed manager, Peter Davenport.

Anthony Williams was drafted in again on loan from Blackburn to replace the injured Lee Martin to become the fourth 'keeper used in the season. These defeats meant that the Silkmen slipped from sixth to 11th position.

February

The club's finances were again causing concern and it was reported that due to dwindling attendances and debts being paid off, the club faced a shortfall of between £22,000 to £30,000 per month, which had to be made up from off-field activities. It also came to light at this time that the club had taken a one-off loan of £60,000 from the Professional Footballers' Association at the end of 1999 to cover payment of players' wages, with the loan to be repaid by the end of March 2000. Under Football League regulations this meant that the club was not allowed to make any new signings, including loan arrangements (although there was an exception for goalkeepers) until the monetary loan had been fully repaid.

This was a good month for results overall but in the first match Rotherham triumphed 2–1 at Millmoor to go top of the table, but then goals by Richie Barker and John Askey gave the Silkmen a home win against Barnet. An excellent victory at Hartlepool saw the Silkmen skating over a muddy playing surface to win 4–1 having led 3–1 at half-time. Goals came from Kieron Durkan, John Askey and a couple from Richie Barker. On a windy day, the final match of the month resulted in a 1–1 home draw against Lincoln City with another goal from John Askey, his 11th of the season to date, leaving the side in ninth position in the League table.

March

This was a disappointing month for results with only one win recorded. Southend has never been a happy hunting ground for the Silkmen and it was no different this season. A single goal by Martin Carruthers gave Southend victory in a Friday evening fixture. The following Tuesday Macclesfield entertained York City, and while Kieron Durkan gave the home side the lead, only seven minutes later Kevin Hulme equalised for the visitors. Only minutes later John Askey scored what looked to be a perfectly good goal and the referee appeared to have given the goal. However, following protests from the York players and consultations between the officials, a full two minutes later the goal was disallowed with play brought back as Simon Davies was adjudged to have stamped on Lee Bullock before the move for the goal had begun. Simon was subsequently dismissed and received a three-match ban.

Another defeat, this time at Mansfield Town, saw the side slip down the table and a Play-off position almost disappeared out of sight. The situation became even more dire when Richie Barker, the season's top scorer, was stretchered off in this match with a serious ankle ligament injury which prevented him from featuring again for the remainder of the season. Yet another defeat looked likely when Peterborough were the visitors and took an early lead in the first half, but tall centre-back Neil Moore equalised four minutes into time added on to take a share of the points.

Brighton & Hove Albion had moved from Gillingham's Priestfield Stadium back to their home town and now played at the Withdean Stadium, an athletics stadium which had been adapted to house the football team. Transport arrangements are unique to Brighton because no one is allowed to travel to the ground by private car to satisfy the local residents' requirement for as little disruption as possible on match days. All car owners have to park on one of two designated car parks, one near the A27 on a dual carriageway and the second at the University in the town centre, and then take the specially laid-on public transport buses to and from the ground using the travel pass attached to the matchday ticket. All matches were all-ticket because of the reduced capacity of the stadium. At that time all the local buses carried the name of a well-known, or former well-known, local personality. How appropriate it was to travel on the bus named 'Richie Barker'. In addition to the almost unique travel arrangements, after matches it is a requirement of the use of the stadium that volunteers pick litter from the surrounding streets to keep the area tidy.

The Silkmen side was somewhat depleted through injury and suspension, resulting in three members of the reserve side and manager Peter Davenport named on the substitutes' bench. With Richie Barker unavailable, this gave Davenport the opportunity to introduce his prodigy striker Damien Whitehead, who scored his first League goal in the match. This was not an encounter for the few Silkmen fans present to remember as the side were soundly beaten 5–2.

But it was a different story the following Saturday when a struggling Shrewsbury side visited the Moss Rose. Although the visitors took a fifth-minute lead, Macclesfield never looked in any danger of losing this match which they won 4–2. Simon Collins and Graeme Tomlinson were on the score sheet but it was young Damien Whitehead who stole the headlines with two goals which he hammered home to lift the side to 12th position having been as low as 16th at one stage in the month. In this match the Shrewsbury 'keeper was Paul Edwards, a cousin of Damien Whitehead.

Damien Whitehead (right) with his cousin, Shrewsbury goalkeeper Paul Edwards.

April

A goalless draw at Leyton Orient was followed by a one-man match-winning performance at the Moss Rose against Plymouth Argyle which saw the Silkmen easy winners, scoring four goals against a solitary goal by the visitors. It was well and truly young Damien Whitehead's match as he scored two goals and was provider for the other two. John Askey opened the scoring in the second minute, converting a pinpoint cross from Whitehead. Kieron Durkan added a second on 15 minutes when he converted another Whitehead cross and on the half-hour Whitehead scored with a brilliant solo effort after beating two men and dummying the 'keeper. In the second half Plymouth pulled a goal back but shortly afterwards were reduced to 10 men. With a minute to go, Whitehead raced onto a John Askey flick before committing the 'keeper and sliding the ball home.

Kieron Durkan making another excellent cross at Carlisle United.

Simon Davies splashing his way forward against Chester City.

Another victory came at Carlisle United, with Damien Whitehead on the score sheet again, heading home in the second half to secure all three points. After this match Damien signed a two-year extension to his contract but ironically failed to score another goal in the remaining matches of the season.

Chester City were the next visitors. Following very heavy rain before the match, the ground had drained fairly well with the exception of the Estate side corners.

Chester were fighting a relegation battle and the match was proving to be a rather dull affair, but there was some joy for the home crowd when John Askey gave the Silkmen the lead in the first half. Proceedings were livened up at the start of the second half when a male Chester fan streaked onto the pitch and after a moment or two running around, belly flopped twice into a pool of water near the away end corner before being escorted off the pitch. Now, whether it was because of this incident or the playing conditions is hard to say, but almost immediately Rae Ingram attempted a back pass which was intercepted by Luke Beckett who scored the equaliser.

A disappointing 3–2 defeat at Torquay, with the home side's winning goal coming with only seconds left to play, meant that the Silkmen's ambitions of reaching a Play-off position were extinguished. Another defeat completed the month when Rochdale ran out winners 2–1, with Macclesfield's 'keeper Lee Martin dismissed for handling his ball outside the area in the second half. In this match Mike Bamber made his senior debut from the substitutes' bench, which must have been one of the shortest debuts ever recorded when he was on the pitch for only 21 seconds.

May

Over recent weeks contract negotiations had been ongoing between the club and manager Peter Davenport but had reached a difficult point before the final match of the season, resulting in Davenport not travelling to Halifax Town. John Askey, Steve Wood and chairman Eddie Furlong took on the joint responsibility to select and manage the team. The highlight of the match was Macclesfield's winning goal scored by captain and defender Darren Tinson, who dashed unchallenged some 50 yards to slip the ball under the advancing 'keeper from 16 yards. It was Darren's first League goal in 127 Football League matches and was a fitting end to a season in which he was the only player to be ever present. Former Silkman Mark Lillis was the Halifax manager, and after the goal had been scored the Halifax fans were calling for his dismissal.

Having reached sixth position early in the season, before plummeting to 21st at one stage, together with injury problems in the final weeks, to finish in 13th position with 65 points was a reasonable outcome overall.

Shortly after the match relations were patched up between the club and Peter Davenport, who signed a new two-year deal. John Askey was voted Player of the Year. John was still a most influential and effective force in the side at the age of 35, completing the season as second-top scorer with 15 goals in all competitions, only two goals behind the leading scorer, Richie Barker.

Richie Barker capped his excellent season by being named in the Professional Footballers' Association Third Division Team of the Year.

Cup Competitions

In the **Auto Windscreens Shield**, the Silkmen received a bye in the first round and travelled to Rochdale for the second round where they excelled in the first half, taking a two-goal lead after only 14 minutes. Rochdale came back strongly in the second half and scored two goals, the second of which came in the 87th minute. At this time there were certain Cup competitions where the golden goal rule applied, where extra-time was played until a goal was scored, immediately ending the match in favour of the scorers. Unfortunately, it was Rochdale who scored a golden goal in the 107th minute to put them through to the third round.

In the competition a modification to the '10-yard rule' was introduced as an experiment for the first time in professional football anywhere in the world. The rule came into force if the award of a free-kick was followed by a player being cautioned for any one of four offences, namely: dissent; delaying the restart of the game by kicking, carrying or throwing the ball away; failing to retreat 10 yards; or any other form of unsporting behaviour.

These offences resulted in the ball being moved forward 10 yards in a direct line with the centre of the goal. Initially, after the ball had been moved forward the 10 yards, it was possible that the free-kick would take place within the penalty area, although the rule was subsequently amended so that the ball could only be moved as far as the penalty box and not taken inside, even if the ball could not be moved forward the full 10 yards. However, this experiment never became law and eventually lapsed.

For the second season running Stoke City were the opponents in the **Worthington Cup**, but there was no repeat of the previous year's victory for the Silkmen. The first leg at the Moss Rose ended in a 1–1 draw but at the Britannia Stadium Stoke ran out easy winners 3–0 to win the tie 4–1 on

Goalmouth action against Hull City.

aggregate. In the second leg, because Steve Hitchen and Simon Collins were out injured and Rae Ingram was suspended, striker Richie Barker played at centre-back leaving John Askey as the sole striker.

It was a hat-trick of senior Cup defeats at the first hurdle when Hull City were victors in the first round of the **FA Cup**. A goalless draw at the Moss Rose was followed by a comprehensive 4–0 win for Hull City, who were three goals to the good after 30 minutes in the replay.

However, Peter Davenport claimed his first piece of silverware when the **Cheshire Senior Cup** was won for a record 20th time. Two goals by Ben Sedgemore ensured victory over Altrincham 2–1 at Wincham Park, Witton Albion's ground. This was the last occasion the Silkmen won the trophy. League clubs did not enter the competition in the 2007–08 season and a new competition solely for League clubs, the Cheshire County FA Premier Cup, was introduced in the 2008–09 season.

The Cheshire Senior Cup.

CHAPTER FOUR: 2000–2001

DAVY AND GIL IN CHARGE

Pre-Season

There was the best possible start for the new season when it was announced that the transfer embargo had been lifted by the Football League following the repayment of the loan obtained from the Professional Footballers' Association in December 1999 to pay players' wages.

Peter Davenport remained as manager having patched up his differences with the board and Alan Preston was appointed assistant manger. With the transfer embargo lifted the management team lost no time in signing Lee Glover, a former Nottingham Forest striker, to work alongside Richie Barker. However, overall there were few pre-season signings with only two further additions – Tony Bullock, a 'keeper signed from Barnsley, and midfielder Gary Twynham from Hednesford.

Similarly there were few departures – Paul Ware and Simon Davies both moved to Rochdale and Graham Tomlinson moved south to Exeter City.

New signing Gary Twynham.

Friendly Matches

The first four matches saw visits to non-League sides Leek Town, Chorley, Northwich Victoria and Hyde United, with the only defeat coming at Chorley, the match finishing 2–0.

There then followed three matches at the Moss Rose against League opposition. In the first match Stockport County won 2–1 including a goal from Chris Byrne. At half-time the score was 0–0 but after the Silkmen had made five substitutions, Stockport proved to be the stronger side and scored two goals in the 67th and 71st minutes to win the match.

For the second consecutive year, the Silkmen triumphed over Port Vale, on this occasion the score was 2–1 with a skilful goal from Lee Glover following a Gerry McMahon free-kick, and the second goal came from Gary Twynham. In this match Lithuanian international Andrejus Tereskinas was seen playing for the Silkmen for the first time, but due to administrative problems relating to his transfer he did not appear in a competitive match for many months.

The final match was a hard-fought encounter against Division One's Crewe Alexandra, who included former Silkmen Neil Sorvel and Efe Sodje in their line up. Newly signed 'keeper Tony Bullock was the key player and made several saves to keep his clean sheet, but the team as a whole fought hard throughout the match and held the visitors to a goalless draw.

SEASON REVIEW

August

In the first competitive match of the season the Silkmen found themselves up against a strong Scunthorpe United side who took all three points with a stunning Lee Hodges goal, who had started his run from the half-way line, but Macclesfield unfortunately let themselves down by missing early chances.

A visit to Shrewsbury kept the Silkmen faithful on the edge of their seats when Steve Jagielka scored twice for the Shrews in the first half, with a Ben Sedgemore goal sandwiched in-between. Referee Paul Rejer had annoyed manager Peter Davenport when he disallowed a goal from a quickly-taken free-kick by Gary Tywnham in the 11th minute because he had not lined up the defensive wall. Davenport told the *Macclesfield Express* 'we were awarded a free-kick, the whistle had been blown and Gary decided to take the kick quickly. It was an absolute nonsense decision.' However, a tremendous finish by Macclesfield brought four corners within two minutes, the last of which was converted by Darren Tinson in the 90th minute to take a share of the points in a match when Shrewsbury were celebrating their 50th year as a Football League club.

The next match was a goalless draw against Hull City, but the month ended with an interesting 4–4 draw at Mansfield Town. It was the first match at Field Mill following extensive building alterations, with ground safety only given clearance at 11.30 on the morning of the match. In the first half the Silkmen were leading 2–1 following goals by John Askey and Ben Sedgemore, but Darrell Clarke equalised on the stroke of half-time which gave Mansfield the momentum at the start of the second half. The home side then took a 4–2 lead but Macclesfield dug in, Richie Barker pulling a goal back, and when Ian Bowling, the Mansfield 'keeper, spilled the ball in the 90th minute, Damien Whitehead was on hand to head home for a share of the points. With only three points accumulated the team completed the month in 17th position.

At the end of the month, following protracted negotiations, no-nonsense, hard tackling left-back Danny Adams was signed from Altrincham for a fee of £25,000.

September

In the League the month started with a 2–0 defeat at Exeter City but the team redeemed themselves only three days later with a 2–0 victory against Lincoln City, with both goals scored by young-gun Damien Whitehead.

But at Hartlepool Macclesfield had to stage a fightback yet again when the home side took a 2–0 lead, but the side battled back into the match and Richie Barker headed home from 10 yards to convert a George Abbey cross and Lee Glover, with nerves of steel, scored a 90th minute penalty to earn a 2–2 draw.

The highlight of the month was the first-ever televised live match at the Moss Rose when Darlington were the visitors. The Silkmen started well, taking an early lead through a Ben Sedgemore goal, and controlled much of the match, but there was a disappointing end when Lee Nogan equalised for the visitors. Before the match, entertainment was provided by the East Cheshire Pipe Band which included in its ranks the club's solicitor, Reg Flowers. Jimmy Read was the matchday mascot, his father being a life-long Macclesfield supporter, and

Young-gun Damien Whitehead (right), scorer of both goals against Lincoln City.

Dave Westbury, the PA announcer, interviewed Jimmy on the pitch and he was allowed to 'score' a goal at the Star Lane End. Half-time entertainment saw two simultaneous football matches (one in each half) when the Macclesfield Ladies Under-12s took on Macclesfield Junior Blues at the Star Lane End, and at the Silkmen Terrace End there was a match between two teams from Macclesfield Boys' Football Club. With the *Macclesfield Express* as one of the matchball sponsors, Vic Barlow, a satirical columnist in the paper, wrote a lighthearted account of his visit to the Moss Rose. He mentioned that Tony Bullock had dyed his hair 'yellow', immediately behind him had sat a gentleman in full Scottish national dress and that a long-lost 'friend' had slapped him on the back in the toilets with the result that his glasses ended up in the urinal!

Finally a 4–1 defeat came at Chesterfield, who were strong candidates for the League title at the time and went on to gain automatic promotion in third position. Nevertheless, there was a marginal improvement in Macclesfield's League position to 16th.

During the month former West Ham United midfielder Kevin Keen was signed having been released by Stoke City, and he went on to form a formidable centre-midfield partnership with Chris Priest.

Vastly experienced midfielder Kevin Keen, signed from Stoke City.

October

October was an excellent month for results overall, starting with three consecutive victories. At Barnet two goals by Lee Glover provided a 2–0 victory which was followed by a 2–1 victory at high-flying Cheltenham Town, with goals coming from Rae Ingram and the evergreen Steve Wood in Macclesfield's 150th League match. In a rather scrappy game the Silkmen won 2–1 against Torquay United at the Moss Rose, the goals coming when when Darren Tinson met a Danny Adams corner to flick the ball home and when Richie Barker took a through ball from Karl Munroe to score the second goal.

A 2–1 defeat at Blackpool was followed by a disappointing 2–2 draw at Rochdale, when the Silkmen had taken a 2–0 lead in the 33rd minute with goals from Lee Glover and Richie Barker, only to see Rochdale score two second-half goals including the equaliser by former Silkman Paul Ware, and the month was wrapped up with a goalless draw against Halifax Town. Nevertheless, the number of points had been doubled to 22 with a respectable 10th position in the League table.

As part of their work in the community, players Rae Ingram, Mike Bamber, Ben Sedgemore and Darren Tinson represented the squad as part of the national NSPCC Full Stop 2000 campaign to raise awareness of child cruelty and neglect. Schools were being invited to accept and raffle a signed football on behalf of the NSPCC and in return nominate a Macclesfield Town player, who would then go to the adopted school to draw the winning ticket and run coaching sessions.

The long-term loan scheme resulted in 17-year-old Andrew Tunnicliffe being signed in October to the end of the season from Manchester City, with City paying his wages while he was on loan at Macclesfield.

November

Results in November were a complete contrast to October. A 3–1 defeat at Southend United saw 'keeper Tony Bullock dismissed in the 17th minute for two bookable offences. He then disgraced himself on leaving the pitch, resulting in him being charged by the Football Association with five offences, and he was lucky to only receive a two-match ban. Ben Sedgemore took over in goal and was hardly tested until late in the match when substitute Ben Abbey gave the home side the lead in the 67th minute, only to see Karl Munroe equalise a minute later. However, goals for the home side in the 89th and 90th minute saw them take all three points.

Against Brighton & Hove Albion, who included striker Bobby Zamora in their starting line up, there was a much improved performance but, despite goalscoring opportunities for both sides, the match ended goalless and following a 2–1 defeat at Leyton Orient on a heavy pitch, the Silkmen dropped to 13th position.

December

December proved to be quite an eventful month, but it started with another defeat, this time at Kidderminster Harriers. Lee Glover had given the Silkmen an early lead only to see Kidderminster score two goals before half-time. Midway through the second half the floodlights failed and the referee had to take the players off the pitch for some 11 minutes. There were no further goals.

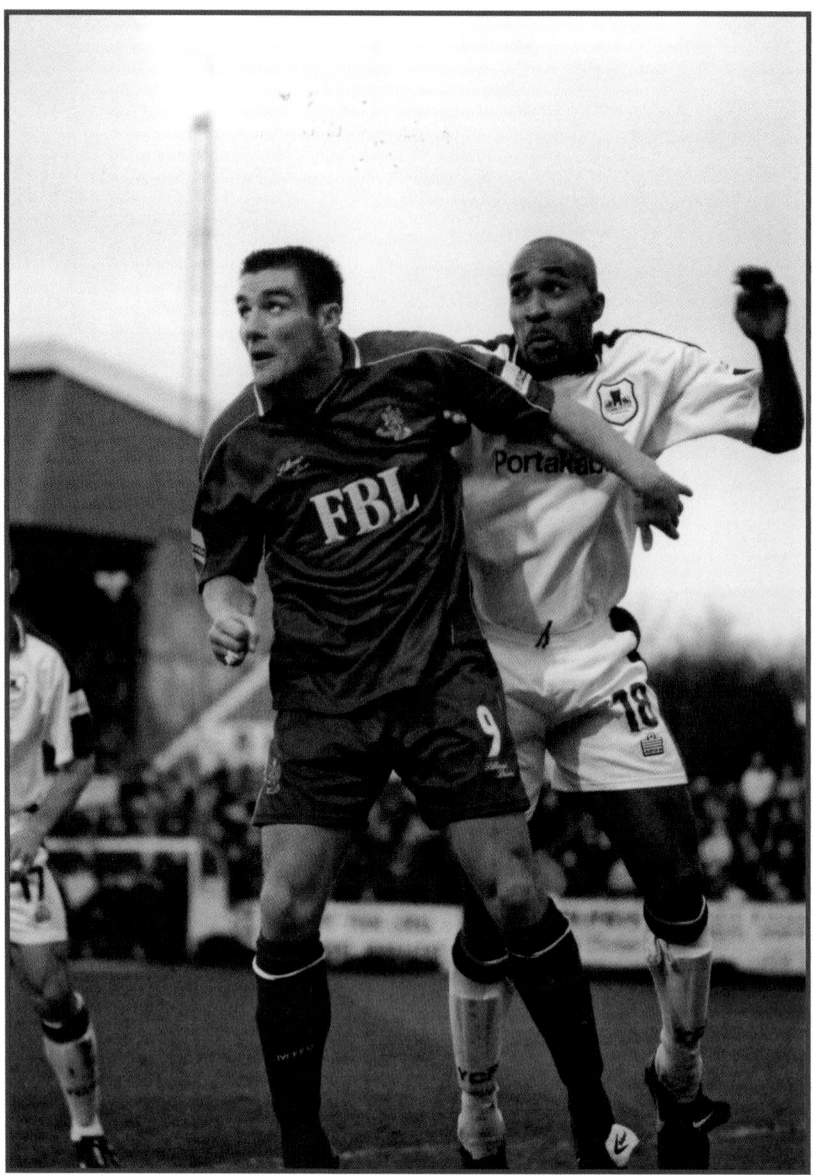

Top scorer Richie Barker (left) was placed on the transfer list when he could not agree terms with the club.

However, a visit to Kidderminster does not solely revolve around football as their refreshments are top class, especially the famous Aggborough soup, which is a meal in itself, and cottage pie.

Just after the match it was announced that striker Richie Barker had been placed on the transfer list because the club and the player could not agree terms, which were said to be the best ever offered by the club.

The next match saw the Silkmen win for the first time in two months, with a Richie Barker strike gaining the points against Carlisle United, but the next two matches ended in defeat against Cardiff City (2–1) and York City (1–0). However, both goals were disputed in the Cardiff match as it was claimed that Lee Martin had been obstructed for the first goal, and even the Cardiff players argued whether the ball had crossed the line for the second goal after the ball had hit the underside of the crossbar and bounced down. Nevertheless, the assistant referee gave the goal.

After the Boxing Day match against York City it was announced that the director of football, Gil Prescott, had been asked to work with the first-team squad, alongside Peter Davenport, to turn around the run of poor results, with

Gil having the final responsibility for team selection. Peter Davenport felt unable to accept the board's decision and his contract was terminated, a move which resulted in Gil Prescott taking control of first-team affairs in addition to his other duties. After taking charge, Gil told the *Macclesfield Express* 'I'm proud to be in charge at the end of the day, though the circumstances don't fill me with pleasure. I'd be happy to finish my career here. Until the board tell me otherwise, I'm happy to stay here.'

Gil immediately set about his task by involving Alan Preston, his assistant manager, John Askey, the reserve-team manager, Norman Bernard, a first-team coach and Mick Holgate, from the centre of excellence, and allowing them to give their input to first-team affairs.

January

The team started the New Year in 15th position with a total of 26 points ahead of Gil's first match in charge away at Scunthorpe. The usual 4-4-2

The popular Gil Prescott was appointed manager in December.

formation was not for Gil, as he favoured the 'Christmas tree' formation with the starting line up as follows:

Bullock
Hitchen Tinson Collins Adams
Wood
Durkan Priest Sedgemore
Keen
Askey

The side took an early second-half lead of 2–1 through goals from Kieron Durkan and Kevin Keen, and victory looked on the cards until Darryn Stamp spoilt the day with an equaliser in the 88th minute.

Having received identical bids for striker Richie Barker from Rochdale and Rotherham, Barker himself decided to join Rotherham, giving him the chance to play at a higher level only seven miles from his home. The transfer fee was set to reach £100,000 dependent on the number of appearances made at Rotherham and them gaining promotion.

A goalless draw at Hull City was followed by a single-goal defeat by Mansfield Town, a match which had been moved to a Sunday in an attempt to bring in more supporters, but there was only a near normal crowd of 1,893. At York City there was a well deserved victory by three goals to one with an own-goal and two goals by Chris Priest to avenge the Boxing Day defeat. However, the month ended with a 5–2 defeat by Cardiff City at the Moss Rose, with Robbie Earnshaw living up to his fine reputation by scoring two of Cardiff's goals. In this match striker Richard Tracey made his debut following a move from Carlisle United and scored with his first touch only a minute after his introduction from the substitutes' bench. A month-end position of 16th followed an indifferent month.

February

A 3–1 victory against Plymouth was secured by the partnership of Chris Priest and Damien Whitehead, who combined for all three goals. With Plymouth leading 1–0, in the 70th minute Plymouth failed to clear a corner allowing Chris Priest to drill home from 15 yards. Three minutes later Damien Whitehead charged down the Plymouth 'keeper's clearance before tapping the ball into an empty net, and to round off the scoring, Whitehead back-heeled the ball for Chris Priest to thump the ball home from 15 yards.

In a scrappy game at Exeter the points were shared in a 0–0 draw, but then two goals from Damien Whitehead secured a 2–1 victory against Shrewsbury Town at the Moss Rose, which turned out to be Ben Sedgemore's last match for the Silkmen before his transfer to Lincoln City for a fee of £12,000.

And then came a 1–0 home defeat at the hands of in-form Hartlepool United, who took their unbeaten run to 12 games. The match was notable for the one and only appearance by the Lithuanian international full-back Andrejus Tereskinas, who had been ineligible to play until the middle of February 2000 because of difficulties in obtaining his work permit. Prior to joining the Silkmen on non-contract terms, Andrejus played for Skonto Riga, even making appearances in the Champions League qualifying rounds, and, at the time, he held the record for the most number of international appearances for Lithuania. Andrejus had made two appearances in the pre-season friendly matches, but after his introduction from the substitutes' bench in the 39th minute replacing the

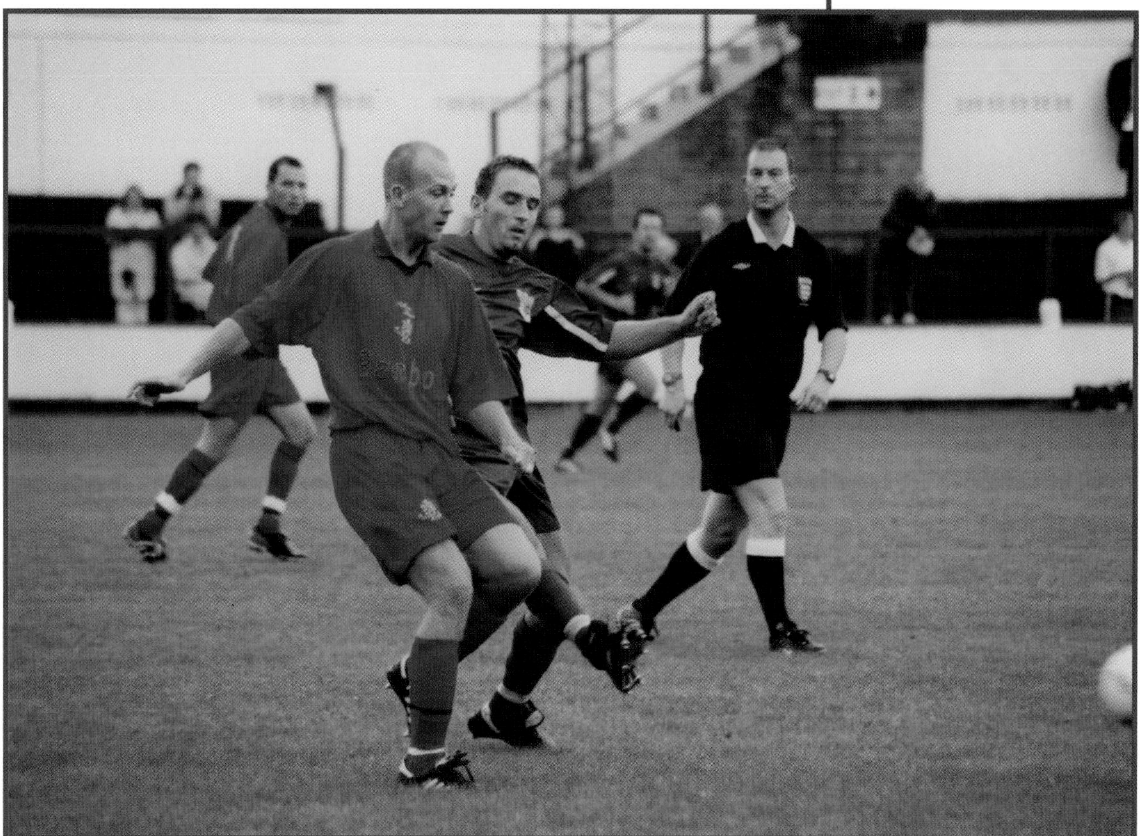

Midfielder Chris Priest (Bee Bo kit) enjoyed a superb match at Plymouth Argyle.

injured Chris Priest his performance was a disappointment, especially as he was asked to play out of his usual position of left-back in a wide left-midfield role.

A Tuesday evening 2–1 victory at Lincoln City saw Darren Tinson scoring in the third minute and Lincoln equalising in the 66th minute, only for John Askey to grab an 89th-minute winner when he headed home a Kieron Durkan cross in front of the travelling fans.

The final match of the month was a tale of two penalties at Darlington. The first was scored by Kieron Durkan in the third minute after the Darlington 'keeper had brought down John Askey. However, there was controversy for the Darlington penalty when Steve Hitchen was rather harshly adjudged to have brought down Clint Marcelle, and Lee Martin saved the resultant penalty only for the assistant referee to say that Lee Martin had moved (albeit very marginally), and Mark Ford made no mistake with the retaken penalty, ramming it home to earn a share of the points.

February was a much more successful month as the team took 11 points and moved up to 11th position.

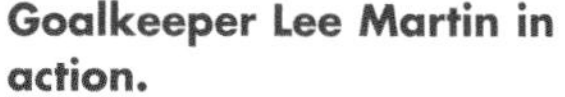

Goalkeeper Lee Martin in action.

March

A 2–1 defeat by high-flying Chesterfield was followed by a 1–1 draw at Cheltenham, a match which the home side could have won in the dying minutes but for Macclesfield 'keeper Lee Martin, who dramatically saved Russell Milton's penalty in time added on.

Prior to the home match against Barnet, the McAlpine Stand on the Estate Road side of the ground was opened by former manager Sammy McIlroy. This all-seater stand has a total capacity of 1,463, of which 413 seats are allocated to visiting supporters, although for this first match only the home end was used. The logos of Adidas and Alfred McAlpine Construction Limited were incorporated on the seating at either end with the letters 'MTFC' on the central seating. The corporate and IT facilities had not been installed at that time. In addition, a cheque for £267,686 was presented to Alan Cash by Sport England for the funding of youth development over a four-year period. Macclesfield celebrated in style with a 3–0 win, with two goals from Kieron Durkan and one from Lee Glover.

The match which was due to be played in the middle of the month at Torquay United was postponed because of a waterlogged pitch at Plainmoor.

Before the transfer deadline two players left Macclesfield and two players joined the squad. Gregor Rioch moved to Shrewsbury Town and Tony Bullock moved to Lincoln City. Chris Shuker, a wide midfield player, came in on loan from Manchester City and 'keeper Steve Wilson was signed on loan from Hull City.

First-half goals from Richard Tracey and John Askey ensured a 2–1 win over Blackpool, but a 1–0 defeat at Carlisle left the Silkmen in 12th position. In the Carlisle match Karl Munroe was dismissed for the second consecutive match, resulting in a seven-match ban.

April

Alan Preston, the assistant manager, left the club by mutual consent in April and at the same time John Askey joined the coaching staff but still remained as a player.

On the match front there was a good start with a 1–0 home win against Kidderminster Harriers courtesy of a Chris Shuker goal. However, Darren Tinson went off injured during this match and as he did not appear in the following match it was the end to a run of 97 consecutive first-team appearances. The re-arranged match at Torquay saw the home side win 2–0, but there was some amusement for the travelling fans when the registration numbers of 11 illegally parked cars were announced over the PA system, including that of the Macclesfield chairman!

A goalless draw against Rochdale saw Lee Martin brilliantly save another penalty, on this occasion from Gary Jones, but Halifax Town were easy victors 3–1 at the Shay. On-loan and very experienced 'keeper Steve Wilson made his Macclesfield debut (Lee Martin was ill with 'flu) against Southend United at the Moss Rose and kept a clean sheet in the 1–0 win courtesy of a Lee Glover penalty, but in the next match a Bobby Zamora hat-trick ensured that Brighton & Hove Albion had an easy 4–1 win at the Withdean Stadium.

May

In the final match of the season the East Cheshire Pipe Band performed before the kick-off and Tom Pendry MP made the presentation of a symbolic cheque for £1.38 million by the Football Trust towards the cost of the McAlpine Stand and ground redevelopments. Leyton Orient secured a Play-off position with a 2–0 win to leave the Silkmen in 14th position at the end of a disappointing season overall; although Gil Prescott had steadied the ship and towards the end of the season there were injuries to some of the key players, including Rae Ingram and Kieron Durkan.

Striker Lee Glover – the Silkmen's penalty taker.

Defender Darren Tinson – Player of the Year.

The Player of the Year award went to Darren Tinson, who had only missed one match during the season and had proved, yet again, his outstanding ability as a strong central-defender, and Lee Glover completed the season as top scorer.

Cup Competitions

In the first round of the **Worthington Cup** a Dean Holdsworth goal gave Bolton Wanderers a 1–0 lead in the first leg at the Moss Rose, but it was a completely different story at the Reebok Stadium in the second leg when Macclesfield defeated the previous year's semi-finalists. Goals from Ben Sedgemore, Karl Munroe and Richie Barker gave the Silkmen a 3–0 lead, only for Michael Ricketts to pull a goal back for the aggregate score to stand at 3–2, leaving the Silkmen to see out a nervous final 12 minutes for one of their best-ever victories. In the second round the Silkmen had taken a 1–0 lead at the Riverside Stadium but goals in the 87th and 90th minutes gave Middlesbrough the upper hand in front of a crowd of 5,144, their lowest-ever attendance. In the second leg, Ben Sedgemore scored from the penalty spot but it was a hat-trick by the Columbian striker Hamilton Ricard, his first in English football, which gave Middlesbrough victory by an aggregate score of 5–2. Paul Ince, later to become manager at Macclesfield, played in both legs of this tie.

The first round of the **FA Cup** saw Oxford United visit the Moss Rose and take a second-half lead to win the tie, but not before the Oxford fans had unhooked the goal netting twice, the second instance resulting in a five-minute delay before Lee Glover's 89th-minute penalty miss.

There was no luck in the **LDV Vans Trophy** again. Having received a bye in the first round, Chesterfield won the second round 4–2 on a frost covered pitch.

There was a fascinating and very open match in the semi-final of the **Cheshire Senior Cup** against Stockport County. Stockport were leading 3–2 at the interval but with Lee Martin, the Silkmen 'keeper, injured in the first half central-defender Paul O'Neill took over in goal. Macclesfield managed to draw level at 4–4 but despite a fifth goal for the Silkmen by Rickie Lambert, County scored a further four goals to win 8–5.

Player of the Year

1997–98
Steve Wood

1998–99
Steve Hitchen

1999–2000
John Askey

2000–01
Darren Tinson

2001–02
Danny Adams

2002–03
Steve Wilson

2003–04
Matthew Tipton

2004–05
Paul Harsley

2005–06
Danny Whitaker

2006–07
Kevin McIntyre

2007–08
Terry Dunfield

2008–09
Paul Morgan

CHAPTER FIVE: 2001–2002

A NEW MANAGER AND THE RESERVE TEAM TRIUMPH

Pre-Season

In complete contrast to the previous season there were several new signings, including the welcome return of midfielder Chris Byrne, who moved from Stockport County. Chris had made his mark for the Silkmen in the Conference Championship season in 1996–1997 when his goals, including a hat-trick in the final match, played a big part in the push for promotion. Goalkeeper Steve Wilson, on loan at the end of the previous season, signed permanently from Hull City, and trainee Michael Welch was given his first professional contract.

Bermudan international striker Kyle Lightbourne was signed from Stoke City and other pre-season signings were Andy McAvoy (Hartlepool), Richard Eyre (Port Vale) and Steven Hodgson (Manchester City).

Among the players released were Simon Collins and Andrejus Tereskinas. The players who moved to other clubs were Rae Ingram (Port Vale), Kieron Durkan (Rochdale) and Steve Wood (Stalybridge). Both Kieron and Rae had made a

Goalkeeper Steve Wilson, who was signed from Hull City.

'Goodbye Woody' after eight successful seasons.

significant contribution during their time at the Moss Rose but the greatest loss was that of Steve Wood, who had been at the club since the start of the 1993–1994 season and made 333 appearances (League and non-League) and scored 68 goals. A character both on and off the pitch, Steve was a firm favourite of the fans, being voted Player of the Year on two occasions, and he was top scorer for two consecutive seasons – quite an achievement for a midfielder.

Moving from the Manchester United Centre of Excellence, Andrew Balderstone, son-in-law of Sir Bobby Charlton, was appointed first-team physiotherapist.

Top 10 Total Player Appearances
(Since August 1997)

Player	Appearances
Darren Tinson	297
John Askey	206
Danny Whitaker	202
Matthew Tipton	184
Steve Hitchen	175
Steve Wood	172
Danny Adams	169
Chris Priest	169
Steve Wilson	154
Kevin McIntyre	153

Friendly Matches

A visit to the club's near neighbours Congleton is always appreciated. In this pre-season match both teams gave as many players as possible the opportunity of some time on the pitch, Macclesfield using a total of 19 players and winning the match 2–0. Stoke City provided a sterner test at the Moss Rose, but they only managed to win by a single Brynjar Gunnarsson goal. A young Macclesfield XI then travelled to Kidsgrove where neither side could score.

Preston North End ran out easy winners 4–0 with goals from Michael Keane, Iain Anderson and two from £4 million-rated Jon Macken, showing that they were easily two Divisions better than Macclesfield.

A goalless draw at Altrincham did not do justice to the fact that this match was long-serving Graham Heathcote's Testimonial. However, at half-time there was a five-a-side match with Altrincham Veterans playing Macclesfield Veterans who included George Shepherd, Graham Tobin, Nigel Shaw and John Timmons in their line up. At full-time numerous former Altrincham players were introduced to the crowd before playing a 30-minute match.

There was a much better performance when the whole team played as a cohesive unit, beating Tranmere Rovers 2–0 with goals from Kyle Lightbourne and Richard Eyre. The last match finished goalless against Bury but this was another encouraging performance by the Silkmen. With two good performances under their belt the future looked reasonably good, but how deceptive pre-season performances can be...

SEASON REVIEW

August

Swansea City were the first visitors to the Moss Rose and by now manager Gil Prescott had reverted to the more conventional 4-4-2 formation with the following line up:

Martin
Hitchen Tinson Ridler Adams
McAvoy Keen Byrne Eyre
Glover Lightbourne

The visitors got off to a flying start with two goals in the first 22 minutes, but a first-half penalty gave the home side some hope. In the second half Chris Byrne almost equalised but a late penalty gave the visitors a 3–1 victory. With the fitting-out of the President's Bar and the McIlroy Suite complete, these facilities were used for the first time at this match when 125 guests were invited for a pre-match meal.

As part of the 2001 Japan Festival, an event held every five years, the Silkmen were hosts to a team from Tsukuba University. Prior to the match there was a presentation to the Japanese team of a framed certificate in Japanese to commemorate the match. The certificate had been prepared with the help of AstraZeneca staff in Japan. A mixture of Silkmen youth and reserve-team players matched the ability of the University side and both sides created scoring opportunities, the Japanese side showing speed and skill, especially their 'keeper who was extremely acrobatic. In the end a penalty scored by Rickie Lambert secured the match for the Silkmen.

The first away match of the season at Rochdale was evenly contended with both sides hitting the woodwork and both 'keepers on top form, but the match ended 1–1 with goals from Rochdale veteran Tony Ford and a Lee Glover penalty for Macclesfield.

The Tsukuba University squad.

A lacklustre match at Rushden & Diamonds ended in a goalless draw, and the month ended with a 4–0 defeat at Mansfield, leaving the Silkmen without a win in 23rd position.

September

The Silkmen fans were treated to an absolutely thrilling match against Scunthorpe, who opened the scoring in the sixth minute before Richard Tracey converted a chip from Lee Glover to equalise. Scunthorpe then took the lead for the second time but on the stroke of half-time Lee Glover converted a penalty to make the score 2–2. In the second half Scunthorpe took the lead for the third time, but the Silkmen were not to be outdone, with play sweeping up the field allowing Lee Glover and Richard Tracey to combine again when Glover played a one-two with Tracey before rounding two players to score with a left-foot shot to equalise for the third time. With Macclesfield in the ascendancy, Richard Tracey headed home from close range in the 86th minute to secure the first win of the season.

There then followed two goalless draws, first away at Halifax Town and then at home to Hull City where Steve Wilson was delighted to have kept a clean sheet against his former employers.

A Tuesday evening visit to Oxford United's new Kassam Stadium brought the second

Goalscorer at Oxford, Bermudian International Kyle Lightbourne, in celebratory mood.

Lee Glover (number 10, above) and Richard Tracey scored match-winning goals against Scunthorpe United in September.

win of the season with a powerful display and goals from both strikers, Lee Glover and Kyle Lightbourne. Having kept a clean sheet in the previous three matches, Plymouth ended this run when they won 2–1. The month ended with two drawn matches, the first against Darlington (1–1) in which both teams worked hard, and the second at bottom-placed Exeter (0–0) where both sides tried their best to grab a winning goal. Overall September was a much better month which lifted the side to 16th position.

October

There was a disappointing start to the month with the team losing 1–0 to Kidderminster Harriers; however, everyone was shocked when Gil Prescott relinquished control of the first team so that he could concentrate on his duties as director of football. Gil stated that it was necessary for the manager of the first team to be able to concentrate solely on that role, which he had been unable to do. Kevin Keen was appointed caretaker manager.

Kevin had a dream start with a 2–0 victory at Bristol Rovers with Macclesfield playing excellent passing football and fully deserving the win, but Kevin was then faced with three consecutive defeats. In another disappointing performance by the Silkmen, Lincoln grabbed all three points with a 90th-minute goal. Worse was to come in the following game when Karl Munroe lost possession in the middle of the field, allowing Adam Boyd to score the winning goal for 10-man Hartlepool United. And in their 200th League match Macclesfield contrived to lose at York City to a 94th-minute goal. This poor set of results left the Silkmen languishing in 23rd position.

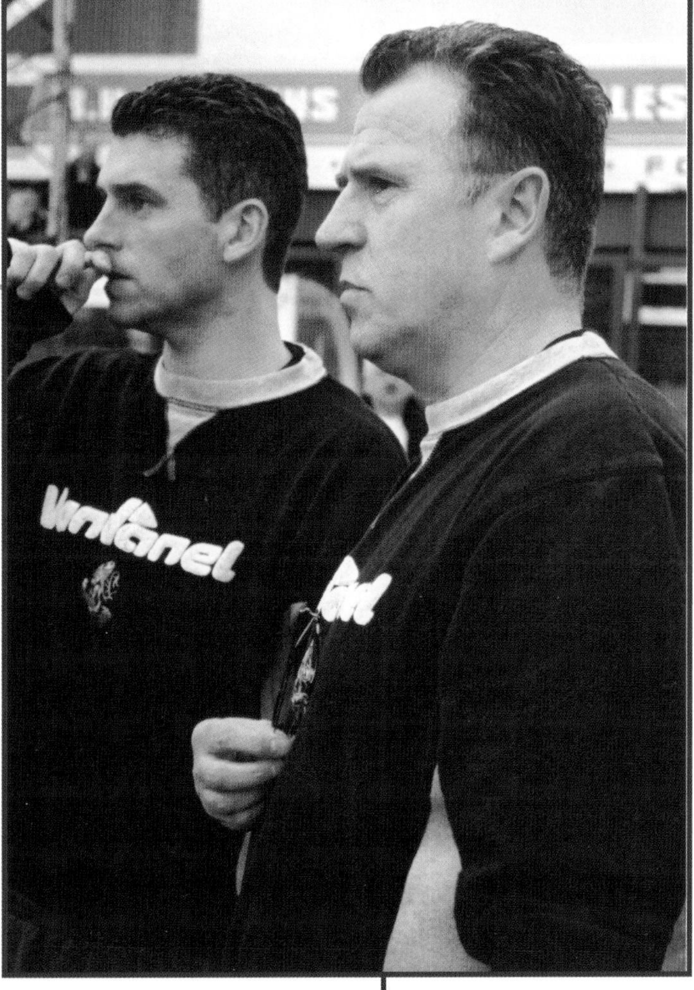

David Moss (right), newly appointed manager, with first-team coach John Askey.

November

Kyle Lightbourne rescued a point against Carlisle at the beginning of November when he converted a Kevin Keen corner for a 1–1 draw.

David Moss was then announced as the surprise appointment as manager. He had enjoyed a successful playing career at Luton Town under David Pleat where Brian Horton was a fellow player and, more recently, he had been assistant manager at Stockport County, Huddersfield Town and then Manchester City under manager Brian Horton. Kevin Keen and John Askey remained as first-team coaches.

Kevin Keen's final match in charge was at Southend United, where the home side took a one-goal first-half lead, after Macclesfield's Karl Muroe had been dismissed for two bookable offences. With the Silkmen looking at another defeat, following permission from the chairman, David Moss went into the dressing room at half-time to take charge, but despite a determined second-half defensive display by the Silkmen, Southend scored two late goals to win 3–1.

And then, at long last, the friendly match against a Northern Ireland XI took place which had been arranged as part of Sammy McIlroy's release to become the Northern Ireland manager. Past and present players formed the Macclesfield team which was (past players' 'current' teams in brackets):

> Price (Telford), Abbey, Adams, Priest, Howarth (Cheltenham), Sodje (Crewe), McAvoy, Byrne, Whitehead, Askey and Matias (Walsall). And on the substitutes' bench: Bullock, Bamber, Shuttleworth, Eyre, Munroe, Wolley, Sorvel (Crewe), Barker (Rotherham), Morris, Whittaker, O'Neill and Hodgson.

The Northern Ireland team's initial line up was:

> Taylor, Dixon, Capaldi, Duff, Burns, McCann, Carson, Toner, Quinn, Feeney and Jones.

This was a most enjoyable game with plenty of passing football played. Northern Ireland scored twice through Feeney and Quinn but Neil Sorvel pulled a late goal back for the Silkmen. All the Macclesfield returnees received an excellent welcome from the crowd but the biggest cheer went up for Sammy McIlroy when he played for the final 20 minutes. The only disappointment of the evening was that the crowd only amounted to 1,278, which included a significant number of Northland Ireland fans who thoroughly enjoyed themselves on the Silkmen Terrace and were often seen marching up and down to their drummers.

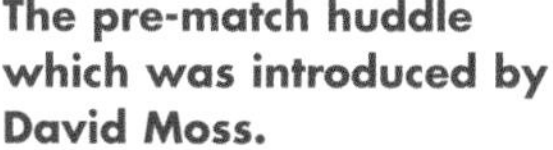

The pre-match huddle which was introduced by David Moss.

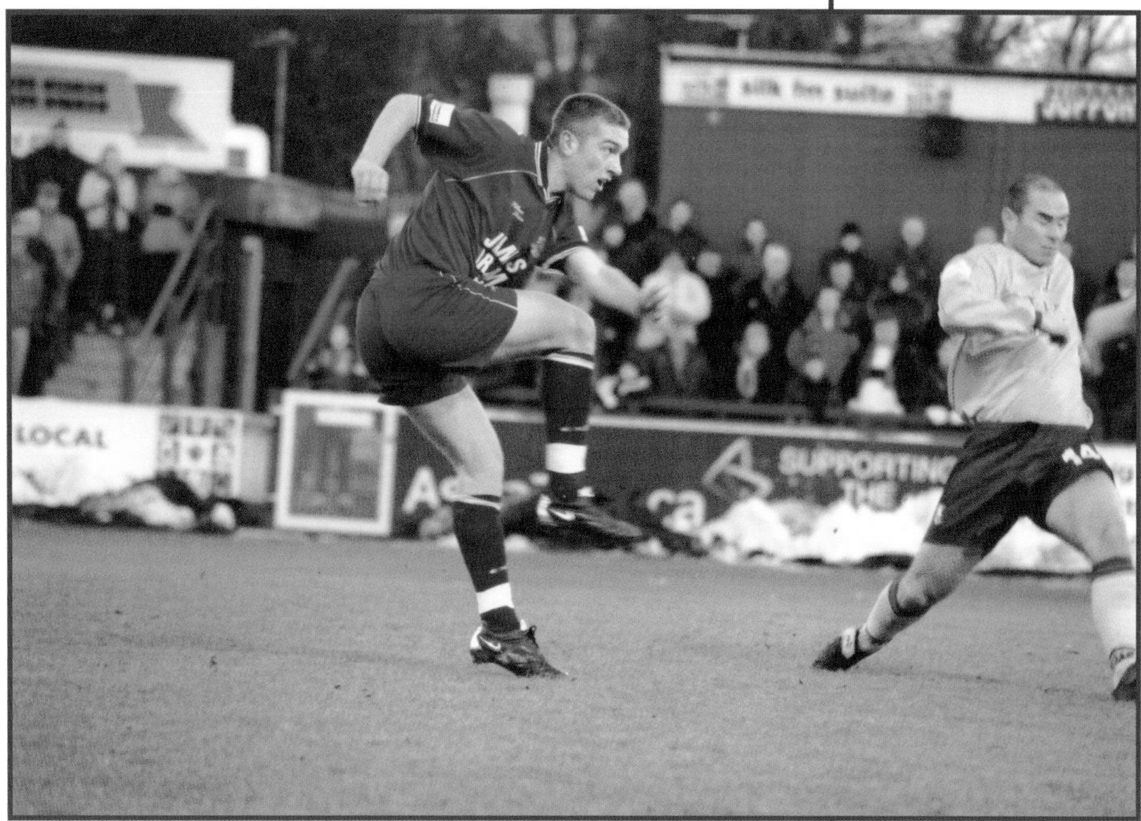

Rickie Lambert scored a hat-trick against Luton Town.

Only days later there was an interesting 'Meet the Manager' session in the McIlroy Suite, in which David Moss set the scene for his managership. Naturally ambitious for his first appointment as a number one, a position which he had wanted for quite some time, he acknowledged that he must have realistic targets, the first of which was to stay in the Football League. He would not be frightened to use youngsters and liked to use wingers in a 4-4-2 formation when he has the players to do so, encourages full-backs to go forward on the overlap and wants five in the box whenever possible. He stated that he was keen on discipline, such as players arriving on time for training, being clean shaven and only having a day off when they had earned it. In addition, he wanted lounge suits to be worn at home matches and training suits for away matches. No backroom staff were to have an alcoholic drink before a match and he did not like baseball caps worn back to front! But there was no mention of the pre-match huddle which he was to introduce.

Back in the League David Moss must have wished he had never joined when Cheltenham secured a 4–1 victory at Whaddon Road, but his first win came, ironically, against Luton Town at the Moss Rose. This was the year that Rickie Lambert developed into a top-class player, and he scored a stunning hat-trick in this match with a header, a 35-yard volley and a fierce drive from the edge of the box, and his hat-trick, along with Chris Byrne's goal, gave a 4–1 victory which was well deserved and lifted the side out of the relegation zone.

December

Rickie Lambert was in fine form again on a visit to Torquay, scoring a further two goals to give the Silkmen a 2–1 victory. In the next League match Leyton Orient, the visitors, took an early lead but Jeff Smith, on loan from Bolton

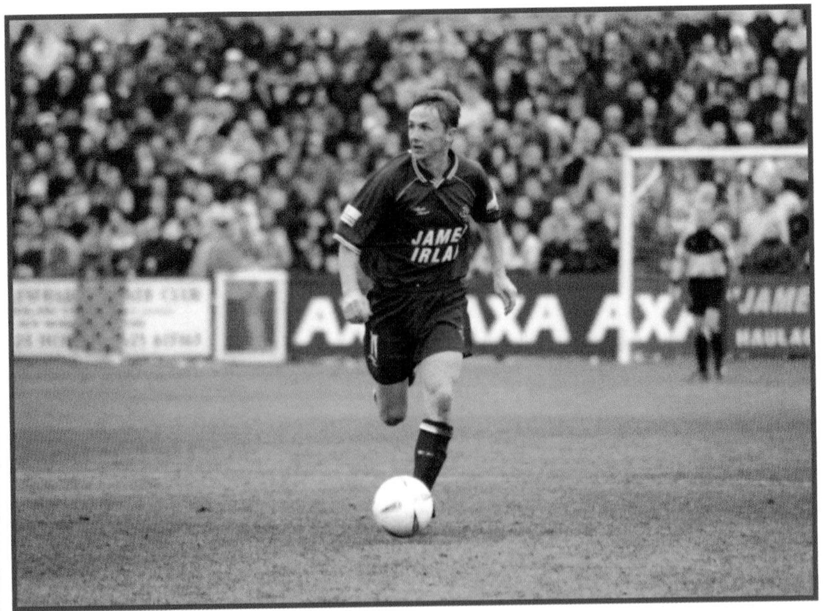

Kevin Keen made his 600th career appearance against Mansfield Town.

Wanderers, equalised in the 43rd minute, but then Chris Byrne scored what turned out to be the winning strike only a minute later to give the Silkmen another 2–1 victory.

The match at Shrewsbury just before Christmas was preceded by a carol service. Macclesfield were by far the better team in the first half and took a 1–0 lead through a Lee Glover goal; however, Shrewsbury staged a fightback in the second half when Luke Rogers equalised. There was another 1–1 draw on Boxing Day when Halifax Town were the visitors. After they had taken the lead they were reduced to 10 men, but just as it looked as though the Shaymen were going to take all three points, Jeff Smith equalised in the 89th minute.

However, the year ended with a defeat by Mansfield Town at the Moss Rose when Allen Tankard scored the one and only goal of the match in the 90th minute after a battling display by both defences, but at least the League position had improved marginally to 20th position. This match saw the vastly experienced midfielder Kevin Keen achieve his 600th career appearance.

January

Two wins and two defeats in January improved the League position to 17th. The visit to Spotland was Rochdale's new manager's first match in charge which future Silkman Kevin Townson won for him with the one and only goal in the match.

In a rather pedestrian affair, Chris Byrne's goal in the second half gave the Silkmen victory at Swansea City which was followed by another win, on this occasion against high-flying Shrewsbury Town. All the goals were scored in the first half, the Silkmen taking a 2–0 lead through a 40-yard chip by Kyle Lightbourne and an Andy Tretton own-goal, although Luke Rogers pulled a goal back for the Shrews.

Unfortunately the month ended in defeat at Rushden & Diamonds, who cruised to victory 2–0.

Off the pitch, Lee Glover took part in the ITV programme *Britain's Brainiest Footballer* hosted by Carole Vorderman, answering questions on history to reach the second round, but in the end he finished fourth, with only the top three going through to the next round.

Local boy Danny Whitaker scored on his debut against Exeter.

February

The visit of Exeter saw local boy Danny Whitaker burst onto the scene, scoring on his debut some 25 minutes after his introduction from the substitutes' bench, but by then Exeter were already two goals to the good including one from former Silkman Graeme Tomlinson. Since the club's elevation to the Football League, Danny was the first local boy to progress through the ranks of the club without experience gained through a professional football club apprenticeship scheme, having played for local schoolboy and county sides and then Wilmslow Albion. There was a second defeat at Lincoln City when the home side won by a single goal which came from a controversial penalty.

In the next match Steve Hitchen scored his one and only goal for Macclesfield with a left-foot shot to give the side a half-time lead, but Scunthorpe turned up the heat in the second half and Steve Torpey scored the equaliser.

Midfielder Chris Byrne in goalscoring form during February.

Matthew Tipton (right), future top scorer, signed in February.

There then followed three consecutive victories. Rickie Lambert's towering header and a lob from the edge of the box by Chris Byrne ensured a 2–1 victory against visitors Bristol Rovers, who had taken an early lead. Yet another winning goal from Chris Byrne, this time against Kidderminster Harriers, gave the Silkmen an away victory, and a Rickie Lambert goal from a very acute angle provided an away win at Hull City.

However, it was back down to earth soon afterwards with a single-goal defeat when the visitors Oxford United secured their first win since October. However, there had been a small improvement in the League position with the team standing at 16th.

During the month David Moss made his first permanent signing when former Welsh under-21 international striker Matthew Tipton moved from Oldham Athletic.

Top 10 Total Goalscorers
(Since August 1997)

Matthew Tipton	54
Jon Parkin	36
John Askey	34
Danny Whitaker	32
Richie Barker	26
Lee Glover	24
John Miles	22
Steve Wood	22
Gareth Evans	20
Kyle Lightbourne	17
Kevin McIntyre	17

March

Runaway leaders Plymouth Argyle came to the Moss Rose to find the Silkmen in good form, but after the interval they brought the match to Macclesfield and took the lead in the 71st minute. But Macclesfield never gave up and in the 90th minute John Askey crossed from the right side for Chris Priest to score from 10 yards out for a share of the points.

At Darlington it was substitute John Askey who converted a Chris Priest cross to score the only, and winning, goal of the match, but the story was different at Leyton Orient when the O's took the lead and extended it further just before half-time from the penalty spot. In the incident leading up to the penalty decision the ball had hit Danny Whitaker on the shoulder and the rebound had been lashed home by Orient's Kevin Nugent. The referee disallowed the goal, awarded a penalty for handball instead and gave Danny Whitaker his marching orders.

A disappointing home performance against Torquay saw the visitors win 2–0, but the month ended on a high note with two victories. The first came at Hartlepool with Matthew Tipton's first goal for the club and a Rickie Lambert goal ensuring a 2–1 win, and then the second win came against lowly York City, where Matthew Tipton was on the score sheet again, along with Lee Glover, giving another 2–1 win and an improved League position of 13th.

April

On April Fools' Day the Silkmen travelled to Carlisle and took a two-goal lead only to see Carlisle pull a goal back with a penalty early in the second half. Matthew Tipton proceeded to miss a penalty and then Carlisle scored twice in the 90th minute, firstly equalising and then winning the match with a penalty. But in the final match of the season (there was an early finish because of the World Cup) a late Matthew Tipton goal sealed all three points for the Silkmen against visiting Cheltenham Town. David Moss had achieved his initial target of retaining the Silkmen's Football League status, finishing in 13th position which was quite an achievement having been in the relegation zone in November.

Danny Adams won the Player of the Year award and Lee Glover was top scorer for the second consecutive year.

The Moss Rose playing surface was named 'Best Pitch in the Third Division,' which was a great credit to the groundsmen, Mark Patterson and Mark Mathers.

Groundsmen Mark Patterson (centre-left) and Mark Mathers receive their award.

Danny Adams – Player of the Year.

Reserve Team

The reserve team was first formed prior to the 1998–1999 season and was initially managed by Geoff Lutley and then by Norman Barnard, but for the 2001–2002 season John Askey was in charge for most of the time. This was probably the strongest second-string squad fielded by the club and included players with first-team experience and those who were just about to be promoted to the senior side. Players with senior experience included George Abbey, John Askey, Chris Byrne, Lee Martin, Karl Munroe, Paul O'Neill, Richard Tracey and Damien Whitehead. And those who were about to make the senior side included Rickie Lambert (who finished as top scorer), Michael Welch and Danny Whitaker.

Success was achieved right from the start with a final tally of 14 wins, including seven consecutive victories, three draws and only three matches lost.

Some of the best results were the following victories:
3–1 Rochdale – two goals from Rickie Lambert and an own-goal.
5–0 Hull City – goals from John Askey, Danny Whitaker (2) and Rickie Lambert (2).
3–0 Carlisle United – goals from Damien Whitehead, Danny Whitaker and an own-goal.
3–0 Mansfield Town – goals from Kyle Lightbourne, Andy McAvoy and Richard Eyre.

The final match of the season was watched by over 200 supporters in which the Silkmen Reserves beat Hartlepool United 3–1 to win the Avon Insurance League Division Two by two points. Unfortunately, they never had the opportunity to test themselves at the higher level as the First and Second Divisions were amalgamated and split into East and West Divisions.

Captains Matt Woolley and Paul O'Neill show off the Avon Insurance Championship Trophy.

The trophy and medals were presented at the last senior match of the season with Paul O'Neill, who had shared the captaincy with Matt Woolley, collecting the trophy.

Cup Competitions

Bradford City were the visitors in the first round of the **Worthington Cup** when the Silkmen were not outplayed and took a second-half lead through a Lee Glover goal. Nineteen minutes later Andy Tod equalised for the Bantams but it took a 115th minute extra-time goal by Stuart McCall to give Bradford passage to the second round.

Thirty-one Macclesfield fans travelled to Darlington for the first round of the **LDV Vans Trophy** and saw the Silkmen take an early lead from a Lee Glover penalty. However, Darlington scored two late goals to win and the Silkmen failed at the first hurdle in this competition for the fifth consecutive year.

But there was much more excitement in the **FA Cup**. In the first round, Conference side Forest Green Rovers twice came from behind at the Moss Rose with two penalties to earn a replay.

Prior to the replay there was a League fixture at Cheltenham Town when the general manager of Forest Green Rovers came to see the Macclesfield fans to enquire whether segregation was required at the replay. He was advised that as there were never any crowd problems with Macclesfield supporters there was no need for segregation but that he should confirm this with the chief executive of Macclesfield Town. The result was that there was no segregation.

On a cold and damp evening the replay was quite an eventful affair, with former Silkman Mark Cooper giving Forest Green Rovers the lead in the first half, but Kevin Keen equalised for the Silkmen only four minutes later. The score remained at 1–1 at the end of 90 minutes and in extra-time the Silkmen were lucky to remain in the competition when the Conference side had a goal disallowed and Mark Cooper missed a penalty. With the score remaining at 1–1, a marathon penalty shoot-out then took place. Each team had missed one penalty, and with the penalty count standing at 10–10, Kevin Logan missed the 12th penalty for Forest Green Rovers but Lee Glover made no mistake to give

Sports Stadium Services at work.

Match of the Day studio.

the Silkmen victory 11–10. At the time, the number of penalties required to settle this FA Cup tie (24) was a record for the competition.

In the second round, four goals in eight minutes, two from Lee Glover and two from Chris Byrne, disposed of Swansea City who scored a late consolation goal at the Moss Rose.

West Ham United were the opponents in the third round at the Moss Rose, and this draw led to some frantic preparations. Unfortunately it had started to snow during the previous match on 29 December and continued afterwards, making it impossible to put the ground covers in place, leaving a layer of snow some 2in deep on the pitch. There was some concern as the BBC had scheduled to televise the tie on Sunday 6 January 2002 and the club certainly needed the income from the tie. A hardy bunch of volunteers cleared the snow from the pitch, and on the Thursday before the match the Football Association deployed outside contractors, Sports Stadium Services, to cover the whole of the pitch with plastic sheeting with hot air blowers underneath. The snow which had been removed from the pitch had been dumped on the terraces and this was removed using equipment supplied by Scott Plant Supplies.

All this work ensured that the match could go ahead and it was played in front of a crowd of 5,706 at the Moss Rose and a television audience of 4.4 million. Barry Davies was the match commentator with Joe Royle as his co-commentator. In the Moss Rose 'studio'

Chris Priest (right) challenging Sebastian Schemmel.

Flash point – Steve Macauley has a lot to say.

situated in the current office area, which had not been fitted out at the time, were Ray Stubbs, Mark Lawrenson and Sammy McIlroy.

The Silkmen held out until the 45th minute, when Jermain Defoe scored for the Hammers. Early in the second half the Silkmen were unlucky to have a goal disallowed, but it was the Hammers who went on to win with a further goal from Jermain Defoe and a third goal from Joe Cole.

Players Scoring on their Debut for MTFC

(Since August 1997)

Efe Sodje	9 August 1997	Torquay United
Colin Holt	26 September 1998	Reading
Richie Barker	7 August 1999	Northampton Town
Richard Tracey	27 January 2001	Cardiff City
Danny Whitaker	2 February 2002	Exeter City
David Eaton	12 October 2002	Kidderminster Harriers
John Miles	29 March 2003	Kidderminster Harriers
Matty McNeil	7 March 2006	Carlisle United
Francis Green	11 August 2007	Bradford City
Martin Gritton	18 August 2007	MK Dons

CHAPTER SIX: 2002–2003

WELCOME TO AMAR AND BASHAR

Pre-season

Preparations for the forthcoming season were hampered by the demise of the ITV Digital organisation jointly owned by Granada TV and Carlton TV. Protests were organised and four Macclesfield Town supporters, including Mike Rance, together with Lincoln fans with their famous siren, peacefully demonstrated outside Granada TV in Manchester. Eventually a new television rights contract was agreed with Sky TV, but the new deal left Macclesfield with a shortfall of £67,000.

In all, four players were released pre-season. Barry Shuttleworth joined Altrincham, Andy McAvoy moved to Spennymoor United, Damien Whitehead signed for Leigh RMI and Kevin Keen, who had been told that the club could not afford to retain his services, left to become the Under-17s coach at his old club, West Ham United.

Several of the current players signed new contracts but, due to financial constraints, new signings were thin on the ground. Lee Hardy, a left-sided midfielder, joined from Oldham Athletic, Paul Aldridge (son of John) signed from Tranmere Rovers and striker David Eaton, having been released by

New signing Neil Robinson, whose fee was paid for by the supporters' organisations.

Everton, initially signed non-contract forms and was eventually given a permanent contract at the end of October. The Macclesfield Town supporters' club and the Silk Alliance initially contributed £6,000 towards the transfer fee of £12,000 for the purchase of striker Neil Robinson, who moved from Prescott Cables. The two groups had pledged to raise funds to cover the remaining £6,000.

There was one major departure from the backroom staff when the club could only offer long-serving Gil Prescott a part-time role because of the overall financial position. Gil opted to move away and became the centre of excellence co-ordinator at Oldham Athletic with an involvement in some scouting, reporting his findings to the first-team coach, former Silkman Tony Philliskirk. On leaving Gil told the *Macclesfield Express* 'I will not say anything bad about Macclesfield Town. I had nine great years there...the supporters there were brilliant to me, and I would like to think that I always gave an honest day's work for an honest day's pay.' Gil readily gave his time to the supporters and never failed to go and speak to the fans at every single away fixture. His forte always was, and always will be, spotting young talent and scouting overall, and his post-match notes on every single opposing player were legendary.

During the pre-season preparations, Chris Fear, the Macclesfield commentator on Silk FM and more latterly on Silkmen World, died at the early age of 59 from stomach cancer. Chris was a friendly man whose commentaries were always interesting but not always about the play, with the quality of the pies on offer often brought into his musings.

But it was not all doom and gloom. The first wedding reception was held in the McIlroy Suite on 20 July 2002 for Darren and Nicky Hutchins. *Any Sporting Questions* was broadcast on Radio 5 Live from the McIlroy Suite with John Inverdale in the chair, assisted by Jimmy Arnfield, Kevin Sheedy, Steve Smith from Sale Rugby Club and ladies' cricketer Clare Taylor. Questions from the audience were answered by the panel with John Inverdale giving a very professional performance.

There was a well supported cricket match on a hot and sunny day at Macclesfield Cricket Club where the cricket club side scored 205 for 8 in their allotted 30 overs with the football club replying with a total of 174 all out. Playing for the football club were, Colin Garlick, Frank Peate (with a runner when batting), Rob Bickerton, Matthew Tipton, Paul O'Neill, David Moss, Mark Patterson (club groundsman who also worked at the cricket club), Matthew Lenton, John Askey, Danny Whitaker and Andrew Balderston. There were some good knocks from Paul O'Neill (35), David Moss (33), Matthew Lenton (23), Matthew Tipton (20) and John Askey (15). However, the executive of Colin Garlick and Rob Bickerton failed to deliver.

Friendly Matches

An ambitious programme of 10 matches was arranged to be played between 17 July and 3 August but, in the end, due to player injuries and the size of the squad three of the non-League matches had to be cancelled. All the matches actually played against non-League sides resulted in victory as follows – Abbey Hey 3–1; Congleton Town 1–0; Stafford Rangers 3–2, where Neil Robinson impressed and former Silkman Ryan Price was in goal for Stafford; Leek Town 1–0; Kidsgrove Athletic 6–0; and Witton Albion 2–0.

The home matches were against Port Vale and Crewe Alexandra. Port Vale won the encounter 2–1 which included an unfortunate, but spectacular, headed own-goal by Michael Welch. In the last match, Macclesfield produced a fine

Karl Munroe renews his acquaintance with Efe Sodje in pre-season action against Crewe Alexandra.

defensive display but with Lee Glover, Chris Byrne, Lee Hardy and Neil Robinson all out of contention it was never going to be an easy task against higher League opposition, and it was a Kenny Lunt goal which gave the visitors the win. At the match there was a warm welcome back for former Silkmen Efe Sodje and Neil Sorvel.

SEASON REVIEW

August

In the opening League match York City grabbed a point in the fifth minute of time added on from a hotly disputed corner which David Moss believed should have been a throw-in, Matthew Tipton having earlier given the Silkmen the lead in the first half. At Leyton Orient the home side cruised into a three-goal lead in the first half, and although goals from Lee Glover and Kyle Lightbourne brought the side back into the match they could not find the equaliser.

A much more determined Macclesfield side beat Hartlepool at Victoria Park by two late goals. In the 85th minute Danny Adams scored his first goal for the club and a minute later Danny Whitaker started and finished a 50-yard move to slot the ball home from a tight angle for the only win of the month.

There then followed three straight defeats. A Hector Sam goal, coupled with an outstanding performance by 'keeper Andy Dibble, gave Wrexham a 1–0 away win. At Lincoln the home side won 3–0 and Bournemouth secured a 1–0 win at the Moss Rose when the ball was deflected off the referee into the path of the scorer Alan Connell. A difficult start to the season left the Silkmen in 23rd position.

Defender Danny Adams scored his first goal for the Silkmen against Hartlepool United.

It is always sad when a well-known supporter dies but even more so when the fan is relatively young. This month the visually impared Stuart Starkey died at the age of just 22. Stuart travelled all over the country to support his beloved Silkmen and, wherever he was, tuned his radio into the local radio station so that he could listen to the commentary. And he was not averse to letting players know his opinion in a loud voice!

September

A much improved performance in the home match against Bristol Rovers saw the Silkmen take an early two-goal lead to win 2–1. Games at Southend have never proved fruitful, and although this match ebbed and flowed, a single goal in the first half gave Southend victory. During this match Chris Byrne injured ligaments in his knee and at the time it was estimated that he would be out of action for six weeks.

There then followed a Tuesday evening trip to Hull City who were still playing at their Boothferry Park ground at that time. Michael Welch was well known for his long defensive clearances and he used his ability to good effect when he scored the opening goal with a shot some 40 yards out which flew over both sets of players and thundered into the back of the net for one of the most spectacular goals in the Silkmen's time in the League. Kyle Lightbourne and John Askey also featured on the score sheet to give the Silkmen a 3–1 victory in front of a crowd of 8,703.

Upon his appointment David Moss had initially stated that he wanted to use a 4-4-2 formation whenever possible, but although he used this formation from time to time he seemed to settle on a 5-3-2 formation with attacking wing-backs. The starting line up for the Scunthorpe match typified his approach:

Wilson
Welch Tinson Ridler
Hitchen Adams
Welsh Whitaker Priest
Tipton Lightbourne

The Silkmen squandered a number of early chances which allowed the visitors to take a three-goal lead. But although Macclesfield pulled two goals back in the last 10 minutes they just could not find the equaliser, giving the visitors a 3–2 win. At Rochdale, Macclesfield's only goal came from Andy Welsh, on loan from Stockport County, but the home side made their chances count and won 3–1. At least the month's results lifted the side out of the relegation zone to 21st position.

October

October was a wonderful month with only one blot on the landscape. It started with a 2–1 home win against Boston United, with several players carrying injuries, and Andy Welsh was on the score sheet again. At Kidderminster Harriers Welsh opened the scoring to give the Silkmen a 1–0 half-time lead. It was an entertaining match with both sides playing good football. The match was

Andy Welsh celebrates his goal at the Moss Rose.

David Eaton (tangerine strip) scored on his debut at Kidderminster Harriers.

sealed for the Silkmen when David Eaton came on from the substitutes' bench, making his first senior appearance, to head home from six yards to score with his first touch.

At Carlisle, Macclesfield were on the back foot from the beginning when the home side took a second-minute lead; however, they fought back and took the lead with goals from David Eaton and Chris Priest, only for Carlisle's Brendon McGill to equalise, earning his team a draw, but in a match which was not at all

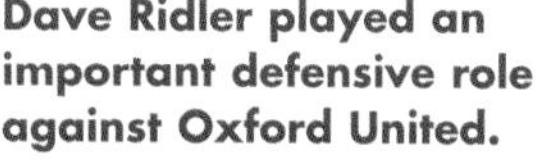

Dave Ridler played an important defensive role against Oxford United.

physical it was disappointing that Macclesfield had six players booked. The only defeat of the month came at Bury when Andy Preece and Silkman-to-be Danny Swailes gave the home side a 2–1 win, Macclesfield's goal coming from Kyle Lightbourne.

The month ended with a 2–1 victory against Oxford United, all the goals coming in the second half when Macclesfield took a two-goal lead in the 88th minute only for Oxford to pull a goal back in the 90th minute. But perhaps this was a match when luck fell the Silkmen's way as earlier Dave Ridler had cleared the ball off the goal-line from a free-kick and Oxford had had a goal disallowed for offside. This set of results left the supporters in a much happier frame of mind with the side moving up five places to 16th position.

At the end of the month Paul Lake, a former Manchester City player and brother of former Silkman Mike, was appointed the first-team physiotherapist. Since the departure of Andy Balderstone, Martin Ollier, the physiotherapist for the youth team and centre of excellence, with the help of 'keeper Lee Martin (who later became physiotherapist at Huddersfield Town) and doctors Mike Whiteside and Mike Hughes, had covered the vacant physiotherapist position.

November

November was just as bad a month in the League as October was good, with Macclesfield picking up just one solitary point.

Rain throughout the match, with a strong wind blowing down the pitch from the Star Lane End made for extremely difficult playing conditions which saw the visitors, Shrewsbury Town, score two breakaway goals to Macclesfield's 80th-minute goal by Danny Whitaker.

Then came the shocking news that talented attacking midfielder Chris Byrne had been shot in the thigh, an injury which put his playing career at serious risk. The shooting took place in a side alley in Hulme, Manchester, and the police were treating the attack by three hooded men as an attempted robbery of Byrne's BMW car. Chris had written himself into the history of the club with his performances in the 1997 Conference Championship squad and, more recently, as the scorer of winning goals, but his lifestyle off the pitch was, unfortunately, in complete contrast to his professional football career. It was some months later that it was sadly confirmed that Chris would never again play professional football.

A visit to Swansea City resulted in a 1–0 defeat, but in the next League match at the Moss Rose Torquay United took a 3–0 lead inside the first 10 minutes. Having left striker David Eaton on the bench, David Moss introduced him in the 22nd minute in place of defender Michael Welch, a move which proved productive nine minutes later when he pulled a goal back. Goals by Steve Macauley, who was back for his third loan spell, and Kyle Lightbourne, his 100th career goal, gave the Silkmen a fortunate point.

At Cambridge the score was 1–1 at half-time but Macclesfield were reduced to 10 men when Danny Whitaker was sent off, and two goals in four minutes gave the home side a 3–1 win to leave the Silkmen in 19th position.

December

It looked as though stout defending had earned the Silkmen a point against visitors Rushden & Diamonds until a Lee Hardy back-pass was intercepted, allowing the visitors to score a late winner. Striker Colin Little had been signed on loan from Crewe Alexandra and made his debut in this match, only to be substituted in the ninth minute with a re-occurrence of a hamstring problem. A goalless draw followed at Darlington with Michael Carr making his debut, and he was unlucky to be dismissed for two bookable offences.

By now David Moss had changed the formation to a more attacking option utilising three forwards in an attempt to improve results. The line up for the Lincoln match was:

Wilson
Hitchen Tinson Welch Adams
Abbey Carr Priest
Eaton Tipton Lightbourne

Nevertheless, Lincoln left the Moss Rose with all three points having scored a late goal, and in the final match of the year at Exeter City, with several players injured, the Silkmen could only name four substitutes. However, a battling performance gave the Silkmen a share of the points in a 1–1 draw and retained 19th position.

With no League victories since the end of October, some of the supporters were expressing their concerns about the lack of overall success of the team.

Darren Dunning (right) gave an inspired performance against Bournemouth.

After the draw at Exeter, David Moss said in the *Manchester Evening News* 'There are still 22 games ahead and I haven't even considered relegation because I know that won't happen. If we show that sort of character for the rest of the season we will be fine.'

January

It certainly was a 'Happy New Year' when the first victory since 29 October 2002 was achieved at Wrexham by a 3–1 scoreline in another battling performance. An own-goal by Wrexham's Shaun Pejic had given the Silkmen the lead but Lee Trundle equalised for the Welsh side. In the second half Karl Munroe made a telling pass to Danny Whitaker, who ran 35 yards with the ball before passing to Matthew Tipton on the edge of the box, who turned and shot past the 'keeper some 20 seconds after the re-start. David Eaton scored a late goal when a back-pass by Pejic was mishandled by 'keeper Andy Dibble, allowing David Eaton to slot the ball home.

In a further attempt to improve results Canadian international Martin Nash was signed from Rochester Raging Rhinos and striker Neil Ross transferred from Stockport County for a fee of £30,000. Steve Macauley returned from Rochdale on loan and midfielder Darren Dunning was signed on loan from Blackburn Rovers.

At Bournemouth, David Moss threw Darren Dunning into the line up and heaped praise on him for inspiring the team, but in reality Macclesfield were two goals up at half-time only to see the home side score two goals to level the score. The League leaders Hartlepool United were the next to visit the Moss Rose, and although they outclassed the home side they only took the three

Michael Welch scored a spectacular goal at York City, seen here climbing high at Bury.

points by a single goal. The return match against Exeter ended in a 1–1 draw again, Danny Whitaker having given the Silkmen a second-half lead only to see Sean Divine equalise for Exeter in the fourth minute of time added on but, at least, a League position of 19th had been retained for the third consecutive month.

February

There were only three matches played in the month with the match scheduled at Shrewsbury postponed due to a frozen pitch, but good results were hard to achieve. Despite a spectacular 30-yard free-kick which Michael Welch drilled home, York City were the victors 2–1, with future Silkman Jon Parkin on the score sheet for York.

Visitors Swansea City lifted themselves off the bottom of the table with a comprehensive 3–1 victory, and having taken a 77th-minute lead at Bristol Rovers the Silkmen could only hold onto their lead for three minutes to earn the only point of the month, slipping to 22nd position.

March

In a busy month with a total of eight matches, some of which followed earlier postponements, results gradually improved but not without the odd hiccup along the way. David Moss changed the formation on a regular basis and this month was no exception with both 4-4-2 and 5-3-2 formations used.

Two goals in the second half gave Macclesfield the lead against Southend but when the visitors pulled a goal back with two minutes to go there was a lot of nervous tension around the ground, but the Silkmen held out for a 2–1 win. Hull City won the next encounter at the Moss Rose with a single goal scored just seconds before half-time.

The best win of the month came in the next match against Leyton Orient when a goal from Danny Whitaker and two from Matthew Tipton gave Macclesfield a 3–1 home win. A goalless draw against Bury was a hard-fought match which either side could have won, but Carlisle took all three points in the following game at Brunton Park with an early goal.

The month finished on a high note with two victories, the first at Oxford where Matthew Tipton scored the only goal, and the second a home win against Kidderminster Harriers with two goals in as many minutes, including a debut goal by recently signed on-loan striker John Miles from Crewe Alexandra. Defender Matt Haddrell also made his debut, having been signed from Vauxhall Motors for a fee which could reach £35,000. Moving up to 18th position in the League did not mean that the team were safe from relegation as they were only three points above the relegation zone.

During the month Amar and Bashar Alkadhi were appointed directors of the club after making an initial investment of £100,000. These two gentlemen have interests in the telecommunication industry in the UK and overseas, and while they are based in London they have strong connections in Macclesfield. Their involvement in the club came about when they asked their accountant to ascertain football clubs in which they could become involved. Their accountant came up with several clubs including Macclesfield Town, suggesting that they really would not want to invest in the club. However, as Amar's partner (now wife) Suzanne was the daughter of a Macclesfield supporter and niece of Roy Higginbotham, associate director and life president, they concluded that

John Miles (left) scored on his debut against Kidderminster Harriers.

Macclesfield Town Football Club was certainly the right choice. Since then they have continued to invest in the club, firstly ensuring that it was on a sound financial footing by repaying several outstanding debts, and subsequently ensuring that there were sufficient funds for the day-to-day operation. Through their investments they have become the owners of the club. As evidence of their commitment to the club, much of the funds invested have been translated into share capital (unlike many investors in football clubs who merely offer loans), such that Amar and Bashar cannot just leave the club and demand repayment of their investment.

April

A 1–1 draw at the start of the month against Cambridge United was followed by a 2–2 draw at Torquay. In this match John Miles scored again and with a Kyle Lightbourne goal the Silkman led 2–1, only for Martin Gritton to equalise for Torquay. Prior to this match the officials at Torquay had made a presentation to the match referee, Mr P. Rejer, to celebrate his retirement as an official at the end of the season.

John Miles was the hero again at Shrewsbury but it was George Abbey who opened the scoring with his first senior goal, although Shrewsbury equalised only nine minutes later. John Miles then put the Silkmen in front only to see the Shrews equalise again three minutes before half-time. Shrewsbury pressed Macclesfield throughout the second half but in the 90th minute John Miles broke free to score the winner with an excellent solo effort. Another win by way of a Danny Whitaker goal ensured the retention of the club's Football League status in the home match against Darlington.

However, despite safety being reached the month still ended on a disappointing note with defeats at Rushden & Diamonds (3–0) and Boston United (2–1).

May

There was an emotional farewell at the end of John Askey's long playing career in the last match of the season at home to Rochdale, but not before the visitors had made the Silkmen work for their victory. In this entertaining match, the first half was a tale of two penalties with Danny Whitaker missing his and Lee McEvilly scoring his for the visitors. Macclesfield equalised through an own-goal but Stephen Hill put the visitors in the lead for the second time. It began to look as though Rochdale were going to take all three points until the introduction of John Askey from the substitutes' bench in the 73rd minute and Matthew Tipton in the 77th minute. The two of them combined for John Askey to level the scores in the 88th minute. Deep into time added on, Matthew Tipton struck a drive from 25-yards into the right-hand corner of the net to win the match for Macclesfield and send the fans delirious.

And so John Askey's playing career came to end, scoring in his last match just as he had done in his very first appearance in December 1984 at Morecambe. John made a total of 672 appearances in all competitions for the Silkmen and scored 155 goals. John still remains a valued member of the backroom staff and is currently manager of a successful youth team.

Steve Wilson was voted Player of the Year, and Matthew Tipton and Danny Whitaker were joint-top scorers.

'Gentleman' John Askey (left) played his last game in May.

Steve Wilson – Player of the Year.

A James Irlam truck in club livery.

Off the Field

Before the arrival of Amar and Bashar Alkadhi, the club needed to raise funds in every possible way. One method used over the years was for supporters to purchase shares in the club, and the most recent scheme was named 'I Care I Bought a Share' and 215 people invested £23,832 in the club.

Club chaplains were appointed for the first time that season with Revd Jeremy Tear and Revd Dean Shaw taking the role in a joint capacity.

During their sponsorship of the club, James Irlam had one of their trucks painted in the Macclesfield Town Football Club livery in place of their normal colour of red, and the vehicle was parked outside the ground for each home match. As part of their fundraising events, The Silk Alliance, one of the supporters' organisations, had Corgi model trucks manufactured with the James Irlam MTFC livery, selling them at £12 each and raising £10,000, which was handed to the club at the match against Bury on 15 March 2003. Each truck had an individual number with several key numbers auctioned off, and the highest bid for a truck numbered 1 came from David Irlam, who presented it to Gary, the driver of the 'MTFC' truck.

Cup Competitions

For the sixth consecutive season the Silkmen were knocked out of the **LDV Vans Trophy** at the first hurdle. On this occasion they were eliminated by Second Division Tranmere Rovers in the second round, having received a bye in the first round. Matthew Tipton scored in the fourth minute and it took Tranmere until the 67th minute to equalise. With the score level at 1–1 the tie had to be decided on the golden goal rule in extra-time. Unfortunately, it was Tranmere who scored in the 117th minute to progress to the next round.

In the first round of the **Worthington Cup** Kyle Lightbourne gave the Silkmen a half-time lead at the Moss Rose, but they had to defend stoutly throughout the second half with Steve Wilson making some excellent saves, and it seemed only a matter of time before Second Division Barnsley would equalise, which they did in the 84th minute. With the score standing at 1–1 after 90 minutes, 30 minutes of extra-time was played. There were no further goals

Lee Hardy presses forward against Watford.

in the first half of extra-time but a barnstorming 14 minute hat-trick by Danny Whitaker in the second half saw the Silkmen progress to the second round with a 4–1 win.

The second-round draw provided another home tie, on this occasion against First Division Preston North End. Again an early goal by Matthew Tipton gave the Silkmen the lead but Preston equalised later in the first half. This was an exciting match which ended in total disappointment for the Silkmen faithful when Preston scored the winning goal in the fifth minute of time added on.

The first round of the **FA Cup** found the Silkmen at Hull City, where they triumphed 3–0 with goals from Matthew Tipton, Kyle Lightbourne and Danny Whitaker. The second round was televised live by Sky TV from the Moss Rose with a 17.35 kick-off against non-League Vauxhall Motors of the Unibond Premier League. The non-League side matched the Silkmen until two late goals gave the home side victory.

The third-round draw provided another home tie, on this occasion against First Division Watford – although it was nearly Manchester United. There were just four balls remaining in the draw, but Allan Mullery drew out Portsmouth to visit Manchester United, just leaving the two balls for Macclesfield and Watford in the draw. An above average crowd of 4,244 witnessed the match which Watford won with two clinical strikes by Heidar Helguson and on-loan Jermaine Pennant.

Defenders Darren Tinson and Danny Adams strive to win the ball.

CHAPTER SEVEN: 2003–2004

IT TAKES THREE MANAGERS

Pre-season

There was an encouraging start to the campaign when season ticket sales had reach 900 before the end of June, the highest since the second season in the Football League, and this against a background of the team operating in the lower half of the League in the previous season. Season tickets were again on offer for the Under-16s at the low price of £23.

Before the season got underway full-back George Abbey made his international debut for Nigeria against Ghana in the LG Cup. In the final of the competition he was involved in two of the goals when Nigeria beat Cameroon 3–0 after extra-time to win the Cup, with George earning the Man of the Match award for his performance. Later in the season, George was ever present for Nigeria in the African Nations' Cup Finals, gaining a third-place-winners' medal.

Backroom appointments included John Askey as first-team assistant manager, while still retaining his position as manager of the reserve side, and goalkeeping coach Mark Prudhoe who signed on a part-time basis and is best remembered for his time at Stoke City where he made almost 100 appearances.

Defender George Abbey represented Nigeria in the LG Cup.

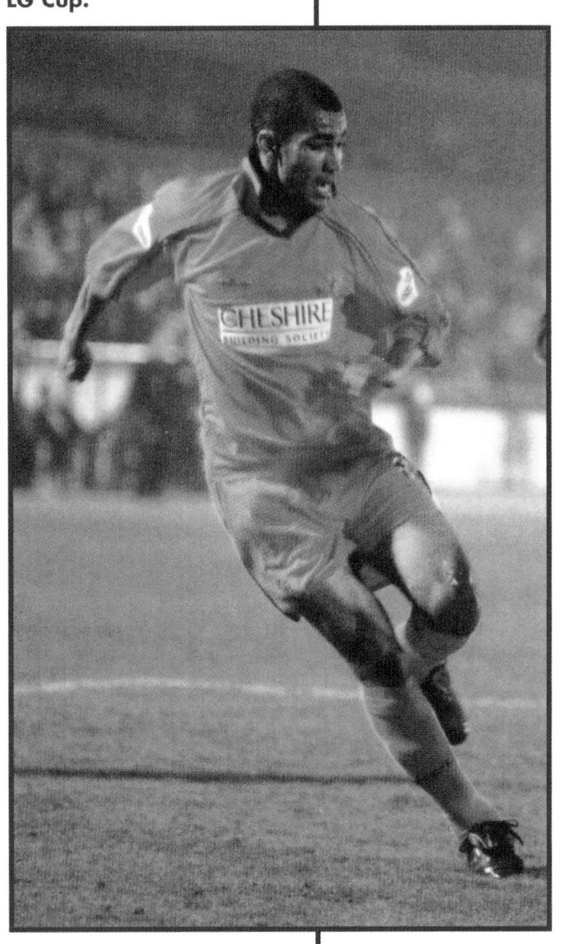

There were the usual comings and goings on the playing staff this season. Both John Miles and Colin Little, who made quite an impression during their loan spells at the end of the previous season, signed permanent contracts. In addition, striker Martin Carruthers (Scunthorpe United), midfielder David Flitcroft (Rochdale) and another experienced midfielder Tommy Widdrington (Hartlepool United) all signed in the summer and young 'keeper Boaz Myhill came on loan from Aston Villa to gain some first-team experience. Youngsters Michael Carr and Steven Brackenridge were both given their first professional contracts.

In total there were seven departures including David Eaton, Lee Hardy, Kyle Lightbourne, Paul O'Neill and Lee Martin, who moved to Huddersfield Town (where his career had started) as joint goalkeeping coach and physiotherapist. But there was one major departure when David Moss released long-serving defender Darren Tinson, who took the opportunity to move to Shrewsbury Town. Darren was the last of the former Conference players to leave the club and made a total of 297 appearances in all League competitions, a record for any player since the Silkmen were promoted to the Football League, and also made 66 non-League appearances. Moving to the Moss Rose in 1996, Darren had formed the backbone of the defence, either at full-back or in his preferred position of centre-back where he was a commanding figure. Also, he was the first player to reach 100 Football League appearances in the match against Hartlepool United in November 1999.

Loan signing goalkeeper Boaz Myhill.

Another cricket match was held against the town's cricket club but, on this occasion, the weather was overcast and cool which probably accounted for a rather disappointing spectator turnout. The football club's team included director Mike Rance and chief executive Colin Garlick, who kept wicket. The cricket club batted first and scored 176 runs for three wickets in the allotted 25 overs, although their batsmen had to retire on reaching 25 runs. Unbelievably the football club also scored 176 runs, the last wicket falling to the last ball, to tie the match. The football club did not have the 25 run restriction, which enabled David Moss to score 54 runs and Matthew Tipton 55 runs.

Friendly Matches

Macclesfield's first-ever fixtures on foreign soil came in a two-match tour of Norway. The first match was against Oslo-based Follo Football, and the Silkmen won through a Colin Little second-half goal. The second match also resulted in victory, this time with second-half goals from George Abbey and Chris Priest against KFUM Oslo (KFUM being the Norwegian for YMCA), in a match

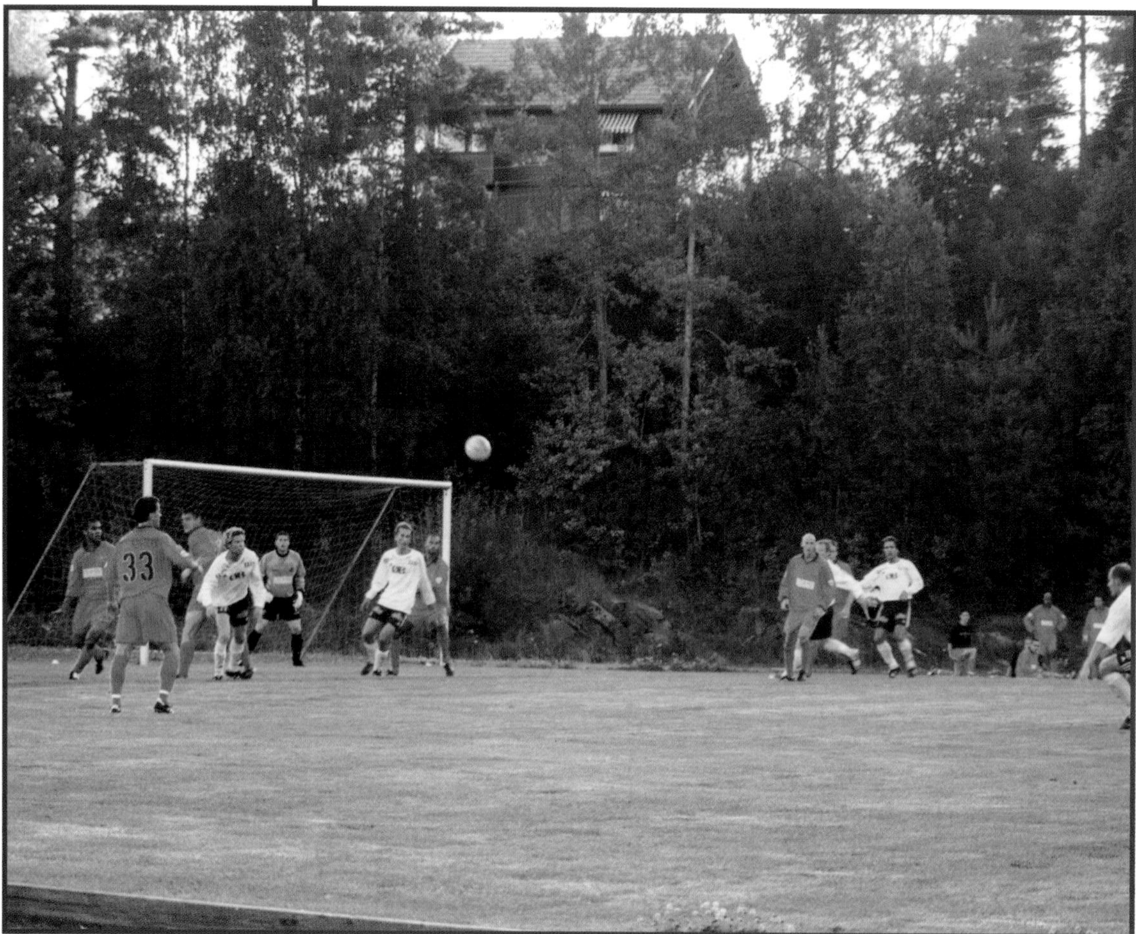

Action against Follo Football in the Silkmen's first-ever match on foreign soil.

played on astroturf. The players and staff had a difficult journey home when the hold door of the aircraft would not close, resulting in alternative flights being arranged to Heathrow and many of the players then having to drive north in hire cars. But some players were more fortunate and managed to obtain flights to Manchester via Amsterdam.

Two days after the second match in Norway, Sheffield Wednesday came to the Moss Rose and were well supported by a large contingent of fans which boosted the attendance to 2,136. Martin Carruthers gave the Silkmen an early lead but Wednesday's Albanian-born striker Shefki Kuqi scored a hat-trick – equalising in the first half, giving them the lead late in the second half and then sealing victory with a penalty in the 90th minute.

An under-19s side were beaten 2–0 at Buxton and there was also a 0–0 draw at Kidsgrove Athletic. Other than for the 'keeper, two different teams were fielded in each half at Leek Town where the Silkmen won 4–0. As part of the transfer deal for Matt Haddrell there was a visit to Vauxhall Motors, who had narrowly missed out on winning promotion to the Conference the previous season. The Silkmen easily won 5–1. A mixed side comprising youth, reserve and senior players was then beaten 3–1 at Congleton. To accommodate Mossley, whose match against Oldham Athletic had been cancelled, the Silkmen visited Mossley as an additional friendly fixture which they won 3–0. Another match played as part of a transfer deal, on this occasion for Neil Robinson, saw the Silkmen beat Prescott Cables 3–1. An excellent overall team performance with fluent passing football saw a Matt Haddrell goal defeat visitors Stoke City, who included 'keeper Ed De Goey who had only signed for the Potters from Chelsea the previous day.

SEASON REVIEW

August

On an extremely hot and energy sapping day, the season started with a goalless draw against visitors Boston United, but at Cambridge in the following game the Silkmen were second best and suffered a 3–1 defeat. Then after failing to put away their chances Macclesfield had to settle for a point against visitors Torquay United in a 1–1 draw. In the next match David Moss was left in dismay when the Silkmen were two goals up in the first 15 minutes at Bristol Rovers only to see the home side reply with two goals in three minutes to take a share of the points.

Having waited all month for a win, it came along in fine style when newly promoted Yeovil were beaten 4–1 at the Moss Rose, with Macclesfield adopting a more determined style of play than seen in the opening matches. Martin Carruthers and Danny Whitaker scored two goals each, the best of which was a brilliant 25-yard strike by Danny. After a poor start to the month, a credible 14th position had been achieved.

Martin Carruthers was in good form in the opening matches of the season.

September

A repeat performance of August's results left the supporters waiting for the first success of the month until the final match. But before that a half-time lead of 2–1 could not be held at Field Mill, when Mansfield scored two goals in the second half, both of which resulted from poor defensive play by Macclesfield, to win 3–2. In the home match against Kidderminster Harriers, on-loan 'keeper

Colin Little (centre) scored a late equaliser against Kidderminster Harriers.

Boaz Myhill was the star player in keeping the Silkmen in the match, but he could not stop the visitors taking a 1–0 lead in the first half. But the Silkmen never failed to give up the cause and Colin Little equalised in time added on to earn a 1–1 draw.

For some reason David Moss changed the formation from 4-4-2 to 5-3-2 at Swansea City, who were by far the stronger side and won 3–0. Another change in formation to 5-2-3 at Northampton had Boaz Myhill keeping the Silkmen in the match again, although it finished in a goalless draw. There was another goalless draw against visitors York City, but the game came to life in the second half when Moss reverted to a 4-4-2 formation, with Steve Macauley hitting the woodwork and Martin Carruthers unfortunate to have a goal disallowed.

In the home match against Rochdale the Silkmen proved to be the better side throughout even when they went a goal behind, which had been scored by former Silkman Chris Shuker. A fortunate own-goal provided the equaliser, but the winner came from Danny Whitaker after John Miles had tapped a free-kick on the edge of the box to Danny, who curled his shot round the wall and past the 'keeper to score a superb goal. Nevertheless, the side had slipped to 18th position.

October

For the third consecutive month only one victory was achieved, leaving the Silkmen fans frustrated and disappointed.

More defensive errors allowed Leyton Orient to gain a 2–0 home win; although, after this match David Moss acknowledged that he had released one of the club's best centre-backs in Darren Tinson. In the next match against Doncaster, initially Macclesfield were on top, Martin Carruthers having given them an early lead, but the visitors equalised on the stroke of half-time and then went on to play with grit and determination after the interval, eventually winning 3–1, which resulted in some of the Silkmen fans collectively expressing their dissatisfaction.

The one bright moment of the month came at Carlisle when Matthew Tipton's free-kick curled up and over the wall to leave 'keeper Matt Glennon helpless to give the Silkmen a 1–0 victory, leaving Carlisle United firmly rooted to the foot of the table. This was followed by disappointment at Lincoln City when Macclesfield twice came from behind with goals from Matthew Tipton, but they were then reduced to 10 men following the dismissal of Karl Munroe, and Lincoln City scored the winning goal well into time added on for a final score of 3–2. During the match, Lincoln City's drummers were in good form but their famous air-raid siren was missing for some reason.

Michael Welch was dismissed in the 26th minute of the home match against Southend United giving the Silkmen an uphill task, and the visitors made the most of their one-man advantage by taking a 2–0 lead in the second half. Substitute Colin Little scored a well-taken consolation goal in the 90th minute, but this was too little too late and with Macclesfield losing their fourth League match of the month they slipped another two places to 20th. Both during and at the conclusion of this match, there were loud calls for the dismissal of manager David Moss.

After the match the board announced that David Moss had been dismissed and so his time at the Moss Rose had come full circle, starting and finishing with matches against Southend United. His record as manager at Macclesfield was: Played 102, Won 34, Lost 43, Drawn 25, thereby winning a third of his matches, a record which has been equalled by many other managers.

Michael Welch sees red.

David Moss was reported to be a decent sort of person but one who just could not deal with the day-to-day criticism from a section of the fans – which comes with the territory of the job – and he spoke out, blaming them for the team's overall performance. Unfortunately, because of his negative comments, David Moss will never be remembered with affection by many at the Moss Rose. However, it has to be remembered that he steered the side to safety at the end of the previous season.

It was quickly announced that Silkmen legend John Askey had been appointed caretaker manager and chairman Rob Bickerton stated that the time had come when everyone had to pull together, and the directors were reportedly especially proud of the community spirit within the club.

November

In John Askey's first match in charge the Silkmen travelled to Hull City's new Kingston Communications Stadium, which was sponsored by the only municipally-owned telecommunications company in the country which, even before privatisation, never fell within the monopoly of the Post Office. This match proved to be an entertaining encounter with play moving from end to end. Having taken a sixth-minute lead through a Martin Carruthers goal, Hull were allowed to equalise only two minutes later. The Silkmen were reduced to 10 men just before half-time following the dismissal of Colin Little, and they continued with their spirited approach but could not stop Hull taking a second-half lead. In the end a well-taken free-kick by Danny Whitaker gave Macclesfield a share of the points in the 2–2 draw, which was considered a good result against the current leaders of the division.

A physical Scunthorpe side made it difficult for the Silkmen at the Moss Rose in a match which saw both sides having four players booked and the Scunthorpe manager dismissed to the stand. Coming from behind on two occasions through goals from Danny Whitaker and Matthew Tipton, the Silkmen took a share of the points again. In the next match, Macclesfield took the lead at Oxford, but poor defending let them down again with the home side winning 3–1.

Immediately on taking up the managerial role, John Askey had reverted to a 4-4-2 formation, and the following starting line up (for the match against Bury) is a good example of his typical team selection:

Wilson
Abbey Welch Munroe Adams
Carragher Widdrington Priest Whitaker
Tipton Carruthers

In the Bury match John secured his first victory as manager, when Macclesfield's excellent passing allowed them to have the majority of the possession, but it was Matthew Tipton's first-half goal which secured all three points, and although Bury looked dangerous on the break, good defensive work paid dividends.

December

The month started on a high note when Macclesfield ripped apart Huddersfield Town on their first visit to the Moss Rose with a comprehensive 4–0 victory.

Steven Brackenridge (left), seen here at the Moss Rose, scored his first senior goal at Darlington.

From the start the home side looked as though they meant business and took the lead in the 13th minute when John Miles's weaving run caused havoc in the visitors' box before Matthew Tipton picked up the ball and blasted it into the roof of the net. There were no further goals until the 67th minute, when John Miles ran onto a Chris Priest pass and scored with a left-foot shot. Twelve minutes later Huddersfield were reduced to 10 men when Nathan Clarke was sent off for a professional foul in the area, with Matthew Tipton stepping up to convert the resultant penalty. The final goal came two minutes from the end when Chris Priest picked up a Matthew Tipton cross to force a parry from the Huddersfield 'keeper, which he then hammered home for the fourth goal.

In the week following this match it was announced that John Askey had been appointed as full-time manager, to the delight of the supporters.

Second-half substitute Steven Brackenridge scored his first senior goal (and Macclesfield's 350th League goal) in a 1–0 win at Darlington in the Silkmen's first visit to Darlington's new 25,000 all-seater stadium which was then named the Reynolds Stadium. Cheltenham Town took control of the next game on Boxing Day at Whaddon Road in driving rain by taking a three-goal lead, but the Silkmen pulled two goals back, first though young Steven Brackenridge (on the score sheet for the second consecutive match) and then through Matt Haddrell's first senior goal. But even though the home side were on the rack in the closing minutes the visitors could not find the equaliser.

The year ended with Macclesfield's 300th League match when Mansfield Town were the visitors. This was an exciting match in which both teams played with pace and enthusiasm, and while Mansfield, in a Play-off position, often looked the stronger side, the Silkmen still managed to carve out chances on goal. The visitors took a second-half lead but just when it looked as though they had secured all three points, Matthew Tipton lashed the ball home with almost the last kick of the match to give the Silkmen a 1–1 draw. There was a marginal improvement in the League position this month to 19th.

January

Early in the month two players left the club. With other central midfielders preferred, David Flitcroft had not made an appearance for some two months and this resulted in his release. Shortly afterwards he signed for Bury. Having made only a handful of appearances in the current season, full-back Steve Hitchen was also released later and joined Bangor City, where Peter Davenport was manager.

A disappointing performance at Boston United led to another defeat, on this occasion 3–1, but at the Moss Rose two splendid goals by Colin Little and John Miles provided a much needed win over Bristol Rovers.

After six years at the Moss Rose, Steve Hitchen was released.

Two poor performances led to a 1–0 home defeat by Cambridge United and a 4–1 defeat at Torquay United, but the month ended with a better performance and a 2–2 draw at Yeovil, although the Silkmen had taken the lead twice and Yeovil's equaliser was hotly disputed, the Macclesfield players claiming that the ball had not crossed the line. On slipping to 20th position, good results were becoming even more of a priority.

February

In February John Askey signed three players who would make quite an impact in the seasons to come. Full-back Graham Potter came from Boston United, hardworking midfielder Paul Harsley transferred from Northampton Town and striker Jon Parkin arrived from York City. However, Matt Haddrell left the club as he had not been able to settle into professional football as well as he would have liked.

In recent matches the Silkmen's poor run of form had not been helped by several key players missing matches through injury, including Tommy Widdrington, George Abbey, Danny Adams, David Smith, Matthew Tipton and Steve Macauley, which left the manager frustrated at not always being in the position to select his best side. In addition, it was interesting that in line with remarks made by former manager David Moss, John Askey found it necessary to mention the importance of the fans backing the players as negativity from the terraces in recent weeks had affected the team, proving that the much-used term 'the crowd is the 12th man' is so right. Later in the month, he was delighted with the support given to the team at Carlisle and took the time to congratulate and thank the fans.

There was disappointment when Macclesfield took an early lead against visitors Cheltenham Town only to see them score two goals in as many minutes to win the match, after Steve Macauley had been ordered off the pitch by the referee and had to return to the dressing room for medical attention.

In a physical game against a Doncaster side flying high in the League, Macclesfield showed more fight and determination but lost by a single goal; however, the result could have been worse, had Steve Wilson not made one of his famous penalty saves when Doncaster had to re-take a penalty.

By now there was a 'new-look' Macclesfield side following the recent signings, resulting in the following line up against Carlisle United with John Askey trying out the 5-3-2 formation:

Wilson
Munroe Macauley Carragher
Abbey Potter
Whitaker Widdrington Harsley
Parkin Tipton

Both sides fought hard in this relegation match, and although Macclesfield had the better of possession in the first half, it was the visitors who took the lead against the run of play. During his time at Macclesfield, wing-back Graham Potter always found space to move forward and this match was no different when he equalised some five minutes later. It was Carlisle's turn in the second half to dominate play but the Silkmen held on for a point. The last match of the month resulted in a 1–0 defeat at Southend to leave the Silkmen in the relegation zone in 23rd position.

Wing-back Graham Potter (number 2) celebrates scoring his first goal for the Silkmen only nine days after signing.

March

At the beginning of March there was a welcome return of centre-back and former Silkman Steve Payne, who moved from Chesterfield for an undisclosed fee. Danny Adams moved to Stockport County also for an undisclosed fee having given sterling service as a no-nonsense, hard-tackling full-back, but he felt that it was time for another challenge. Forward Neil Robinson, who had been on loan at non-League Southport where he had recently scored seven goals in four matches, moved there permanently during the month.

A 1–0 defeat at the Moss Rose by Darlington was followed by Huddersfield Town avenging their 4–0 defeat at the Moss Rose the previous December with an equally resounding 4–0 win on their own ground.

But the next two matches brought better news, firstly with a 2–1 home win against Swansea City with the Silkmen taking a 2–0 lead, only for Swansea to pull a goal back in the 74th minute despite having been reduced to 10 men, leaving a nervous final 16 minutes. In the second match, two goals from Matthew Tipton and one each from Martin Carruthers and Paul Harsley secured an excellent win at Kidderminster Harriers.

Northampton then completely outclassed Macclesfield when they won 4–0 at the Moss Rose, and following a goalless draw against Lincoln City, where many long and high balls were played by both teams, there were anxious faces all round with the side remaining in 23rd position and three points adrift from safety.

Hardworking midfielder Paul Harsley on the left.

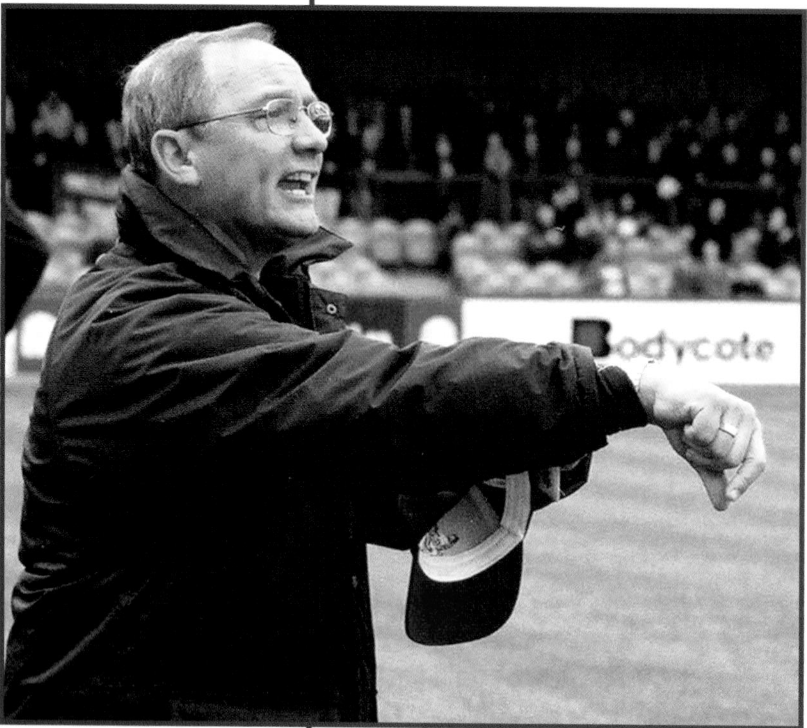

Brian Horton was appointed manager with the brief to save the Silkmen from relegation.

April

Enter Brian Horton, who had previously been manager at Manchester City and Port Vale, to embark on what looked an impossible task of retaining the Silkmen's Football League status in the final seven matches of the season. John Askey returned to the position of assistant manager.

What a start it was for Brian Horton with three wins on the bounce. The first came away from home at relegation threatened York City, where Jon Parkin scored on his first visit back to his former employers and together with a goal from Graham Potter sealed the 2–0 win. Then, in the next match, second-half substitute Martin Carruthers scored the only goal when Leyton Orient were the visitors, and the third victory came at Rochdale, who had taken an early lead, but two second-half goals by Matthew Tipton, the second a disputed penalty, ensured a 2–1 win. By now 18th position in the League had been attained.

High-flying Hull City had their promotion party spoilt at the Moss Rose when Matthew Tipton scored an equaliser to draw 1–1, but a 1–0 defeat at Scunthorpe saw the Silkmen fall back to 22nd position to set the nerves tingling.

In the penultimate match of the season Macclesfield found luck on their side for a change when they won this match with two bizarre own-goals, although the visitors, Oxford United, did pull a goal back. The second of the two own-goals came from Matthew Tipton's 20-yard curling shot, which looked to be going into the far corner until Jefferson Louis stuck out his right boot to deflect the ball over his own 'keeper. Matthew Tipton attempted to claim the goal which would have brought his season tally to 20 but the Dubious Goals Panel ruled against him. However, the 2–1 win ensured that with one match to play Football League status had been retained with York City and Carlisle United both relegated.

With neither side having anything to play for, the final match of the season against Bury did not come to life until Macclesfield's Matthew Carragher had been dismissed, and with Steve Payne having been substituted following injury in the first half, the central defence was left weakened, resulting in Bury scoring two late goals.

It had taken three different managers to see the Silkmen complete the season in 20th position, with Brian Horton plucking the proverbial rabbit out of the hat in the 11th hour.

Matthew Tipton was voted Player of the Year and he also finished as top scorer with 19 goals in all competitions. The playing surface at the Moss Rose was voted the best in Division Three and the Silkmen came top of the Nationwide Third Division Fair Play League.

Youth Team

Under the direction of coaches Steve Carroll and Colin Brookes the youth team completed the season in seventh position in their League and fifth in the Merit Division, but for the first time ever they reach the third round of the FA Youth Cup.

In the first round at the Moss Rose against Blackpool, they took a 3–1 lead but with only minutes to go the visitors pulled a goal back, yet the young Silkmen held firm to progress to the second round. A visit to York City in the second round saw the home side having the better start, but towards the end of the first half Macclesfield began to assert themselves and after the interval were rewarded with a well-taken goal to win the tie.

The third round took place at the Moss Rose against Walsall with the following team – Deasy, Murray, Smart, Wright, Cropper, Teague, Reid (Byrne), Bailey, McDonald, Grandison and Matranga (Bunting), with Whyte the unused substitute. Macclesfield put the visitors under pressure in the first half but Walsall opened the scoring five minutes before half-time with a disputed goal when Macclesfield had pushed up leaving three Walsall players behind the defence. In the second half, McDonald equalised for the Silkmen but 20 minutes into the second half, with the play some 60 yards up the pitch, the referee spotted his assistant waving his flag. After discussion with his assistant, the referee cautioned both Deasy, the Macclesfield 'keeper, and a Walsall player for an offence in the penalty area. Having pulled the play back, the referee then awarded a penalty to Walsall which was converted to win the match.

Cup Competitions

In the first round of the **Worthington Cup**, Sheffield United were the visitors for the live televised match by Sky TV. Macclesfield came out of the starting blocks in a determined fashion, hitting the woodwork on two occasions before Sheffield opened the scoring, although Danny Whitaker equalised on the stroke of half-time. However, the second half belonged to the Blades with the majority of the play in the Macclesfield half, with Sheffield winning the tie through a late penalty.

For the seventh consecutive season Macclesfield were knocked out of the **LDV Vans Trophy** at the first hurdle, on this occasion by Chesterfield 2–1, and all the goals were scored in the first 15 minutes.

In the first round of the **FA Cup** Macclesfield took control of the home tie against Boston United, enjoyed plenty of possession and passed the ball fluently to win 3–0, with two goals coming from Martin Carruthers and a late goal from Colin Little.

The second-round tie against Cambridge United proved to be an eventful encounter. At the Moss Rose Matthew Tipton put the Silkmen ahead with a 22nd-minute penalty only for Cambridge to equalise a minute later. In the second half George Abbey was dismissed but the resultant penalty was saved by Steve Wilson, who went on to make a second penalty save to earn the Silkmen a replay.

At the Abbey Stadium John Miles gave the Silkmen the lead, but they were reduced to 10 men when Karl Munroe was dismissed just before half-time for a second bookable offence. Cambridge put Macclesfield under pressure in the second half and scored the equaliser. Extra-time saw Macclesfield score against the run of play but Cambridge equalised with only a minute remaining. In the penalty shoot-out Steve Wilson proved his shot-stopping abilities again but it was Danny Whitaker who scored Macclesfield's fifth penalty to win the tie 4–2 on penalties.

The third round failed to pair Macclesfield with a 'big' name and they had to settle for a trip to Swansea City. A team weakened through suspensions, injury and illness was undone by two goals by Lee Trundle, although Matthew Tipton pulled back a second-half goal, but the Silkmen could not find another goal, ending the club's FA Cup campaign for another season.

Twelve Year View

Season	League	League Position	Pts	Gls	League Cup	FA Cup	FL Trophy
1997–98	NWL3	2nd	82	63	R1	R2	R2
1998–99	NWL2	24th	43	43	R2	R3	R1
1999–2000	NWL3	13th	65	66	R1	R1	R2
2000–01	NWL3	14th	56	51	R2	R1	R2
2001–02	NWL3	13th	58	41	R1	R3	R1
2002–03	NWL3	16th	54	57	R2	R3	R2
2003–04	NWL3	20th	52	54	R1	R3	R1
2004–05	CCL2	5th	75	60	R1	R2	R3
2005–06	CCL2	17th	54	60	R2	R1	NA Final
2006–07	CCL2	22nd	48	55	R1	R3	R1
2007–08	CCL2	19th	50	47	R1	R1	R2
2008–09	CCL2	20th	47	45	R2	R3	R1

CHAPTER EIGHT: 2004–2005

THE YEAR OF 'THE BEAST'

Pre-season

Having secured Football League status at the end of the previous season, manager Brian Horton was awarded a five-year rolling contract, with John Askey kept on as his assistant. Ian Brightwell, the former Manchester City defender, was signed from Port Vale to manage the reserve team.

Season ticket prices were increased for the first time in two seasons, but a re-structure of the cost for young supporters saw the introduction of free entry for those aged under six years, and despite quite a large rise in the cost for all other categories of season tickets early sales were good, with well over 700 sold in June providing a useful increase in income.

With the introduction of new sponsors, the Football League Divisions were re-designated. The fourth tier of English football, formerly the Nationwide League Division Three, was re-named the Coca-Cola League Two.

During the summer eight of the playing staff were released by the club including full-back George Abbey, who moved up a League to play for Port Vale; central-defender Karl Munroe, who moved to Northwich Victoria; central midfielder Chris Priest, who signed for League of Wales side Bangor City; and striker Martin Carruthers, who initially moved to Boston United.

New signing Tony Barras (left) in pre-season action.

Signings included young defender Michael Briscoe from Coventry City, vastly experienced former Northern Ireland international goalkeeper Alan Fettis from Hull City, defender Mark Bailey from Lincoln City, another experienced defender Tony Barras from Notts County and veteran striker Mike Sheron from Blackpool. In addition, regular scorer for Everton's reserve and youth teams Tommy Rooney, cousin of Wayne Rooney, signed a one-year contract.

Friendly Matches

Hussam Fawzi, said to be the 'Iraqi Kevin Keegan'.

Towards the end of May Macclesfield hosted an international match, when the Iraq national side played an England National Game XI managed by former Stevenage Borough chief Paul Fairclough. A crowd of 2,636, a third of whom were Iraqi supporters in fine voice, witnessed a brilliant evening's football. In the first half the Iraqi side took the lead when Jassim Swadi Faydah scored with a header, but the England side drew level just before half-time when Barnet player Liam Hatch headed home from a corner. However, the second half belonged to the touring side, with goals coming from Ahamed Abbas (2), Karim Ajeel and Hussam Fawzi, to give the Iraqi side a 5–1 win. Playing for the Iraqi side was Jassim Fayadh who later signed for the Silkmen, but after making seven appearances for the reserves scoring three goals, and just two appearances for the senior side, Jassim had to return to Baghdad to be with his family during the troubles there.

For the Silkmen there were the usual visits to non-League sides commencing with the fans' favourite Congleton Town, where there was an unusual kick-off time of noon to avoid clashing with the town's carnival event. Matches at Leek Town and Buxton followed.

A two-match tour to Scotland firstly saw the Silkmen draw 3–3 at Clyde with goals from Matthew Tipton, Jon Parkin and Neil Morgan, a new signing who went on to feature regularly in the reserve side. The second match at Dumbarton saw a comprehensive 4–0 win, with Jon Parkin, Danny Whitaker (2) and John Miles on the score sheet.

This left time for just two home pre-season matches, the first of which ended in a 0–0 draw against Derby County with the following team: Fettis (Wilson 45), Bailey (Carr 55), Potter, Welch, Barras, Briscoe, Widdrington (Morgan 73), Harsley, Miles (Whitaker 59), Tipton (Ross 81), Parkin. The match was noteworthy for the brilliant saves made by all three 'keepers involved, Alan Fettis and Steve Wilson for the Silkmen and former Silkman Andy Oakes who was, at that time, Derby County's first-choice 'keeper. The second match saw visitors Huddersfield Town win with a late goal when Chris Brandon beat the offside trap, although the Silkmen had put in an encouraging performance and matched the visitors until the winning goal was scored.

SEASON REVIEW

August

What a start to the season with three straight wins and a leaner, fitter Jon Parkin appearing regularly on the score sheet.

For the first time in eight attempts victory was achieved at Brisbane Road when two goals from Jon Parkin and one from Matthew Tipton gave the

Silkmen a 3–1 win against Leyton Orient, leaving manager Brian Horton ecstatic and predicting that his side would be the Coca-Cola League Two surprise package. It was certainly a day for celebration for Matthew Tipton as this match was his 100th appearance for the Silkmen and his 200th career League appearance.

A 2–1 home win against Shrewsbury Town, with goals from Jon Parkin and Tony Barras, was followed by the third win when Swansea City were the visitors to the Moss Rose. Jon Parkin, playing his 100th career League match, scored the only goal in the 17th minute having controlled a Mark Bailey cross on his chest before striking home from 10 yards, and the result put the Silkmen temporarily top of the table. It seemed that Horton's defensive formation was a winning formula with the following starting line up for the Swansea match

Fettis
Welch Briscoe Barras
Bailey Potter
Harsley Widdrington Whitaker
Parkin Tipton

About this time Jon Parkin was given the nickname of 'the Beast' and after each of his goals, Andy Worth's voice would ring out over the PA system 'feed the Beast and he will score', which roused the supporters into voicing their delight. Initially Jon was somewhat unhappy with this nickname but gradually he realised that it placed him apart, and even to this day the media continue to refer to Jon as 'the Beast'– in the nicest possible way.

The second half of the month was not quite as successful. A hard-fought match at Boston saw Jon Parkin score a late equaliser in a 1–1 draw which was followed by another battling performance in the home tie against Scunthorpe

Striker Jon Parkin scored in all the opening matches of the season.

United. In an exciting match the Silkmen took the lead with a Paul Harsley goal, only for the visitors to take a 2–1 lead early in the second half. However, Matthew Tipton's 71st-minute penalty gave the Silkmen a share of the points. Three of the four 'keepers involved in this match had all played for Hull City at one time – Alan Fettis and Steve Wilson, who was on the substitutes' bench, and Scunthorpe's Paul Musselwhite. The Silkmen had never won a match at Roots Hall and the last match of the month continued the sequence when Southend ran out 2–1 winners to leave the Silkmen in fifth position in the League.

September

The month started badly at Chester City, where the Silkmen never really got going and were punished well into time added on when the home side scored from a corner, leaving the Silkmen fans somewhat aggrieved as the corner resulted from a sequence of play when there had been a bad foul on 'keeper Steve Wilson which was not recognised by the officials.

However, the status quo was restored when Grimsby Town visited the Moss Rose for the first time, although the visitors took a first-half lead and had the better of the play, until Brian Horton made a double substitution and brought on Paul Harsley and John Miles. Harsley scored with his first touch and Miles put the Silkmen in the lead only four minutes later with full-back Graham Potter sealing victory with a third goal.

At Kidderminster Harriers it was a tale of two second-half penalties, when Matthew Tipton missed the first for the Silkmen but only two minutes later Richard Appleby converted for the Harriers to win the match. For the second

Paul Harsley (right) celebrates with John Miles after scoring at Grimsby Town.

time in recent matches the Silkmen fans felt aggrieved as the offence clearly took place outside the penalty area. To rub salt into the wounds, Graham Potter had been dismissed for the foul which gave the Harriers the penalty and this was the third occasion at this early stage of the season that the Silkmen had lost to a side at the bottom of the League.

Before the final match of the month against Darlington, at the Moss Rose, there was a minute's silence in memory of football legend Brian Clough, who had died earlier in the week. In the match a brilliantly worked goal saw defender Mark Bailey score his first goal for the Silkmen giving them a 1–0 victory, and despite losing two matches during the month a League position of sixth had been achieved.

October

October was a disappointing month for results and the side were lucky to retain sixth position. A 2–1 defeat at Bury was followed by a defeat by the same margin against Notts County, another side in the doldrums before the start of the match.

However, the middle of the month saw an improvement in the results with a battling performance against high-flying Yeovil Town at Huish Park gaining victory 2–1 through a Terry Skiverton own-goal and a late winner by Jon Parkin. The following Tuesday a pacy Cambridge United side were held to a 1–1 draw at the Moss Rose, with Matthew Tipton scoring the equaliser early in the second half. A 22-yard volley by Mike Sheron, coupled with some find saves by 'keeper Alan Fettis and stout defending, gave the Silkmen a 1–0 home win against Oxford United. Completing the month a visit to Spotland saw Rochdale run out easy winners 3–0.

Veteran striker Mike Sheron (number 14) celebrates his goal at Mansfield Town.

November

Only three League matches were played in November due to Cup competitions. Mike Sheron was on the score sheet again when he scored the only goal in a 1–0 victory at Mansfield Town, however Macclesfield looked out of sorts two weeks later in the home match against Cheltenham Town when the visitors won 2–0 through two second-half goals in a match full of errors. Goals from Graham Potter a minute before half-time and Jon Parkin a minute before full-time gave the Silkmen a 2–0 victory at Rushden & Diamonds in a match where they only had three shots on target, but this win ensured that sixth place had been retained.

Brian Horton was delighted after the win at Rushden & Diamonds, saying 'We've got 30 points, which can be a bit of a landmark, and we have got there quickly so I'm delighted.' During the month Brian Horton stated that he wanted to strengthen the squad and started the process by signing midfielder Neil MacKenzie on loan from Mansfield Town.

December

Matt Carragher chalked up his 400th career appearance at Bristol Rovers.

Brian Horton then went on to make two important signings. Firstly, hardworking central midfielder Alan Navarro came on loan from Tranmere Rovers and secondly, left-sided player Kevin McIntyre moved on a free transfer from Chester City.

Two late goals by Jon Parkin, the second of which was Macclesfield's 400th League goal, gave the Silkmen a home victory against Lincoln City, but not before the visitors caused consternation when they pulled a goal back in the 90th minute. In the next match both defences ruled as a scoreless draw was fought out at Bristol Rovers, a game in which Matthew Carragher made his 400th career appearance.

There was disappointment at the Moss Rose against Northampton who won the encounter 3–1, scoring a goal on the break and two through defensive errors by the Silkmen, but full-back Graham Potter was on the score sheet again when he netted Macclesfield's only goal. On Boxing Day there was another goalless draw, this time at Grimsby Town. However, the match flowed from end-to-end and with the Silkmen defending well and 'keeper Steve Wilson making numerous saves throughout the match a share of the points was well deserved.

The year ended in thrilling style when Danny Whitaker gave the Silkmen a sixth-minute lead at the Moss Rose against Wycombe Wanderers, only to see the visitors equalise in the 90th minute. However, Macclesfield never gave up and, deep into time added on, new signing Alan Navarro scored from 20 yards to give the Silkmen their first League win against the Chairboys, old foes from the Conference days.

What a pleasant change to be looking at the top end of the table at the turn of the year with the team in fifth position. Not only that, but also on current form, the supporters were all believing that a Play-off position at the end of the season was attainable.

January

Driving rain in the first half and a swirling wind throughout the match did not provide the best of playing conditions when Chester City were the visitors for the first match of the year. Mike Sheron gave the Silkmen an early lead when he scored his 150th career goal, and while the home side had opportunities to extend their lead they found themselves defending for much of the second half, resulting in Chester scoring two goals in four minutes to complete the season double over the Silkmen. Away in the North East, Macclesfield were no match for a Darlington side which included seven players who had previously played for Middlesbrough, the Silkmen losing the match 3–1.

Some breathing space arose when the match against Notts County was postponed due to their involvement in the third round of the FA Cup. Tommy Widdrington, who had suffered a loss of form, left the club for Port Vale and Brain Horton made another extremely important double signing in central-defenders Dave Morley and Danny Swailes. Dave moved from Doncaster Rovers for a fee of £15,000 and Danny moved from Bury, at a time when they were desperate for funds, for a club-record transfer fee of £40,000. Their signing signalled the start of a run of eight matches unbeaten.

Danny Swailes (left) and Dave Morley signed at the same time, strengthening the central defence.

Following the new signings the line up for the home match against Kidderminster Harriers was as follows:

Fettis
Swailes Morley Welch
Harsley Potter
MacKenzie Navarro McIntyre
Tipton Parkin

The Silkmen as a whole were a dominant force throughout the match and secured victory with a goal each from the strike force of Matthew Tipton and Jon Parkin. At Wycombe Wanderers it was the proverbial game of two halves, with Macclesfield dominating the first half and taking the lead through a Jon Parkin goal, and Wycombe having the upper hand in the second half, resulting in Roger Johnson scoring the equaliser.

In the next match five goals were put past Notts County at Meadow Lane. Jon Parkin scored a hat-trick, firstly firing home at the second attempt after a block, then seizing onto a long ball from Michael Welch to strike into the top corner of the net and finally converting a penalty after Danny Whitaker had been brought down. To allow Jon to score his hat-trick, the usual penalty taker, Matthew Tipton, generously handed the ball to Jon. The other goals were scored by Matthew Tipton, who converted a Paul Harsley corner, and a header by Michael Welch.

In the following match, the visitors Bury took an early lead but this was cancelled out when transfer-listed Michael Welch scored the equaliser just after the break, but it was that man again, Jon Parkin, who secured all three points when he scored in the 89th minute to break Matthew Tipton's club League season record. This result left the team still, frustratingly, in fifth position.

Jon Parkin scores against Bury to break Matthew Tipton's goalscoring record of the previous season.

Top Scorers by Season

Season	Player	Goals	Season	Player	Goals
1997–98	Steve Wood	13	2003–04	Matthew Tipton	19
1998–99	Graeme Tomlinson	8	2004–05	Jon Parkin	26
1999–00	Richie Barker	17	2005–06	Clyde Wijnhard	12
2000–01	Lee Glover	10	2006–07	Kevin McIntyre	10
2001–02	Lee Glover	13	2007–08	Francis Green	11
2002–03	Matthew Tipton	14	2008–09	Gareth Evans	13
	Danny Whitaker	14			

Matthew Tipton with the matchball having scored a hat-trick against Rochdale.

February

Success continued in February with a 3–1 home win over League leaders Yeovil Town with goals from Matthew Tipton and two from Graham Potter when he drove both shots through a melee of players. In the next match against Cambridge United at the Abbey Stadium another victory was chalked up by a single goal late in the match. Forgotten player John Miles was introduced in the second half and it was his perfect cross from which Graham Potter scored the winner.

Victory over a local rival is always sweet, and a magnificent hat-trick from Matthew Tipton helped the Silkmen overcome Rochdale 3–0 at the Moss Rose. His goals came in the eighth, 12th and 90th minutes with a powerful 20-yard volley, a six-yard tap-in and the conversion of a cross from Paul Harsley.

The following match at Oxford United was postponed due to a light covering of snow on the pitch and an adverse weather forecast. In the last match of the month Bristol Rovers were beaten 2–1 at the Moss Rose, with two goals from goal machine Jon Parkin, to complete a run of six consecutive victories which lifted the team into an automatic promotion spot. With the League table looking as follows everyone's thoughts were now looking at automatic promotion at the end of the season.

	Matches Played	No. of Points
Yeovil Town	34	65
Scunthorpe United	35	60
Macclesfield Town	**34**	**60**
Swansea City	35	60
Southend United	35	60
Lincoln City	35	55
Northampton Town	33	52

For the team's performance Brian Horton was named the Coca-Cola League Two Manager of the Month for February.

March

A second-minute goal by on-loan Danny Crowe for Northampton Town saw the home side win by a single goal, bringing to an end the sequence of eight undefeated matches by the Silkmen. This match saw a very special landmark in the history of Macclesfield Town as it was their 4,000th competitive League match since the inception of the club. It was unfortunate that the milestone took place away from home as it really should have been celebrated the previous week for the home match against Bristol Rovers, but the postponement of the Oxford match a few days earlier meant that the actual 4,000th match was at Northampton.

Paul Harsley celebrates his goal against Leyton Orient sandwiched between Jon Parkin and Kevin McIntyre, with Matthew Tipton looking on.

Life was better at Shrewsbury Town when rejuvenated John Miles came on from the substitutes' bench to score a late winner, with his shot taking a massive deflection on the way. Another victory was secured at the Moss Rose when Leyton Orient were the visitors. Having taken the lead in the first half through a Jon Parkin goal, the visitors equalised early in the second half and always looked dangerous, winning more corners and having more shots at goal, but after Matthew Tipton had converted a penalty for Macclesfield they never looked back and sealed victory with a third goal scored by Paul Harsley.

With England playing a World Cup Qualifying match the following day, the next match at Swansea City was brought forward by a day and played on the Friday evening. The home side were on top throughout and scored a goal in each half to win the encounter. To make matters worse Jon Parkin was dismissed late in the second half for violent conduct, for which he

Mark Bailey rises high to score a rare goal and then joyfully celebrates with Tony Barras.

received a three-match ban, and 'keeper Alan Fettis sustained a hand injury. With the goal machine out of the reckoning doubts were raised at this stage of the season whether an automatic promotion position was still attainable.

The month ended with a 1–1 draw at home against Boston United but Macclesfield had the assistant referee to thank for awarding them their goal, which was scored by Mark Bailey as the referee had indicated that play should continue after an alleged infringement. Having reached the dizzy heights of an automatic promotion position, by the end of the month the team had slipped back to fifth position.

April

Steve Wilson was in his best shot-stopping form and with the defence holding firm a goalless draw ensued at Glanford Park against Scunthorpe United. The re-arranged match at Oxford United followed with the Silkmen on the back foot almost from the start when the home side took a third-minute lead. Steve Wilson again played a blinder to keep the Silkmen in the match but it was left to John Miles, whose ability to change the direction of a match helped him score a late equaliser for a share of the points.

Jon Parkin returned for the match at Lincoln City but Macclesfield's poor run of form continued when the Imps ran out 2–0 winners. Another defeat came at the Moss Rose when Southend United were the visitors, taking all three points, winning 2–1 and launching themselves to the top of the League table.

However, in the next match at the Moss Rose Macclesfield scored three of the best goals of the season against a poor Mansfield side. Jon Parkin was back on form and scored the first from 25 yards, and Matthew Tipton scored the second after Paul Harsley had won the ball in midfield and set up Matthew Tipton, who picked out Jon Parkin who then planted a cross onto Matthew Tipton's head to finish with a glancing blow. The third goal came from Dave Morley when he headed home from a Mark Boyd corner. The visitors scored one goal but it was the home side who ran out 3–1 winners.

Due to a pre-season injury Silkmen favourite defender Steve Payne had been unable to make any appearances for the senior side, although he had played some part in the reserve side's campaign, resulting in him being released so that he could seek out another club.

The final match of the month ended in disappointment when Cheltenham earned a 3–0 home win to leave the Silkmen in sixth position.

May

Needing just one point in the last match of the season to be sure of a Play-off place, an uncertain first half against Rushden & Diamonds had the Silkmen supporters anxious and frustrated at half-time. However, on the hour Jon Parkin scored the only goal of the match after which Macclesfield looked more comfortable and took the game to the visitors, only to be frustrated by some excellent saves by their 'keeper. The result ensured that the Silkmen completed the League programme in fifth position, a slot which they had occupied for much of the season and guaranteed them a place in the Play-off competition for the first time ever.

Lincoln City were the Silkmen's Play-off semi-final opponents as they had completed the season in sixth position. The first leg took place at Sincil Bank with a 17.15 kick-off in front of 7,032 spectators. Before the match all the fans

Jon Parkin scores the winning goal against Rushden & Diamonds.

Macclesfield fans supporting their team at Sincil Bank.

paid tribute to the 56 who had died in the Bradford fire tragedy some 20 years earlier when Lincoln City were the visitors, with a rendition of *You'll Never Walk Alone*.

The Macclesfield team was: Fettis, Bailey, Carragher, Morley, Swailes, Harsley, McIntyre, Whitaker (Townson 78), Parkin, Tipton. Lincoln scored the only goal in the 11th minute when Kevin Sandwith (later to become a Silkman) crossed the ball into the box for Gareth McAuley to head home. Macclesfield were unlucky when an excellent strike by Matthew Tipton hit the crossbar just before half-time.

The second leg took place a week later on 21 May at the Moss Rose with a 12.05 kick-off to accommodate Sky television. The attendance was 5,223 and the Macclesfield side was: Fettis, Bailey (Whitaker 65), Barras, Carragher, Morley, Swailes, Harsley, McIntyre, Parkin, Tipton (Briscoe 75), Townson (Miles

Matthew Tipton claims foul play when Lincoln goalkeeper Alan Marriot brought down Jon Parkin.

Player of the Year Paul Harsley (right) pulls a goal back in the second leg of the Play-off semi-final at the Moss Rose.

60). In a repeat performance of the first leg, Gareth McAuley scored an early goal, giving the Silkmen an uphill task. Macclesfield really did not start playing until the additional pace of Danny Whitaker and John Miles was introduced when they came on from the substitutes' bench in the second half. The Silkmen were then inspired and Paul Harsley pulled a goal back in the 76th minute after which the Silkmen attacked the Lincoln goal, but the assault was too late with Keith Alexander's Lincoln winning 2–1 on aggregate to gain a place in the Final at the Millennium Stadium.

The Silkmen had enjoyed their most successful season since their first season as members of the Football League in 1997–98, providing a much more exciting level of play. Jon Parkin's total of 26 goals saw him finish the season as top scorer and set a club Football League record for the highest number of goals scored by a player in a season, a record which still remains today. The ever-hardworking midfielder Paul Harsley was voted Player of the Year.

Cup Competitions

There was a first-round exit in the **Carling Cup** at Hartlepool United where the Silkmen took an early second-half lead through a Jon Parkin goal but conceded two late goals to lose the tie 2–1.

A 2–1 victory against Chesterfield at the Moss Rose in the **LDV Vans Trophy** was the Silkmen's first-ever success in this competition. In the second round they demolished visitors Mansfield Town 4–0 with goals from Tony Barras, Jon Parkin (2) and Matthew Tipton to celebrate Brian Horton's 1,000th match as a manager. Brian became only the 11th manager in English League football to achieve this milestone – the others before him to reach this landmark were Alan Buckley, Lennie Lawrence, Dario Gradi, Dave Bassett, Graham Taylor, Jim Smith, Brian Clough, Sir Matt Busby, Sir Alex Ferguson and Denis Smith. The third round was another home tie when a well organised Tranmere Rovers side ran out winners 1–0.

In the first round of the **FA Cup** the Silkmen were given an away tie at Conference North side Alfreton Town, which proved to be a lively affair. Danny Whitaker must have thought that he had won the match for Macclesfield when his 25-yard shot took a deflection and flew into the net in the 86th minute, but Alfreton's tall striker, Mark Sale, had other ideas when two minutes into time added on, Alan Fettis having been blatantly barged off the ball, he equalised from close range. In the replay 10 days later, two extremely well-taken goals by Jon Parkin and Mike Sheron ensured progression into the second round. Hull City were the opponents but the Silkmen only managed to match them for the first 27 minutes, after which the home side scored four goals in 18 minutes to win 4–0 and claim a place in the third round.

Manager Brian Horton (second from the left) presented with a commemorative vase by ex-Nottingham Forest boss Frank Clark to celebrate 1,000 managerial games.

Top 10 Home Attendances

(Since August 1997)

6,381	Manchester City	League	12 September 1998
6,008	Everton	FAC Round 3	3 January 2009
5,982	Chester City	League	25 April 1998
5,706	West Ham United	FAC Round 3	6 January 2002
5,223	Lincoln City	League Two S/F Play-off	21 May 2005
5,122	Notts County	League	28 February 1998
4,553	Stockport County	League	26 December 2006
4,451	Stockport County	League	14 April 2007
4,325	Preston North End	League	10 April 1999
4,244	Watford	FAC Round 3	4 January 2003

CHAPTER NINE: 2005–2006

BACK DOWN TO EARTH

Pre-season

As usual there were several changes in the playing staff including some surprises among the nine players who left the club during the summer months. Perhaps one of the most unexpected releases was central-defender Matthew Carragher, who had performed well, especially in the role of sweeper, although he had played out of position at full-back towards the end of the season which did not suite his style of play. Another surprise release was Graham Potter, who arguably was one of the best left-backs seen at the Moss Rose in recent years, and to score six goals from the full-back position had been quite remarkable. Both Matthew and Graham decided to retire from professional football with Graham eventually taking up the position of football development manager at Hull University. Goalkeeper Steve Wilson, having proved his shot-stopping abilities more than once, occasionally keeping Alan Fettis out of the team, secured a move to Tranmere Rovers. Others who left were Michael Welch, who moved to Accrington Stanley; Steven Brackenridge; Steve Owens; and Tommy Rooney.

There were five new signings. David Beresford, a pacy left-sided player, who had spent time on loan at the Moss Rose in the 2003–2004 season, made the move from Tranmere Rovers. Right-winger Martin Bullock came from Blackpool and left-back Kevin Sandwith, who was provider for Lincoln City's goal at Sincel Bank in the previous season's Play-off semi-final, made the move from Lincoln City. Another player who had previously been on loan at the Moss Rose was forward Kevin Townson, who moved permanently from Rochdale, and lastly Scottish striker Allan Russell moved south of the border from St Mirren.

It was decided that the club would not operate a reserve side for the forthcoming season, with manager Brian Horton justifying the decision inasmuch that he could not afford to have players injured as he was working with a smaller squad, and it was wrong to have members of the youth team playing two matches each week. He also said that other Football League sides successfully operated without a reserve side but that friendly matches would be arranged to accommodate those members of the squad who were not playing on a regular basis.

New signing, right-winger Martin Bullock in pre-season action at Northwich Victoria.

Friendly Matches

There were six friendly matches arranged with the usual mixture of non-League and Football League sides. A strong Macclesfield side proved too much for Congleton Town when they ran out easy winners 6–0. A goal in each half helped the Silkmen win 2–0 at Northwich Victoria, but there was a surprise defeat at

Goalkeeper Alan Fettis made several important saves in the pre-season friendly match against Manchester City.

Droylsden 5–1 and Leek Town won 1–0 through a spectacular goal against a Macclesfield side which included several members of the youth team.

On a warm and sunny afternoon Macclesfield faced a depleted Manchester City side as many of the squad had flown out to Thailand where they were to play series of matches the following week. Nevetheless, the City starting line up included Ben Thatcher, David Sommeil, Sylvain Distin, Claudio Reyna and the up-and-coming Micah Richards. The Macclesfield team was Fettis, Bailey (Briscoe 45), Sandwith (Smart 59), Morley, Swailes (Teague 59), Bullock (Barras 45), Harsley (Whitaker 45), Parkin (Townson 21), Miles (Morgan 70), Beresford (McDonald 75), McIntyre (MacKenzie 59). The Silkmen took the lead in the fourth minute with a goal from Jon Parkin but City's speedy triallist Yasser Hussain equalised four minutes later. On 21 minutes disaster struck when Jon Parkin, the previous season's top scorer, was injured and had to leave the field. Later it was revealed that he had sustained a bad knee injury which kept him out of contention until the end of October. Alan Fettis was called upon to make several saves but the match ran out of momentum in the second half.

The final pre-season match saw newly promoted Premiership side Wigan Athletic visit the Moss Rose, where goals from Andreas Johansson, Jimmy Bullard, Gary Teale and Alan Mahon gave the visitors a 4–0 win.

SEASON REVIEW

August

For the second consecutive season the Silkmen travelled to Brisbane Road to play Leyton Orient for the opening match. But unlike the previous season when they ran out winners, this time it was the home side who were the victors. The Silkmen's start to the season could not have been worse when Orient opened the scoring after 63 seconds but a more spirited performance by the Silkmen in the second half saw Paul Harsley equalise, but it proved to be in vain as Efe Echanomi sealed victory for the Orient with a cheeky back-heeled goal in the 90th minute.

Cheltenham Town were the first visitors of the season and bossed the first half, taking a 1–0 lead into the interval, but the Silkmen appeared to have been hampered by an unusual formation of 3-1-5-1. With a half-time change of formation to 4-4-2 Macclesfield's performance improved to provide a lively second half but this did not stop Cheltenham extending their lead in the 82nd minute. However, Macclesfield stepped up a gear and two goals in three minutes by Neil MacKenzie and Martin Bullock gave the Silkmen a share of the points.

The home match against Rushden & Diamonds was postponed when a tremendous storm before the match flooded the corner between the Silkmen Terrace and the McAlpine Stand.

There then followed two away matches, firstly at Barnet where a first-half strike secured them victory, and secondly at Rochdale where the Silkmen took the lead when Kevin Townson, returning to his former club, scored a wonderful solo goal when he collected the ball near the right-hand corner, beat a defender on the bye-line and struck home from the tightest of angles. But two goals in two minutes, both from corners, saw Rochdale take charge of the match. Rochdale went on to score a third goal in the second half to leave the Silkmen in bottom place, a complete contrast to the previous season when they were top of the table at this time.

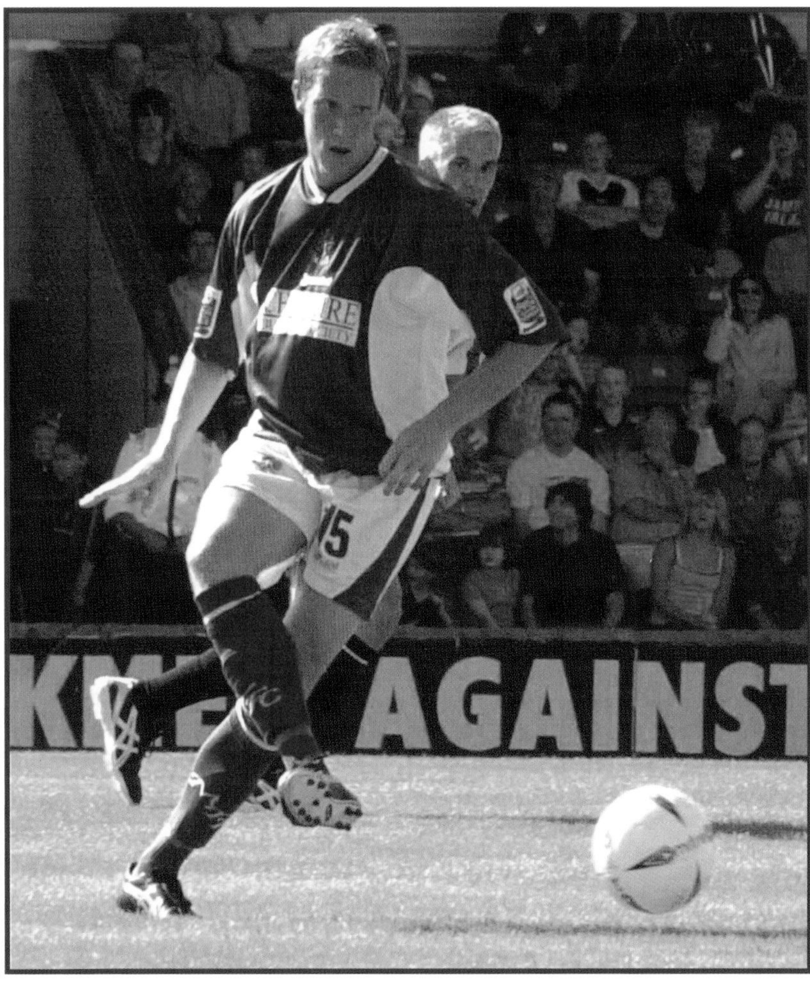

Neil MacKenzie's goal against Cheltenham Town earned a share of the points.

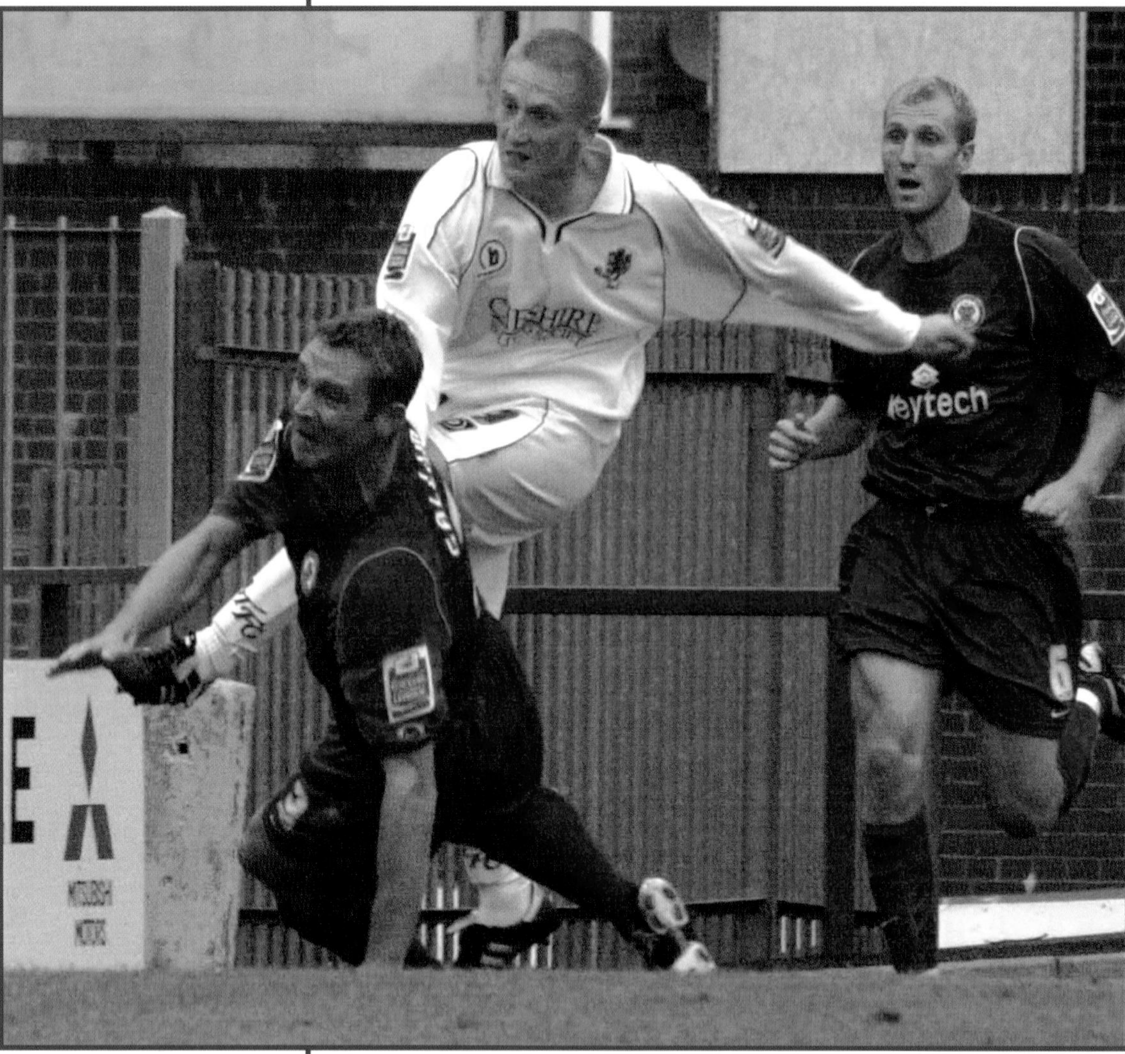

Under pressure, Kevin Townson (centre) scores a wonder goal at Rochdale on his return to his former club.

However, much to the relief of the Silkmen supporters, a first-half goal by Martin Bullock secured a 1–0 win against Bury at the Moss Rose, but not before Bury had applied pressure in the second half when the ball was cleared off the line and 'keeper Alan Fettis had to make several saves. Following this victory the side were in 21st position.

During the month Macclesfield Town players became the first Division Two team to wear Sockatyes tie-ups emblazoned with the club logo, their name and squad number.

September

The first match of the month was played in sweltering heat and Boston United were the visitors. The Silkmen took a two-goal first-half lead but Boston performed the better of the two teams in the second half, pulling a goal back on 48 minutes and equalising on 75 minutes. In this match Paul Harsley made his 300th career League appearance.

At Carlisle, the Silkmen held on until late in the second half when the home side scored twice, leaving Brian Horton fuming and complaining post match 'We're just not strong enough as a unit. We're not playing as a team, we're not defending as a team and it's costing us.'

But back on home soil the re-arranged match against Rushden & Diamonds three days later produced a much needed victory. A rather run-of-the-mill affair in the first half, nevertheless saw Martin Bullock give the Silkmen a first-half lead. The second half was a much more lively affair with end-to-end football and more incidents including a penalty claim, clearances off the line and three goals, two for Macclesfield through a Paul Harsley penalty and a second for Martin Bullock, and a consolation goal for Rushden & Diamonds.

A 4–1 defeat by Northampton Town at the Moss Rose saw Dave Morley making his 200th career League appearance, but a visit to Wrexham saw the Silkmen pick up their first away point of the campaign when Allan Russell scored a wonderful solo goal having latched onto the ball, turned and then beaten two defenders before firing home for his first English League goal to level the score at 1–1.

The month ended with another 1–1 draw, this time against Mansfield Town at the Moss Rose. It was an entertaining match between two evenly matched teams, with Allan Russell on the score sheet again in the first half, but Mansfield came out after the break in determined form and quickly equalised. However, at least 21st position had been maintained. In a move to boost attendances free tickets were handed out at this match to everyone attending to pass on to their family, a friend or a colleague to attend any home League match before 25 December 2005. In addition, each season-ticket holder was given a voucher for a pre-booked one-match upgrade to Vice-President entry.

October

A goalless draw started the month off when Notts County were the visitors, who had their 'keeper, Kevin Pilkington, to thank for keeping them in the

Allan Russell, seen here in action at Rochdale, scored a splendid solo goal at Wrexham.

New signing, defensive central midfielder Alan Narvarro.

match with a string of saves. Alan Fettis, the Macclesfield 'keeper, made his 400th career appearance in this match. There was more woe on the road soon afterwards when Darlington won 1–0 in the following match, which was followed by a 4–0 home defeat by Peterborough United. After this match Brian Horton was so incensed that he placed Tony Barras, Neil MacKenzie, Allan Russell and Kevin Sandwith on the transfer list.

Midfielder Alan Navarro, who had been on loan the previous season, was signed from Accrington Stanley and went straight into the side. In addition, Surinam-born veteran striker Clyde Wijnhard was signed on loan from Darlington and made his full League debut in the next match at Torquay. Following the signing of Clyde, Brian Horton went for a 4-5-1 formation which he used at Torquay as follows:

Fettis
Bailey Morley Swailes McIntyre
Bullock Whitaker Navarro Harsley Beresford
Wijnhard

Paul Harsley gave the Silkmen an early second-half lead which they failed to hold onto when the home side equalised in the 68th minute, and the match ended 1–1 and left the Silkmen in bottom place.

But there was a much better performance when Bristol Rovers were the visitors, Clyde Wijnhard giving the Silkmen an early lead in the second half, only for Rovers to equalise three minutes later. However, in a goalmouth melee 10 minutes later, Paul Harsley forced the ball home from close range to win the match 2–1. There was even better news when striker Jon Parkin made a cameo appearance in this match after injury, coming on from the substitutes' bench in the 90th minute. Nevertheless, the Silkmen found themselves in the relegation zone in 23rd position.

November

With the FA Cup competition occupying the first Saturday in the month the first League match was played at Grimsby Town on Friday 12 November, the match having been brought forward as England were due to play a friendly against Argentina the following day. The Mariners won the encounter 3–1 but Jon Parkin scored his first League goal of the season when he was again introduced from the substitutes' bench.

A much-needed victory came at home against Darlington through a Kevin McIntyre goal. Jon Parkin made his first League start of the campaign and was an influential member of the team, using his physical presence and as provider for the goal. With Jon available for selection in the starting line up, Brian Horton reverted to a two-man strike force of Jon Parkin and Clyde Wijnhard, who would head a 4-4-2 formation.

The month ended in a goalless draw against 10-man Leyton Orient but, at least, the Silkmen had gained one place in the League table to 22nd position.

Recent signing striker Clyde Wijnhard scored his first goal at Bristol Rovers to set him on the road to being top scorer for the season.

December

The month started in turmoil for the supporters when it was announced that assistant manager John Askey had been served with six months' notice to terminate his contract with the club. John, affectionately known as 'Sir John', had been one of the most faithful employees of the club since 1984 as a player, first-team coach, manager, assistant manager and manager of the reserve side. A fans' petition was set up expressing disappointment with the current position and asking for John to be found alternative employment within the club. To everyone's delight there was a happy ending but it was several months before there was a further announcement by the club (which will be covered later).

In contrast, the month of December saw results starting to improve. At Lincoln City, Clyde Wijnhard scored on the stroke of half-time but it was the home side who took the lead in the second half with goals in the 72nd and 79th minute. Macclesfield fought back and Andrew Teague scored his first senior goal two minutes later, and the Silkmen could well have taken all three points but for a superb save by the Lincoln 'keeper Alan Marriott.

Next the Silkmen were off to Cheltenham Town for a disappointing 2–2 draw after Kevin Sandwith and Jon Parkin had given Macclesfield a two-goal

Youngster Andrew Teague scored his first senior goal at Lincoln City.

lead. The home side came back strongly, however, and scored in the 85th and 90th minutes. There was then yet another drawn match at home when Barnet equalised in the 90th minute, Kevin Sandwith having opened the scoring in the first half. In this match Paul Harsley made his 100th appearance for Macclesfield and Danny Swailes made his 200th career League appearance.

On Boxing Day near neighbours Stockport County visited the Moss Rose for the first time in a competitive League match, although they had played at the Moss Rose previously in an FA Cup encounter during Macclesfield's Conference days. And for the first time in their League history Macclesfield scored six goals. They were inspired by Man of the Match Martin Bullock and were the dominant force throughout, but it has to be taken into account that Stockport were reduced to 10 men early on when Tesfaye Bramble was dismissed in the 17th minute. The goals were scored by Clyde Wijnhard (2), Jon Parkin (2), Martin Bullock and John Miles. At least the Stockport supporters retained their sense of humour by chanting 'we want one', and they said later that Macclesfield had done them a favour when their manager was dismissed following the match.

The match on 28 December, which should have been played at Shrewsbury Town, was postponed due to a frozen pitch. The year ended in triumph when Kevin McIntyre's 60th-minute goal provided a home victory against Chester City; however, 'keeper Alan Fettis was injured during this match and was replaced by young Tim Deasy. A League position of 18th made much more healthy reading.

A match full of drama, especially for Macclesfield's young 'keeper Tim Deasy, was played out at Wycombe Wanderers when the Silkmen were in the lead 3–0 in the first 13 minutes, with two goals from Clyde Wijnhard and one from Danny Whitaker, but the home side pulled a goal back before half-time via the penalty spot. In the second half Wycombe scored two more goals to equalise and then Dave Morley put the ball in his own net to give Wycombe a 4–3 lead. Enter Jon Parkin, who levelled the score a minute later and won the match with a towering header in the 81st minute to give the Silkmen a 5–4 win, their highest aggregate score since joining the Football League and their first away victory of the campaign.

Defender Tony Barras had been sidelined for several weeks through a recurring hip problem and was given the choice of a third operation, which would have carried him through to the end of the season but could have caused health problems in the longer term, and so he elected to retire from professional football after a total of 17 years in the game.

In his 150th career League appearance Jon Parkin scored Macclesfield's only goal at Boston, who ran out winners 3–1 to bring to an end the Silkmen's League record run of 10 consecutive matches without defeat. This was Jon's final match for the club as he moved to Hull City the following week for an

Defender Tony Barras decided to retire from professional football after 17 years.

Farewell to high scoring Jon Parkin who moved to Hull City.

undisclosed fee. Preston North End were said to have made a higher offer but Jon, living in York, opted to move to Hull. A tall, robust striker, Jon was much more than a target man and still holds the club's League record for the most goals scored by an individual player in a single season. His 26 goals in the 2004–2005 season ensured that the team remained near the top of the League for the whole season and enhanced the matchday experience, making for a more enjoyable and relaxing time. On leaving Jon said 'I owe everything to Macc. My career was going nowhere until John Askey brought me to the club, but ever since I joined it has just got better and better.'

With Jon Parkin gone, Brian Horton gave Clyde Wijnhard the lone striker's role, although Martin Bullock was used just behind him in a 5-3-1-1 formation, but there were times when a second striker was introduced and Brian would revert to the more conventional 4-4-2 formation. The first post-Parkin match resulted in a 1–1 draw when Oxford United visited the Moss Rose and defended all set pieces with 10 men.

Although 'keeper Alan Fettis had regained full fitness, second string 'keeper Tim Deasy had been injured, and so to ensure that there was back-up for Alan Fettis, Tommy Lee, a 20-year-old 'keeper from Manchester United, was signed on loan.

Promotion chasing Cobblers proved too much for the Silkmen when they visited Northampton Town, who ran out easy winners 5–0; however, a much improved performance saw the Silkmen defeat Carlisle United 3–0 at the Moss Rose with three first-half goals from Danny Swailes, Kevin McIntyre and Danny Whitaker. The re-arranged match at Shrewsbury Town, who included former Silkman Neil Sorvel in their side, turned out to be a disappointing draw, Macclesfield again losing the lead. Nevertheless, the side moved up one position in the League to 17th.

The late Eric Campbell.

There was some sad news during the month as Eric Campbell, the club's assistant physiotherapist, who was also physiotherapist during the Conference days, died after a heart by-pass operation. Eric had been connected with the club for many years and was well liked by everyone. In the McIlroy days he loved refereeing the end of training sessions' five-a-side matches, when he would often give some questionable decisions on purpose. As a permanent memorial to Eric, the home changing room has been named 'The Eric Campbell Dressing Room', a truly fitting reminder of a really genuine person.

February

For once Macclesfield came from behind at Mansfield Town when Danny Swailes converted a Kevin

Sandwith corner for a 1–1 draw, but in truth it was another outstanding display by 'keeper Alan Fettis that gave the Silkmen a share of the points. The following match against Wrexham was postponed due to a frozen Moss Rose pitch.

Macclesfield's 400th Football League match took place at Oxford United, where young on-loan 'keeper Tommy Lee made his Football League debut as Alan Fettis had picked up an injury during training. This was also Clyde Wijnhard's 200th career appearance in English football. A 25-yard free-kick by Kevin Sandwith had given the Silkmen the lead, which they contrived to lose when Oxford scored an equaliser for a second 1–1 draw in the month.

A third consecutive 1–1 draw saw the Silkmen concede the lead for the 10th time in the season after Clyde Wijnhard's penalty had given them the lead in the first half, on this occasion at home to Lincoln City.

Left-back Kevin Sandwith scored from a 25-yard free-kick at Oxford United.

The match at Rushden & Diamonds was described by Brian Horton as Macclesfield's worst performance of the season so far when they lost 1–0 to on-loan Drewe Broughton's 81st-minute goal. Leading scorer Clyde Wijnhard had picked up a knee injury and was unavailable for selection, with John Miles taking his place as striker. The Silkmen were fortunate that the home side had two goals disallowed and were saved further by fine saves by 'keeper Tommy Lee. At least 17th position had been retained.

On-loan goalkeeper Tommy Lee in action against Rushden & Diamonds.

March

With Clyde Wijnhard out of contention for the remainder of the season, 6ft 5in striker Matty McNeil was signed on loan from Conference North side Hyde United as a replacement.

There was another postponement due to a frozen pitch, this time at Bury. Macclesfield's woes continued when their performance lacked energy, ideas and passing ability when Rochdale, the visitors, won 3–1 in a match which completed their double over the Silkmen.

The re-arranged match against Wrexham at the Moss Rose saw the Silkmen lucky to go in at the interval only 2–1 down in a match where central-defender Dave Morley partnered Matty McNeil as the Silkmen's strike force. In the second half, the home side played with more determination and goals from Danny Whitaker and Michael Briscoe gave them a 3–2 win. In the following match a bizarre own-goal and a goal in time added on gave Stockport County a 2–0 win at Edgeley Park.

To bolster the strike force, Marcus Richardson was signed on loan from Chester City to the end of the season, and he made his debut in the 2–0 home win against Shrewsbury Town. This victory gave the Silkmen a seven point buffer from the relegation zone.

April

In April the club announced that they were to retain the services of long-serving John Askey, who had been given six months notice to end his contract earlier in the season, and that a further announcement would be made during the summer about the position he was to fulfil.

Defender Dave Morley started as a striker again in the match at Chester which was goalless at half-time, but on-loan Chester striker Derek Asamoah opened the scoring shortly after the break. On the hour Kevin Townson replaced Dave Morley, and 15 minutes later he headed home the equaliser, only for Man of the Match Asamoah to score in time added on to give Chester all three points. Three days later the re-arranged match at Bury ended in a goalless draw in a match where both teams only managed a total of four shots on target.

In the next home match, Paul Harsley scored from the penalty spot in the first half against Wycombe Wanderers and Danny Whitaker extended the lead in the second half, but Wycombe scored a late goal and put Macclesfield under pressure, but at the final whistle the Silkmen had held out to win 2–1 for their first double of the season.

At Notts County the home side took the lead on the stroke of half-time but after Kevin Townson had been tripped in the box, Paul Harsley stepped up and slotted home the resultant penalty one minute from time to earn a point.

There were no celebrations for Danny Whitaker's 200th career appearance when Torquay United won 2–0 at the Moss Rose, and there was another defeat at Peterborough. Before this match there was drama when the Posh manager resigned 70 minutes before the start of the match at a time when Peterborough were taking part in a television series. The Silkmen went into the interval with the score at 0–0 but they lost the match 3–2 in time added on yet again, having taken the lead, lost it and equalised.

Alan Fettis returned in goal for a nerve-racking match when the visitors Grimsby Town took a first-half lead, but Marcus Richardson bundled the ball over the line some three minutes later. However, Macclesfield withstood the Mariners' pressure to gain a vital point, but this still left the Silkmen with all to play for in the final match of the season with the League table as follows:

	Played	Goal Difference	Points	
Bury	45	12	52	
Macclesfield Town	**45**	**12**	**51**	
Torquay United	45	13	51	
Barnet	45	-14	51	
Notts County	45	15	51	
Stockport County	45	-21	51	
Oxford United	45	13	49	
Rushden & Diamonds	45	31	45	Relegated

May

There was another 90 nerve-racking minutes at Bristol Rovers in the final match of the season. Dave Morley opened the scoring in the seventh minute when he headed home a Kevin McIntyre corner, but Rovers' Lewis Haldane equalised just five minutes later. On-loan striker Marcus Richardson muscled off two challenges to put the Silkmen in the lead again and the score remained 2–1 at half-time. Lewis Haldane equalised for Bristol in the 57th minute and just when it looked as though the match would end in a draw, Marcus Richardson headed home a pin-point cross from John Miles to give the

Dave Morley (far right) celebrates the Silkmen's opening goal at Bristol Rovers.

Striker Marcus Richardson scored the all-important winning goal at Bristol Rovers.

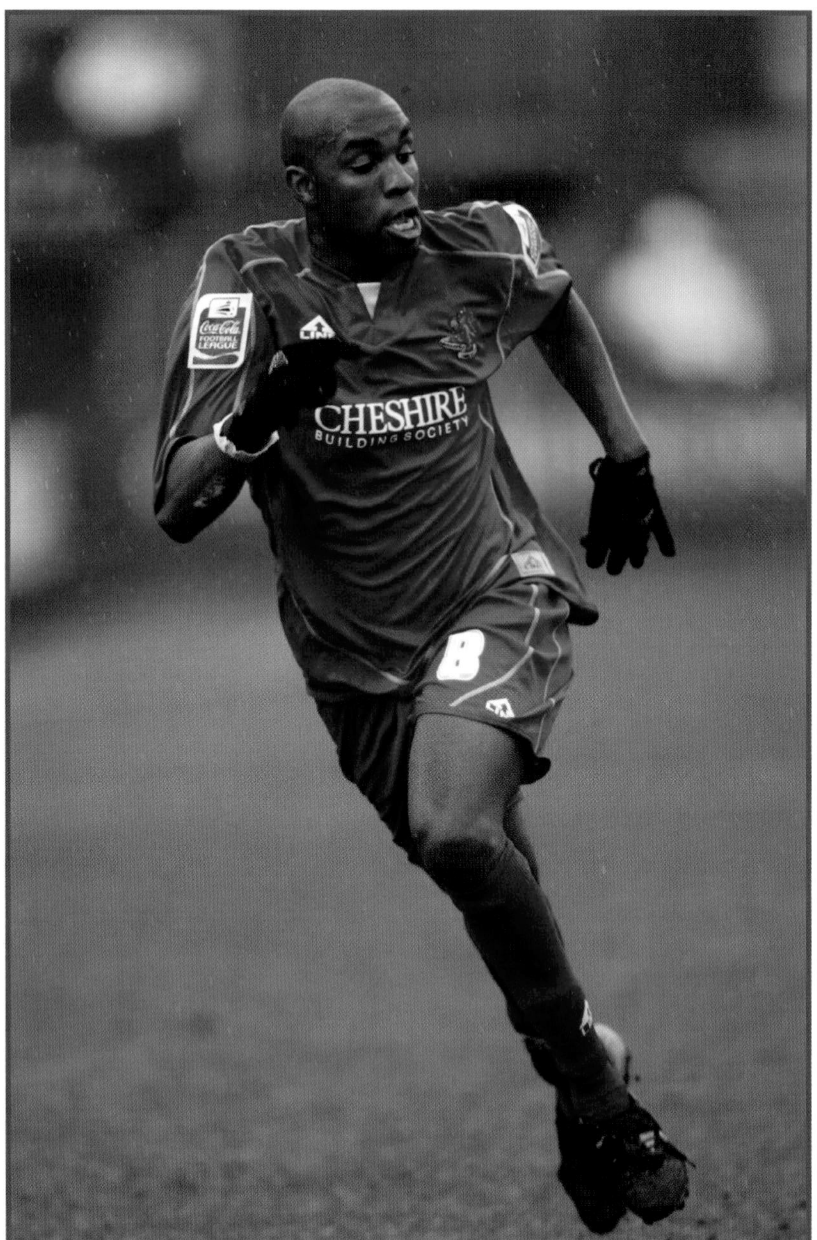

Average Home Attendances

1997–98	2,905
1998–99	3,311
1999–2000	2,304
2000–01	2,064
2001–02	2,123
2002–03	2,110
2003–04	2,390
2004–05	2,277
2005–06	2,275
2006–07	2,428
2007–08	2,309
2008–09	1,897

Silkmen a 3–2 victory and retention of their Football League status, finishing the season in 17th position with 54 points, five points more than 23rd placed Oxford United.

The elation of staying up was dampened when the players could not celebrate with the Silkmen fans at the end of the match because a minority of young Bristol Rovers fans caused a disturbance in front of the away supporters.

After the enjoyment of riding high in the League the previous season, the team really came down to earth with a bang and found themselves unable to climb up the table throughout the season. Nineteen different players scored goals, but it was veteran striker Clyde Wijnhard who was top scorer with 12 goals, all of which were scored between October and February, with the departed Jon Parkin second top scorer with nine goals. Even the players admitted that the side had missed the physical presence and goalscoring ability of Jon Parkin. Danny Whitaker was rewarded for all his hard work in the midfield when he was voted Player of the Year.

Cup Competitions

In the first round of the **Carling Cup** Macclesfield won a fine victory at Nottingham Forest 3–2. Forest took an early lead but goals by Danny Whitaker and Kevin Townson gave the Silkmen a 2–1 lead at the interval. Neil MacKenzie took the score to 3–1 in the 80th minute but Forest's 83rd-minute goal resulted in a tense finish. The second round saw the Silkmen on the road again, this time to the Welsh capital and opponents Cardiff City. Martin Bullock gave the Silkmen the lead in five minutes which they held onto until the interval. Cardiff pulled out all the stops in the second half and took the lead after five minutes, with on-loan substitute Jason Koumas scoring the winner with a superb free-kick.

In the first round of the **FA Cup** Yeovil Town made Macclesfield battle hard at the Moss Rose, but against the run of play Clyde Wijnhard scored the opening goal two minutes after half-time. Danny Swailes was then dismissed for deliberate handball and Yeovil equalised from the penalty spot to set up a replay at Huish Park, where Yeovil took charge and won 4–0.

After the LDV Vans company had gone into liquidation the competition was renamed **The Football League Trophy** which, completely in contrast to their indifferent League form, saw the Silkmen enjoy their best-ever success in the competition. In the first round, a changed formation to 4-4-2 saw a much improved performance by all the players, who worked as a team, passed accurately and defended well to beat Chesterfield Town 2–0 with goals from Clyde Wijnhard and David Beresford.

In the second round, two second-half goals, including a brilliant free-kick by Kevin Sandwith, saw the Silkmen victorious in a 2–1 win at Chesterfield. Then a comprehensive 4–2 win at the Moss Rose in the third round against Conference side Cambridge United saw the Silkmen progress to the Northern area semi-final for the first time, where they faced another Conference side, Hereford United, at the Moss Rose. First-half goals from Danny Whitaker and Paul Harsley gave the Silkmen a 2–0 win and progression to the Northern area final.

The first leg of the Northern area final was played at Carlisle in front of a crowd of 5,706 where Andy Smart scored a stunning 22-yard shot for a valuable away goal, but this only spurred the home side into action, who equalised 11 minutes later from a disputed corner. After the break Macclesfield changed their formation from 5-3-2 to 4-5-1 and looked dangerous on the break, but poor defending allowed Carlisle to score in the 90th minute to take a one-goal advantage into the second leg at the Moss Rose. It was a pulsating match from start to finish played in front of a crowd of 3,598, including over 2,000 Carlisle fans. Macclesfield went two goals up in the first 28 minutes, the second of which was scored by Matty McNeil on his debut for the club, but Carlisle scored a vital away goal just before the interval to level the scores at 3–3 on aggregate. Neither side could score in the second half but in extra-time Karl Hawley scored his second goal of the evening and Carlisle's second away goal. Kevin Townson scored in the last minute of extra-time for Macclesfield to level the aggregate score at 4–4, but Carlisle won the tie on the 'away' goals rule. It was extremely disappointing that Macclesfield had missed out on the opportunity to play at the Millennium Stadium by a whisker. The 'away' goals rule can be seen as favouring the side playing away from home in the second leg, but fortunately today the competition no longer relies on this rule. Instead, if the scores remain level at the end of extra-time, the tie is settled by penalty-kicks.

CHAPTER TEN: 2006–2007

THE GREAT ESCAPE

Pre-season

In a further move to increase attendances on match days, there was a bold decision by the directors when they reduced admission prices to £13 for seated accommodation and £10 for terrace accommodation, with proportionate reductions for concessions. The age for free entry for young people was raised from under six to under 12 years of age, and under 16s only paid £5 per match at the gate or £50 for a season ticket. The cheapest season ticket for adults was set at £210 for early purchase. This move was emphasised by the slogan 'Real football for real fans at real prices' together with a leaflet drop in the town. However, there was a niggling feeling among some of the supporters that the move could be undermined if the quality of the product on the pitch did not improve significantly on that seen in recent times.

The long-awaited announcement of the future role of Silkmen legend John Askey was greeted with approval when he was given the responsibility for youth development in the club and as youth-team manager. Brian Horton remained as manager with Ian Brightwell as the first-team coach.

There were numerous changes to the playing squad over the summer months. Eight players who had featured regularly in the previous season left the club for pastures new. Michael Briscoe moved to Burton Albion, Tim Deasy to Stockport County, Alan Fettis to Bury, Paul Harsley and Danny Whitaker moved up a League to Port Vale, Kevin Townson moved to Northwich Victoria, Clyde Wijnhard initially signed for Brentford but later retired to become a football agent and Kevin Sandwith, who after an indifferent start had made a useful contribution to the Silkman cause, moved to Chester City.

Striker Matty McNeil and 'keeper Tommy Lee, both of whom had been on loan the previous season, signed permanent contracts and another 'keeper, Jonny Brain, moved from Port Vale. Striker Marvin Robinson came from Lincoln City, and utility player Colin Heath (Chesterfield) and midfielder Jamie Tolley (Shrewsbury) also signed. Completing the summer signings were defenders Carl Regan (Chester City) and Jimmy McNulty (Caernarfon Town). In addition, defender Izak Reid was awarded his first professional contract having moved up through the ranks at the club.

Friendly Matches

The Silkmen visited four non-League sides, firstly Congleton, where they ran out easy winners 7–1, followed by a 3–0 victory at Kirkham and Wesham. There was a disappointing display at Southport who won 2–0, followed by a 2–0 victory at Hyde United, and the youth team drew 1–1 at Buxton.

Leicester City visited the Moss Rose when the Silkmen put in a good performance only to lose the match to a late goal by speedy forward Elvis Hammond in front of a crowd of just 665. It was a completely different matter when a crowd of some 5,500 witnessed a Manchester United side play at the Moss Rose. The Macclesfield side was: Lee (Brain), Regan, McNulty (Teague), Swailes, Morley, McIntyre, Navarro (Reid I), Miles (Hadfield), Bullock, McNeil,

Robinson (Heath). The United starting line up was: Van der Sar, Simpson, Lee, McShane, Ferdinand, Gibson, Martin, Jones, Rossi, Rooney and Eagles. Macclesfield played well but it was Wayne Rooney, making his first appearance since his World Cup red card, who opened the scoring at the beginning of the second half with a back-heeled goal, but Danny Swailes equalised for the Silkmen two minutes later. However, it was second-half substitute Frazer Campbell who scored the winner for United. Although the Silkmen had passed this test, could they put this battling performance into practice in the forthcoming League matches?

SEASON REVIEW

August

A difficult start to the season awaited the Silkmen when they travelled to Darlington. They were undone when the home side scored three goals in the first half with Barry Conlon completing his hat-trick in the second half, allowing the home side to run out easy winners 4–0.

The Silkmen's early-season strike force of Martin Bullock (left) and Matty McNeil.

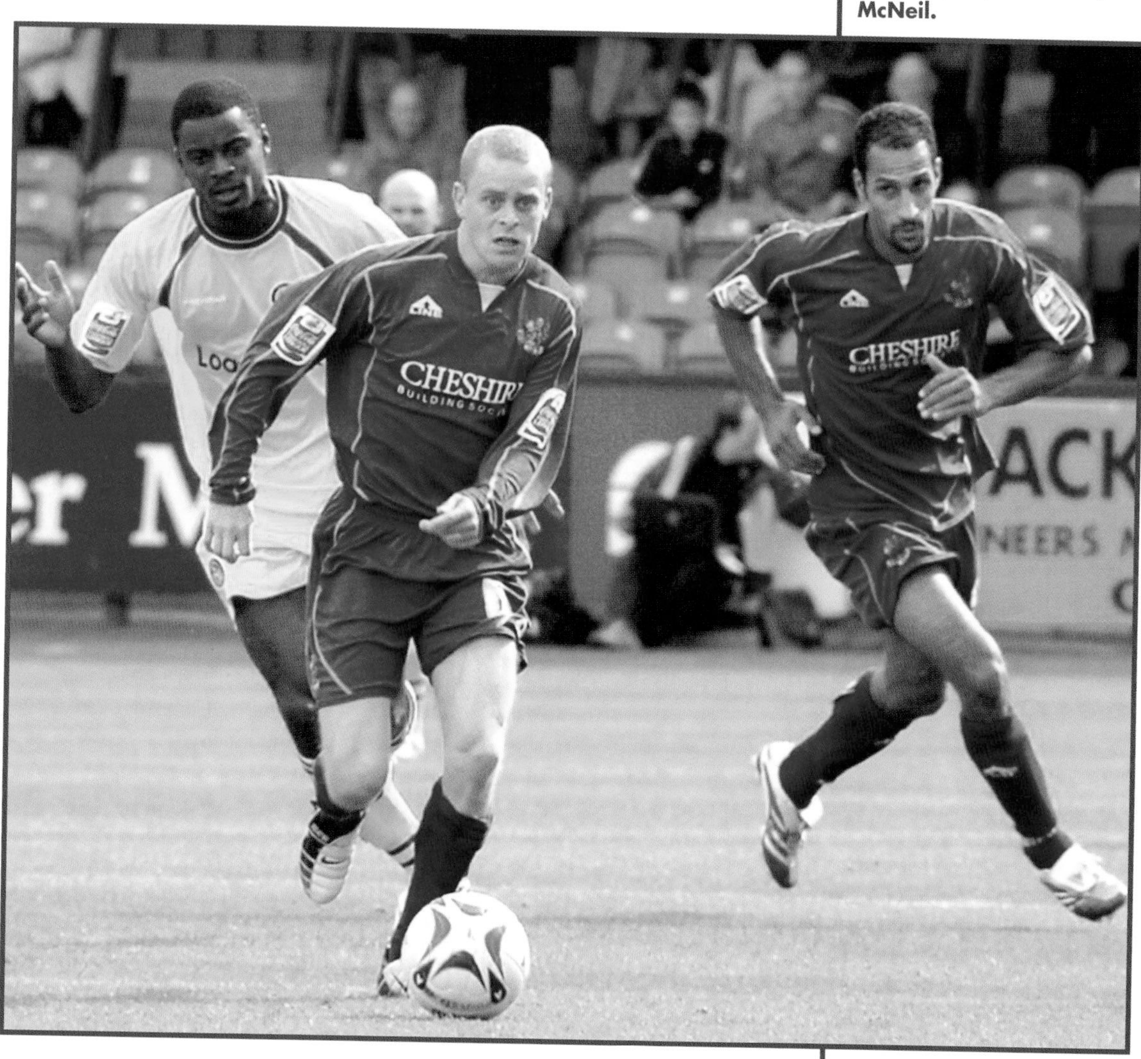

Brian Horton had vowed before the season commenced that he wanted to play a 4-4-2 formation to give full advantage to the wide men. The starting line up for the first home match when the visitors were Hartlepool United was as follows:

Lee
Regan Morley Swailes McNulty
Bullock Navarro Hadfield McIntyre
Robinson McNeil

Although the Silkmen created goalscoring chances, an extremely well disciplined Hartlepool defence kept them at bay and the match ended in a goalless draw.

Another home match saw MK Dons visit the Moss Rose for their first-ever encounter with the Silkmen. Macclesfield made a good start and even hit the cross-bar in the early stages but it was the visitors who opened the scoring in the first half. After the interval Macclesfield played better and when Matty McNeil was brought down in the penalty area, Kevin McIntyre converted from the spot, the first of many penalties he would take during the season. Macclesfield just did not have any luck in this match, having a goal disallowed and the Dons 'keeper only cautioned for handling the ball outside his area, and even worse luck befell them when Danny Swailes put the ball into his own net to give the Dons a 2–1 victory.

Two goals in the first three minutes of the second half together with an own-goal by Andrew Teague gave Peterborough a 3–1 win at London Road, with the Silkmen's consolation goal coming in the 90th minute. Wycombe Wanderers won the last home match of the month with two goals in the first half to leave the Silkmen languishing at the bottom of the table with a solitary point.

With the first transfer window closing on 31 August, further signings were made on transfer deadline day to bolster the strength of the squad. Tall, powerful defender Rob Scott signed from Oldham Athletic and young striker Spencer Weir-Daley signed on loan from Nottingham Forest. As he did not feature in the plans of the manager at Bury, striker and former Silkman Matthew Tipton returned, remaining for the rest of the season. Moving in the opposite direction, Marvin Robinson, who had only been signed in the summer but could not find form, was transferred to Oxford United for an undisclosed fee.

September

Andrew Teague headed home Carl Regan's cross to equalise for the Silkmen at Grimsby Town to pick up only the second point of the campaign. When Barnet visited the Moss Rose there was an uninspiring first half but after the interval the match burst into life with four goals in 15 minutes, two from each side. Matty McNeil and Matthew Tipton scored for the Silkmen, Tipton's goal being Macclesfield's 500th Football League goal, but the Bees stung Macclesfield with a 74th-minute winner with a poorly defended header.

Macclesfield were always chasing the next game at Sincil Bank where Lincoln City won 2–1, and despite the Silkmen laying siege to the Lincoln goal they just could not find an equaliser. Another defeat, this time at Walsall 2–0, left the Silkmen struggling.

The home match against Torquay United was undoubtedly the most exciting match of the month but still ended in disappointment. Torquay took the lead with Macclesfield equalising through Dave Morley but they just could not extend their lead with the Torquay 'keeper having the game of his life. After the

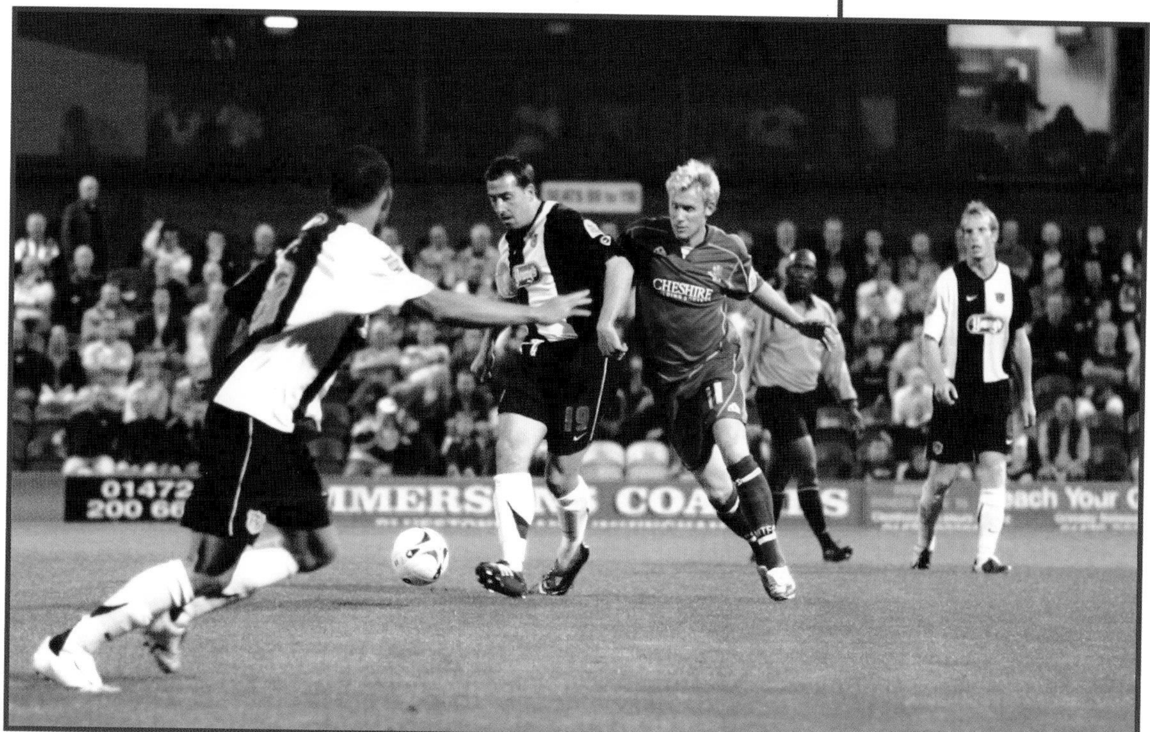

Central midfielder Jamie Tolley (blue strip) challenges for the ball against Grimsby Town.

interval Martin Bullock scored following a brilliant solo effort but Torquay then equalised in the 67th minute and in the 85th minute took the lead 3–2. Just when it looked as though another defeat was on the books, deep into time added on Kevin McIntyre's shot was blocked on the line allowing Danny Swailes to hammer home the rebound to earn a share of the points.

Another draw at Chester saw the Silkmen take an early lead through a Martin Bullock goal, but they could not hold on and former Silkman Kevin Sandwith equalised in the second half. Another defeat at Hereford United 1–0, in a match where the opposition 'keeper had an excellent game, saw the Silkmen finish the month still bottom of the League having accumulated just four points from a possible 36.

The directors then took the decision to dismiss Brian Horton and appointed Ian Brightwell as caretaker manager, a decision which allowed themselves time to find a replacement manager. Brian had been in charge for 131 matches in all competitions at the Moss Rose, winning 47, drawing 35 and losing 49, giving a win rate of 36% in comparison to his career record of 34%.

October

In his short time in charge, Ian Brightwell fared no better than Brian Horton. His reign could not have got off to a worse start at Shrewsbury when they took the lead after just 17 seconds. Spencer Weir-Daley equalised in the second half, striking home from an acute angle after Martin Bullock's quickly taken free-kick, but shortly afterwards Bullock was dismissed for a second bookable defence. Although 10-man Macclesfield almost held out, Shrewsbury scored the winning goal deep into time added on.

On home soil, the Silkmen took the lead against Bury courtesy of a Rob Scott goal, but the visitors then controlled the game and took a 3–1 lead. Speedy striker Spencer Weir-Daley pulled a goal back when he converted a Kevin McIntyre corner, but a frustrating final 15 minutes saw the Silkmen hit

Silkman Rob Scott celebrates after scoring the opening goal at Bury, but opposing central-defender Paul Scott turns his back.

the cross-bar and have a penalty claim turned down only to find themselves on the losing side again.

In Ian's final match in charge at Bristol Rovers, Macclesfield fought hard in a goalless draw, playing with 10 men on two occasions in the same game. Firstly when Spencer Weir-Daley was off the pitch for 20 minutes for stitches and secondly after the dismissal of Danny Swailes.

Paul Ince was appointed player-manager on 23 October 2006, taking up his first ever managerial role. As a player he had a first-class record, appearing 697 times in all competitions at club level and scoring 79 goals, in addition to which he had played for Inter Milan, won 53 full England caps and was the first black captain of the national side. The experienced Ray Mathias was appointed as his

Former England captain Paul Ince is appointed manager.

assistant, and immediately Paul Ince set up a new regime, firstly appointing Duncan Russell as fitness trainer, who had 22 years experience in the Army Physical Training Corps, and Alex Butler as masseur. He also introduced responsibility for a healthy diet and as part of this regime all the players were served lunch prepared by the club's chef following training sessions. Initially, and for many weeks after his appointment, both Paul and the club received a huge amount of publicity in the media, certainly putting Macclesfield Town Football Club well and truly on the map.

When Paul Ince took over as manager the bottom of the League table looked as follows:

	Played	Goal Difference	Points
Wrexham	13	-10	15
Grimsby Town	15	-12	15
Barnet	15	-9	12
Boston United	15	-10	12
Macclesfield Town	**15**	**-16**	**5**

But there was no instant success for the Guv'nor; although the Silkmen played with more determination and aggression in his first match, when Mansfield Town were the visitors and were leading 2–1 in the 81st minute through goals by Colin Heath and Dave Morley. However, Mansfield drew level two minutes later and then proceeded to take all three points, the winner coming from the penalty spot following a handball infringement by skipper Dave Morley, enabling Richie Barker, a former Silkmen favourite, to score his second goal of the match.

To strengthen the squad further, striker John Murphy initially moved to the Moss Rose on loan from Blackpool with his move made permanent the following January, and there was a welcome return for speedy winger and capable crosser of the ball Simon Wiles, also from Blackpool.

Striker John Murphy (centre) in action.

November

Paul Ince earned his first point in charge in the goalless draw at Wrexham where the Silkmen looked more solid at the back, hit the post and had two chances cleared off the line. However, there was disappointment when Boston were the visitors, with Boston taking the lead after three minutes, Colin Heath equalising with a penalty in the 17th minute, only to see the visitors re-take the

Penalty king Kevin McIntyre.

lead a minute later and extend their lead to 3–1 before half-time. Carl Regan scored a consolation goal in the dying moments of the match but the Silkmen's woeful season continued with this defeat against the second-bottom placed side. After the match it was reported in the *Macclesfield Express* that Ince had told his players 'It's the first time [since my appointment] I have been really upset. I'm hurting and I hope you're hurting too. This is a game we should have won, but now we will be written off.'

His words must have had an impact as the next match heralded the start of a 10-match unbeaten run to equal the club's League record set the previous season. The much needed win came when the Silkmen beat Walsall 1–0 in the first-round repay of the FA Cup. This match and the FA Cup run is covered in a separate section under the heading 'Cup Competitions'.

The final match of the month took place at Stockport County where the first half belonged to Macclesfield, who took the lead through a Kevin McIntyre penalty. In the second half, Stockport battled hard and after the Silkmen's defender Andrew Teague and 'keeper Jonny Brain collided, Adam Proudlock was able to walk the ball into the net to equalise. Both players were stretchered off with broken legs and the able 'keeper Asmir Begovic, on loan from Portsmouth, replaced Jonny Brain in goal. Worse followed when Simon Wiles was stretched off as well, which resulted in him returning early to Blackpool.

There was even more bad news the following week when hero goalscorer of the FA Cup replay at Walsall, Jimmy McNulty, broke a leg in training. With only seven points from 19 matches, Macclesfield remained firmly at the bottom of the League some 10 points adrift of second-bottom club Boston United.

December

But things were looking up. Macclesfield had progressed to the third round of the FA Cup with a 'plumb' tie against Chelsea at Stamford Bridge, giving the players a real moral booster, and Paul Ince laid down the gauntlet when he told them that they would have to impress him in the more important forthcoming League Two matches if they wanted a starting-berth at Chelsea.

Even though Macclesfield had been reduced to 10 men when Alan Navarro was dismissed, they battled hard in the home match against Rochdale and won 1–0 through a Matty McNeil goal to win their first League match of the season, and in doing so they became the last League club to earn a win that season. Macclesfield's first away win of the campaign came at Notts County when they went two goals up in the first half with the home side only managing a consolation goal in the 90th minute.

Accrington Stanley were the next visitors to the Moss Rose for their first-ever competitive League match against the Silkmen. They took a 1–0 lead into the interval but the second half came to life with five further goals. Jamie Tolley and Martin Bullock gave the Silkmen a 2–1 lead but Accrington equalised in the 75th minute from a disputed free-kick, but John Murphy restored the Silkmen's lead in the 89th minute only to see the visitors equalise in the 90th minute after Macclesfield failed to retain possession.

Christmas came early to the Moss Rose on 23 December when carols were sung at half-time, and an exciting and entertaining match gave the Silkmen a 2–1 win over Swindon Town. The festive spirit continued at Chester City on Boxing Day when goals from Matthew Tipton, John Murphy and a Kevin McIntyre free-kick saw the Silkmen win 3-0 in another fine performance, moving off the bottom of the League for the first time since the end of August to finish in 23rd Position. The Guv'nor's magic was beginning to work and he was rewarded with a specially engraved crystal football when he won the Performance of the Week award. The month was completed by a last-minute header from David Morley when he converted a Kevin McIntyre corner at Torquay, who by then were in bottom place, four points behind the Silkmen.

January

Heavy rain during the match against Lincoln City on New Year's Day did not put a dampener on what was an exciting and entertaining game from start to finish. Penalty king Kevin McIntyre scored twice from the penalty spot to secure another 2–1 win in a match where Tommy Lee made several wonderful shot-stopping saves and the Silkmen equalled their club League record of 10 consecutive matches undefeated in all competitions.

The next League match came at Barnet, who, the previous week, unlike the Silkmen, had progressed to the fourth round of the FA Cup and as a result were on a 'high', and they won the encounter 1–0. With Tommy Lee suspended and Jonny Brain still recovering from a broken leg, David Rouse, the Silkmen's goalkeeping coach, made his one and only appearance for Macclesfield when he took over the 'keeper's position. Prior to joining Macclesfield, David had held a similar position at Manchester United for eight years during which time he spent a period in Hong Kong but had never made a senior appearance. Therefore he made his Football League debut (and Macclesfield Town debut) at the age of 30 in this match, and while he was named as a substitute for three subsequent matches, his appearance at Barnet remains his one and only senior appearance.

There was much better news when Hereford visited the Moss Rose. Reduced to 10 men early in the first half, the visitors had an uphill task against a dominant Macclesfield side who won the encounter 3–0 with yet another penalty from Kevin McIntyre and two goals from John Murphy, the second of which was made by Alan Navarro, who, when he could easily have taken a shot at goal, unselfishly passed to Murphy. This victory took Macclesfield out of the relegation zone for the first time since August to 20th position having accumulated 29 points.

Unfortunately, the final two matches of the month both ended in defeat. Firstly at Swindon 2–0, when Nathan D'Layrea became the 150th player to be used by Macclesfield in League matches since promotion to the Football League, and secondly when Walsall gained their revenge for the FA Cup defeat earlier in the season by winning 2–0 from goals scored in the second and 90th minutes. The loss agasint Walsall put the Silkmen back into 22nd position.

Before the January transfer deadline Paul Ince made four signings. Striker Robbie Doyle came into the squad but only went on to make two substitute appearances. The other signings all came to the club on loan. For goalkeeping cover Adam Legzdins signed from Birmingham City but never made an appearance. Defender Nathan D'Laryea came from Manchester City where he was a regular in their reserve side, which he had captained on a number of occasions, but he only made one appearance for the Silkmen, and midfielder Ashan Holgate also arrived on loan, and he spent the remainder of the season at the Moss Rose from Swindon Town.

February

An 86th-minute goal by midfielder Alan Navarro cancelled out Darlington's first-half lead to gain a point, and in the next match Navarro,

Midfielder Jordan Hadfield (number 17) scored his first goal against Hartlepool.

who rarely appears on the score sheet, scored the winner in a 2–1 home win against Peterborough.

In a visit to Hartlepool the home side took a two-goal lead on the hour mark, but the Silkman struck back quickly, Jordan Hadfield scoring his first senior goal with a 25-yard strike and then five minutes later Carl Regan forced the ball over the line for a rather lucky goal, but unfortunately the game was lost in the 88th minute when the ball rebounded off Dave Morley into the net, allowing Hartlepool to extend their unbeaten run to 17 matches and go top of the League.

The Silkmen bounced back from the Hartlepool defeat when they entertained Grimsby Town and won 2–1 with first-half goals from the penalty spot by Kevin McIntyre and a scissor-kick by Colin Heath. The result lifted the team to 20th position.

March

Wycombe Wanderers earned an emphatic win at Adams Park by three goals to nil when Jordan Hadfield was dismissed in the second half, but on a more positive note Danny Swailes made his 300th career appearance in this match. In the next match, Matthew Tipton had given the Silkmen a two-goal lead only for Shrewsbury Town to pull a goal back through a Danny Swailes own-goal and then equalise with a strike by Leo Fortune-West.

At MK Dons the Silkmen were no match for the home side, who ran out 3–0 winners and at Bury there was good fortune when it looked as though their 75th-minute goal was the winner until Mr Cool himself, Kevin McIntyre, converted his ninth penalty of the season deep into time added on to earn a share of the points. In this match it was the turn Macclesfield's other central-defender, Dave Morley, to chalk up his 300th career appearance.

In the final match of the month a John Miles and Matty McNeil partnership combined to score two goals. Firstly a lay-off by Matty McNeil to John Miles allowed Miles to calmly slot home for his first goal for 11 months and then John Miles' shot was only parried away by 'keeper Jason White, allowing Matty McNeil to pick up the loose ball and slot home. However, only two minutes later Mansfield pulled a goal back, but despite Mansfield then hitting the post the Silkmen survived to record a vital victory to retain 20th position.

Before the March transfer deadline day, Paul Ince increased his squad further. Ronayne Benjamin signed non-contract forms but only went on to make three substitute appearances on the left-wing and the experienced striker Isaiah Rankin signed on loan from Grimsby Town. In addition, Ciaran Donnelly came on loan from Blackpool but never made the substitutes' bench.

Striker Matty McNeil (left) battles for the ball in the victory against Wrexham.

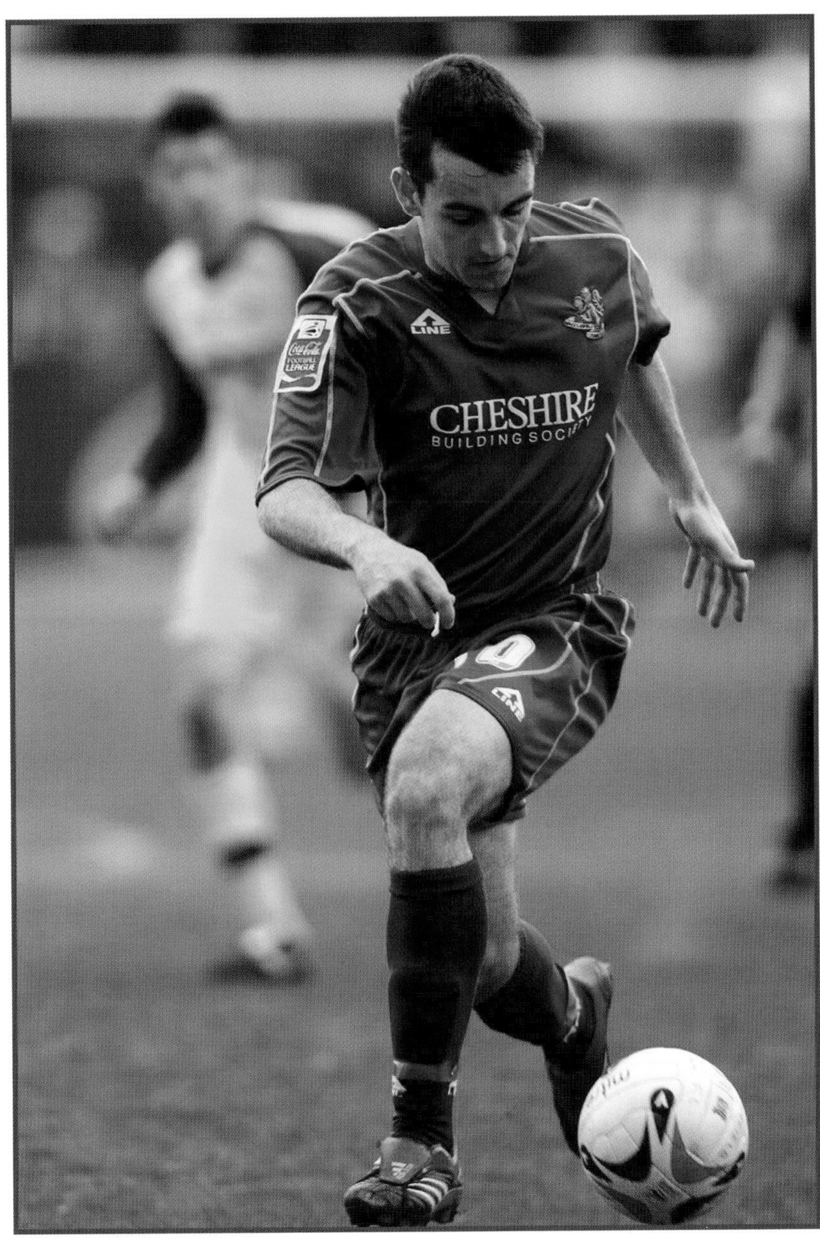

Rejuvenated John Miles scored the second goal in the win against Stockport County.

April

In an entertaining match Macclesfield won the relegation battle with Wrexham at the Moss Rose with goals from Matty McNeil and John Murphy, but on Easter Monday Boston ran out winners 4–1, leaving Martin Bullock nothing to celebrate when he made his 500th career appearance. However, a goal in each half from John Murphy and John Miles gave the Silkmen a valuable 2–0 home win in the derby against Stockport County, in which Matthew Tipton celebrated his 300th career League appearance.

But there then followed three straight defeats which left the nerves jangling and relegation still a possibility despite all the hard work since Paul Ince was appointed manager, at which point the Silkmen had looked doomed. First Rochdale demolished the Silkmen 5–0 at Spotland, and then in a re-arranged match the following Tuesday evening a rugged Bristol Rovers defence kept out the Silkmen at the Moss Rose and stole all three points with a single second-half goal. But the agony and disappointment were far worse in the following match at Accrington Stanley, one of the least well-appointed grounds in the League. Free coaches had been laid on for the Macclesfield fans and a crowd of 3,012, including 829 Macclesfield fans, saw two John Miles goals give Macclesfield a 2–1 lead after 30 minutes, only for Accrington to draw level from a corner on the stroke of half-time. And to make matters worse Stanley scored a third goal early in the second half which turned out to be the winner. This match saw the return of Jimmy McNulty, who played his first match since he broke a leg in training the previous November. Prior to the start of this match there was a minute's applause in memory of 1966 England World Cup hero Alan Ball, who had died the previous week at the age of 61.

For the second consecutive season, the Silkmen were left with the task of retaining their Football League status in the final match of the season,when the bottom of the table was as follows with Torquay United already relegated:

	Played	Goal Difference	Points	
Bury	45	-15	49	
Wrexham	45	-24	48	
Macclesfield Town	**45**	**-22**	**47**	
Boston United	45	-27	46	
Torquay United	45	-27	34	Relegated

May

On the final day of the season Macclesfield entertained Notts County, but Boston United were playing at Wrexham so if Boston won and Macclesfield lost, then the Silkmen would be relegated. However, as long as Macclesfield earned a draw then they would be safe on goal difference even if Boston were to gain a victory. This scenario set up one of the most nerve-tingling ends to a season in which Macclesfield had been involved. A crowd of 4,114 including 638 Notts County fans descended on the Moss Rose on 5 May on a warm and sunny day. The Macclesfield starting line up was: Lee, Regan, Morley, Swailes, McIntyre, Bullock, Navarro, Tolley, Miles, Murphy and McNeil.

John Miles gave Macclesfield the lead in the sixth minute but Notts County equalised in the 38th minute. However, only a minute later Boston took the lead at the Racecourse Ground, leaving the Silkmen in 22nd position. At this stage the nerves of the Silkmen faithful were still on edge and with neither side creating many chances the score remained 1–1. News soon filtered through that Wrexham had equalised in the 56th minute, and then even better news came when Wrexham took the lead in the 87th minute and extended their lead to 3–1 in the 90th minute. By now the Boston board of directors had held an emergency meeting in which they agreed to place Boston United Football Club into administration, as soon as it was clear that they would be relegated from the Football League, thereby incurring the 10-point penalty immediately.

In the meantime, in the 85th minute manager Paul Ince came on from the substitutes' bench to replace Alan Navarro and promptly received a caution from the referee, Mr Hill. At the final whistle the point earned, coupled with Wrexham's win, saw Macclesfield complete the season in 22nd position with 48 points and the retention of their Football League status. The Moss Rose witnessed the very last professional appearance of Paul Ince, who, in such a relatively short time, had brought the club from the brink of relegation to a position where everyone could continue to enjoy life in the Football League.

Paul Ince leaving the field after making his last appearance as a player.

Supporters celebrate 'The Great Escape'.

By a quirk of fate there were four other milestones reached in the match. John Miles made his 150th career appearance (ie. all competitions), Matthew Tipton his 350th and John Murphy his 450th, and the goal scored by John Miles was Macclesfield's 550th Football League goal.

In a break from tradition supporters were allowed on the pitch to witness the end-of-season awards, which were made in the Silk FM Stand. By having the presentations al fresco it meant that far more supporters could witness them

than if the usual celebration had been held in the McIlroy Suite where numbers have to be restricted. Kevin McIntyre gained the Player of the Year award for a consistently fine performance throughout the whole of the season, including finishing as top scorer having converted nine consecutive penalty-kicks and scoring a 10th goal from a free-kick. There were two special awards, firstly to big John Murphy for his splendid goal at Chelsea in the third round of the FA Cup and secondly to Paul Ince for rescuing the Silkmen.

Overall this had been one of the most interesting seasons since promotion to the Football League, but it had also been far from the most enjoyable, especially when in the early part of the season everyone thought that Conference football beckoned. But a good run in the FA Cup, including a wonderful day out at Chelsea, and a record 10-match unbeaten run, gave everyone hope and in the end League football beckoned again, a position which really looked an impossible dream at one stage.

Youth Team

An inexperienced youth team managed by John Askey had a mixed season of fortune. Although they finished at the foot of their League, they faired better in the FA Youth Cup, reaching the third round. In the first round they beat Curzon Ashton 3–2 in a game that was far more comfortable than the scoreline suggests. A narrow win by a single Kristian Dennis goal saw them beat Shrewsbury Town at the Moss Rose, although 'keeper Matthew Cooper had to make some fine saves to keep a clean sheet.

The third-round tie was played on a heavy pitch at the Moss Rose against Everton in front of a crowd of 344. The Everton side comprised, in the main, second-year scholars whereas the Macclesfield side where mainly first-year scholars. In addition, the Everton side boasted five previous England under-16 representatives, a couple from the Republic of Ireland, one Welsh and one Northern Ireland international youth player. In addition, many of the Everton squad had played in the Goodison Park reserve side. Goals by Everton in the 24th, 73rd and a penalty in the 74th minute saw them win 3–0, but the Silkmen youngsters never gave up, to make John Askey a very proud manager.

Cup Competitions

In the first-ever competitive encounter between Leicester City and Macclesfield Town, the Championship side were victorious by two goals to nil at the Walkers Stadium in the first round of the **Carling Cup**.

In the **Johnstone's Paint Trophy** Stockport County came to the Moss Rose and won by a single second-half goal in the first round of the competition.

But the **FA Cup** gave a much needed boost to the Silkmen's season and the first-round result provided the momentum for an improved performance in the League. The first round was played at the Moss Rose against Walsall on Monday 13 November and transmitted live by SKY TV. A minute's silence was held before the match as part of the Remembrance weekend and E-ON distributed numerous clappers before the match as part of their sponsorship of the competition. The match ended in a goalless draw with Macclesfield unable to take any initiative when Walsall were reduced to 10 men for the final 10 minutes. Approximately 10 minutes into the second half the game had to be halted when 36 footballs were catapulted over the Star Lane End stand into the ground. This incident was given nationwide publicity and the pranksters later owned up and apologised, stating that they wanted to give the Macclesfield supporters something to smile about in view of the team's recent poor form. The replay was held eight days later when Jimmy McNulty's first-ever senior goal gave the Silkmen victory, bringing to an end a run of 21 consecutive matches without a win – an unfortunate club record.

The second round saw Hartlepool United visit the Moss Rose. The match turned on a handball incident right at the end of the first half which resulted in

Hartlepool defender Anthony Sweeney being dismissed and Kevin McIntyre converting the penalty to wipe out Hartlepool's lead, which had come about through a Carl Regan own-goal in the eighth minute. The Silkmen won the match in the 53rd minute when John Murphy scored his first goal for the club with a header from eight yards, and for the sixth time in their history Macclesfield progressed to the third round.

Anxious fans had to wait until almost the end of the draw to find out who the Silkmen would meet in the third round. With four balls left, number 10 Chelsea was drawn and then Amir Khan pulled out ball number 50, Macclesfield Town, giving the club a plumb tie. While it has to be acknowledged that it was a far greater achievement for the 1967–1968 Macclesfield non-League side to reach the third round against Fulham, the tie with Chelsea was undoubtedly the most glamorous and certainly the 'big' one of the modern era.

From the end of the draw there was non-stop activity. Continual publicity in the media at both national and local levels gave the club a high profile in the run-up to the Cup tie.

The club certainly pulled out all the stops with free coach transport provided for everyone purchasing a ticket with encouragement for the whole town to support the team, a gesture which cost the club just over £50,000.

Reduced ticket prices were agreed with adults paying £25 and Concessions £12 – a significant reduction on the usual ticket prices at Stamford Bridge. The tie fired the imagination of the town, with Macclesfield's ticket allocation quickly sold out.

An FA Cup T-Shirt emblazoned with 'Let's win it for the boys' was available from the Olympus Trophy shop with the profits going to the four injured players, Jonny Brain, Andy Teague, Jimmy McNulty and Simon Wiles.

Radio 5 Live broadcast an 'FA Cup Evening' from the McIlroy Suite, during which the FA Cup was on display.

Fans at Lyme Green preparing to leave for London.

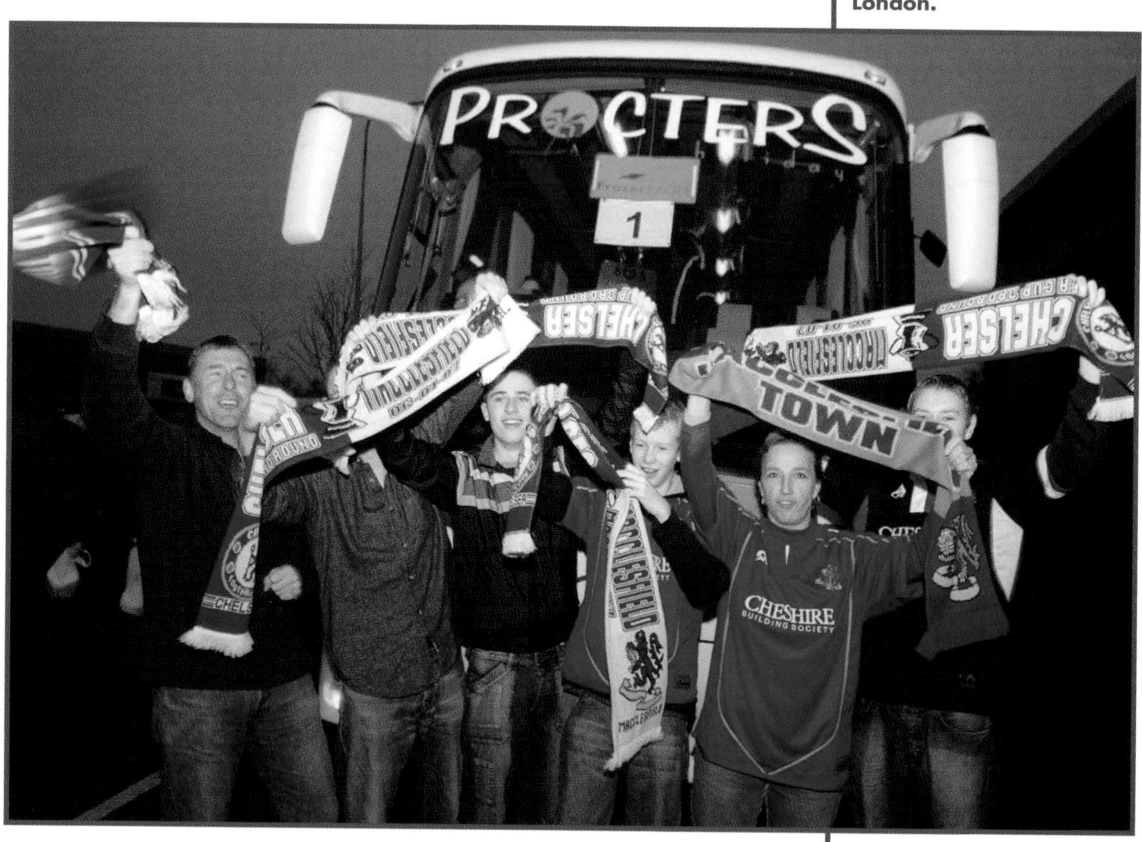

Betbrokers, the world's first sports betting brokerage, announced that they would pay Macclesfield Town Football Club £1 million if the Silkmen beat Chelsea and provided flags which were distributed to each coach on match day.

The biggest press day ever held at the club took place in the McIlroy Suite on 4 January 2007.

On the day of the match there was a hive of activity at Lyme Green Business Park when thousands of supporters were seeking their designated coach, and even the local Member of Parliament, Sir Nicholas Winterton, was among the supporters. There was an air of excitement and anticipation and television cameras

Balloons away at the Shed End at Stamford Bridge.

were working overtime both on and off the coaches preparing for programmes such as *Match of the Day* and *Look North West*. A total of 74 coaches made their way to London and many parked just a short walk away from the ground, enabling many of the supporters to sample the hostelries on the King's Road.

The stadium gradually filled and the crowd of 41,434, including 4,887 Macclesfield supporters, was the largest ever that a Macclesfield team had ever played before and everyone remarked how warm it was in the stadium! It was good to see the three players recovering from broken legs on the pitch before the match in their white tracksuits, albeit using crutches.

The Macclesfield team was: Lee, Morley, Regan, Swailes, Bullock, Hadfield (Tolley 73), McIntyre, Navarro, Heath (Miles 59), McNeil (Jennings 52), Murphy. Subs not used: Reid I, Tipton.

The Chelsea team was: Hilario, Bridge, Carvalho, Cole A (Woods 79), Ferreira, Geremi, Lampard (Morais 71), Mikel, Wright-Phillips S, Kalou (Sahar 76), Shevchenko. Subs not used: Kalambay, Sinclair S.

Before the match Chelsea manager Jose Mourinho revealed that he was going to rest Frank Lampard, but young midfielder Lassana Diarra had arrived 40 minutes late for the pre-match team meeting, which had angered the Chelsea manager with the result that he was omitted from the squad. Of course, Frank Lampard went on to make quite a mark in the match.

Macclesfield played well in the first half but it was star-player Frank Lampard who gave the Premiership side the lead on 16 minutes, but the Silkmen held out and in the 40th minute Chelsea's Ricardo Carvalho failed to clear the ball, leaving big John Murphy clear on goal, and holding his nerve he struck his shot through the legs of the diving 'keeper Hilario to equalise – lifting him to hero status in the eyes of the Silkmen fans.

The Silkmen supporters erupted in joyful celebration of big John Murphy's goal with the electronic scoreboard showing 'Chelsea 1 Macclesfield Town 1', but their joy was shortlived as Frank Lampard restored Chelsea's lead a minute later right in front of the Silkmen supporters at the Shed End. Just before half-time, the match had to be halted as Tommy Lee had sustained a hand injury.

John Murphy scores the equaliser.

But half-time came and with the score at 2–1 and the Silkmen playing well, the supporters were still optimistic.

A minute after the restart, Macclesfield 'keeper Tommy Lee was adjudged to have brought down Andriy Shevchenko in the penalty area and was dismissed by Premier League referee Lee Mason, brother of former Silkman Andy Mason. With no substitute 'keeper on the bench, captain Dave Morley took over in goal with his first task to face the resultant penalty, which Frank Lampard despatched to complete his hat-trick. Reduced to 10 men, Macclesfield had to defend more and more and Shaun Wright-Phillips, John Obi Mikel and Ricardo Carvalho added three more goals for the home side.

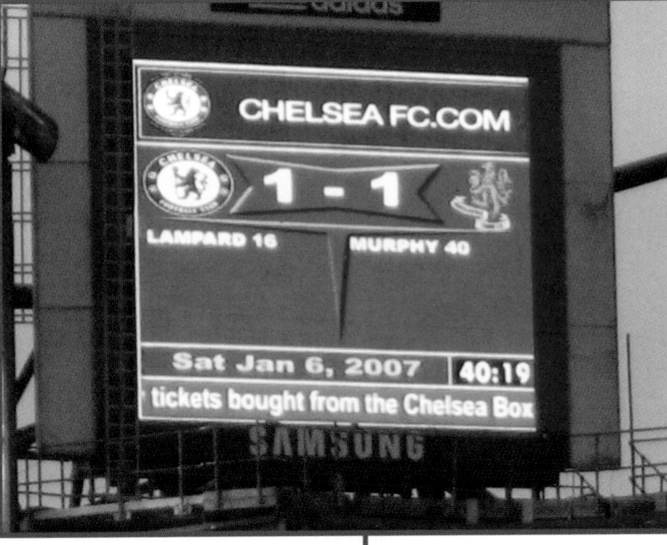

As good as it got.

Chelsea even gave a senior debut to 16-year-old Michael Woods, who became their fourth-youngest-ever debutant. The position became even worse for Macclesfield when John Miles went off injured, leaving Macclesfield to complete the match with nine men. Nevertheless, throughout the second half they still battled hard with Dave Morley making a superb save from a Shevchenko shot and John Murphy having a shot tipped over the bar by Hilario. There was one nice gesture during the match when Jose Mourinho congratulated Jordan Hadfield at the time he was substituted and, at the end of

Tommy Lee lies injured towards the end of the first half.

Jordan Hadfield in action with Frank Lampard.

the match, Mourinho remained on the touchline so that he could shake hands with all the Macclesfield team.

Even though the match ended in a 6–1 defeat the supporters were not downhearted, gave the team a rapturous applause at the end of the match and travelled home a shade disappointed but having enjoyed a wonderful day in the capital. The players remained in London overnight and had an evening on the tiles, including a visit to a casino, returning to Cheshire the next day to continue their campaign to remain in the Football League.

Top 10 Away Attendances

(Since August 1997)

41,343	Chelsea	FAC Round 3	6 January 2007
31,086	Manchester City	League	20 February 1999
15,053	Hull City	League	1 November 2003
14,197	Coventry City	FAC Round 3	2 January 1999
13,981	Stoke City	League	15 August 1998
13,401	Bradford City	League	11 August 2007
11,908	Bradford City	League	3 March 2009
10,500	Burnley	League	28 March 1999
10,316	Preston North End	League	20 October 1998
10,153	Fulham	League	9 January 1999

CHAPTER ELEVEN: 2007–2008

HERE WE GO AGAIN!

Pre-season

The start of the summer close season followed the usual form when manager Paul Ince released six players – Roynane Benjamin and Robbie Doyle, both of whom were signed in the second half of the season; Marvin McDonald and Andrew Smart, neither of whom had featured regularly; together with defender Rob Scott and striker/midfielder Colin Heath. Four players made their own decision to leave, with winger Martin Bullock opting to sign for Wycombe Wanderers, striker/midfielder John Miles moved to Accrington Stanley, striker Matty McNeil made the short move to Stockport County and striker (and goalscorer at Chelsea) John Murphy moved back to his first club, Chester City.

Paul Ince made two signings, bringing in striker Francis Green from Boston United and speedy winger Danny Thomas from Hereford United, with both players joining on a free transfer and a two-year contract.

Then came the announcement on 25 June that Paul Ince had resigned to join MK Dons as their manager, taking with him his assistant Ray Mathias and fitness coach Duncan Russell. During his short stay at the Moss Rose, whenever there was a managerial vacancy announced elsewhere there was always speculation that Ince was a possible candidate, and coupled with his ambition to manage at the

Ian Brightwell (right) is appointed manager with his assistant Asa Hartford.

highest level, it was really no surprise that he wished to move to a club where he could take advantage of their financial position. However, the timing of the move left Macclesfield and Ince's successor with a difficult task.

On leaving, Ince told the official web site: 'This has been a tremendously difficult decision for me. My heart has said stay with Macclesfield Town, but my head has been telling me to go to MK Dons. They have significantly more resources for me to work with, and I am ambitious to make it to the very top. I think I have to go for it.'

As a consequence of Paul Ince moving to MK Dons, midfielder Alan Navarro later moved to join him there, as did centre-back Danny Swailes.

Four days later it was announced that first-team coach and former Manchester City defender, Ian (or Bob as he is affectionately known to everyone) Brightwell had been appointed to the manager's position with ex-Scottish international Asa Hartford appointed as assistant manager. Ian was upbeat about his appointment but acknowledged that some people thought that the club had taken a risk. He told the official web site 'First and foremost I was absolutely delighted to be given the opportunity [as manager]. Since I arrived at the Moss Rose the club has become very close to my heart and it's a real honour to take the club forward. It isn't going to be easy but I've been in the game long enough to know what makes a good manager. I am my own man with some very clear ideas on how I want to take Macclesfield Town forward.'

Needing to sign players quickly, Ian certainly lost no time making striker Michael Husbands his first signing from Port Vale, giving Michael a chance to get his career off the ground. Next ex-Manchester City defender and former colleague of Ian, Richard Edghill came across the Pennines from Bradford City. The most interesting signing was that of Canadian international midfielder Terry Dunfield, a former Manchester City trainee who had lived locally since he was 15 and had recovered from a severe injury incurred when he was at Bury. Terry requested a trial at Macclesfield and having greatly impressed the management team he was given a permanent contract. Another interesting signing was that of no-nonsense central-defender and Maltese international Luke Dimech from Marsaxlokk, Malta. Luke had already tasted English League football previously at Chester City and wanted the opportunity to play at this level again. Others to join the squad were striker Martin Gritton from Lincoln City, Levi Reid, brother of Izak, and just after the season started, former Crewe Alexander Academy striker Gareth Evans. Youngsters Mick Jeffries, Matthew Flynn and Izak Reid were all given contracts of varying lengths and Simon Wiles made another move to the Moss Rose from Blackpool, but still on a loan basis.

Sadly, before the season commenced two well-known supporters died. Paul Jefford was a young man who never enjoyed the best of health but still had the wonderful ability to communicate with everyone and always had a smile on his face. Paul attended as many home matches as he could with his parents, standing on the London Road Terrace where he could acknowledge the players. He was the Junior Blue of the Year in 1998 and always celebrated in style when he scored a goal in the Junior Blues penalty shoot-out.

At the other end of the age spectrum was Wilf Hall. In his footballing days, Wilf had been goalkeeper at Stoke City and then Ipswich Town, who paid Stoke City a fee of £4,700 which enabled Stoke to buy back Stanley Matthews from Blackpool. At Ipswich he won a First Division Championship medal in the 1961–1962 season under the management of Alf Ramsey. He then moved to play for the Silkmen in 1963 and remained an integral part of the club. After retiring from playing he took on many roles

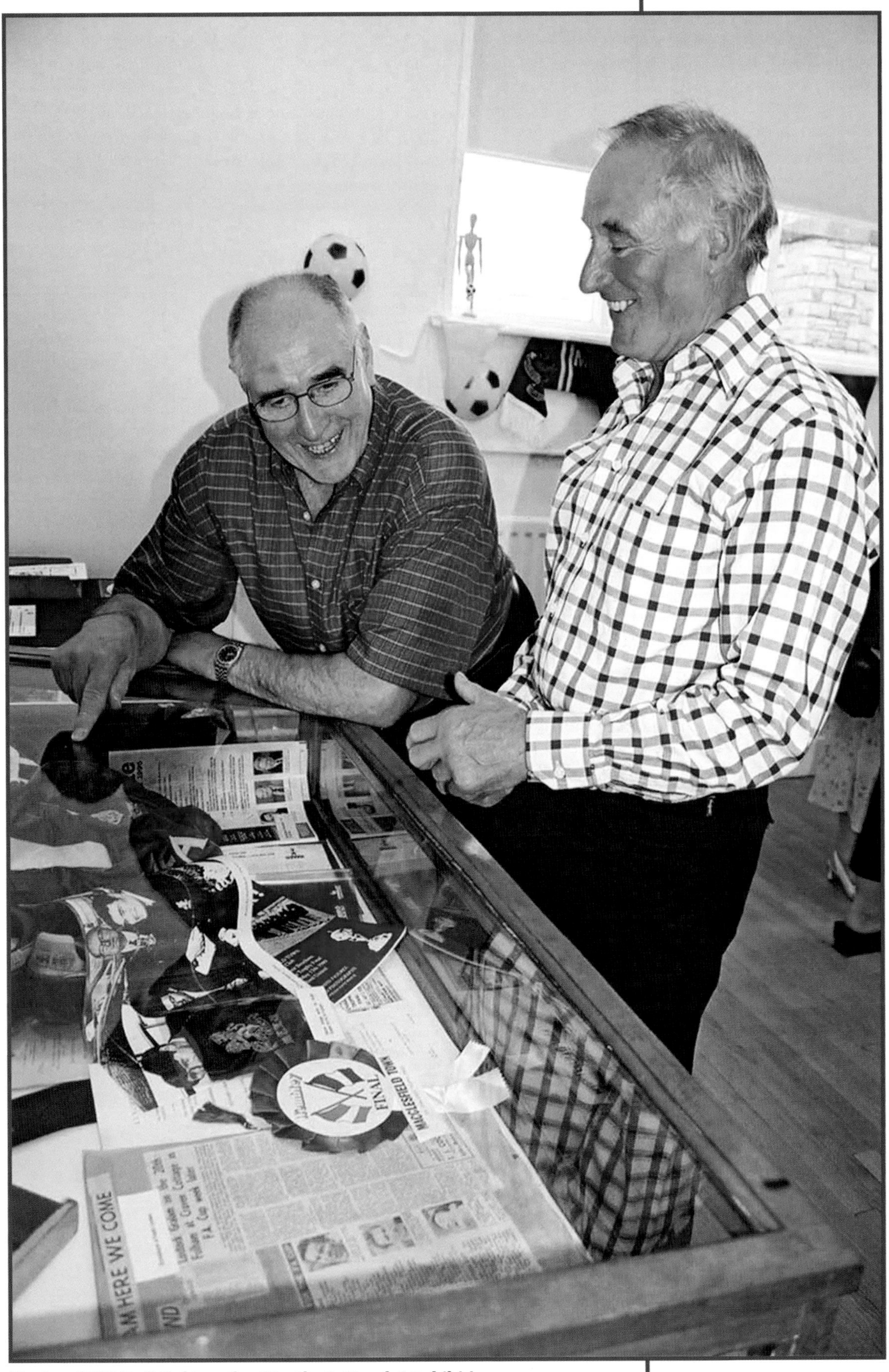

The late Wilf Hall (left) at the 'Hustle & Muscle' Exhibition.

including trainer, groundsman, reserve-team coach, director, programme seller and gateman. In more recent years he was commissionaire in the McIlroy Suite or at the players'/directors' entrance.

The club chaplain, Revd Jeremy Tear, came up with an excellent idea to have a memorial board on which the names of officials/supporters can be recorded as a permanent memory to them. This board is situated in the concourse of the McAlpine Stand, adjacent to the sponsored bricks.

Friendly Matches

Results on the road at non-League venues were disappointing, commencing at Kidsgrove where the score was 1–1 at the interval, but after a total change of playing personnel at half-time the Silkmen proceeded to lose the match 4–3. This was followed by a disappointing performance at Southport where former Silkmen manager Peter Davenport's side won 2–0. With a mixture of trialists and youth-team players the Silkmen managed to draw 2–2 at Buxton, and both the Macclesfield goals were ironically scored by Colin Heath, who had been released by the club. A similar make-up of players lost 3–1 at Marine.

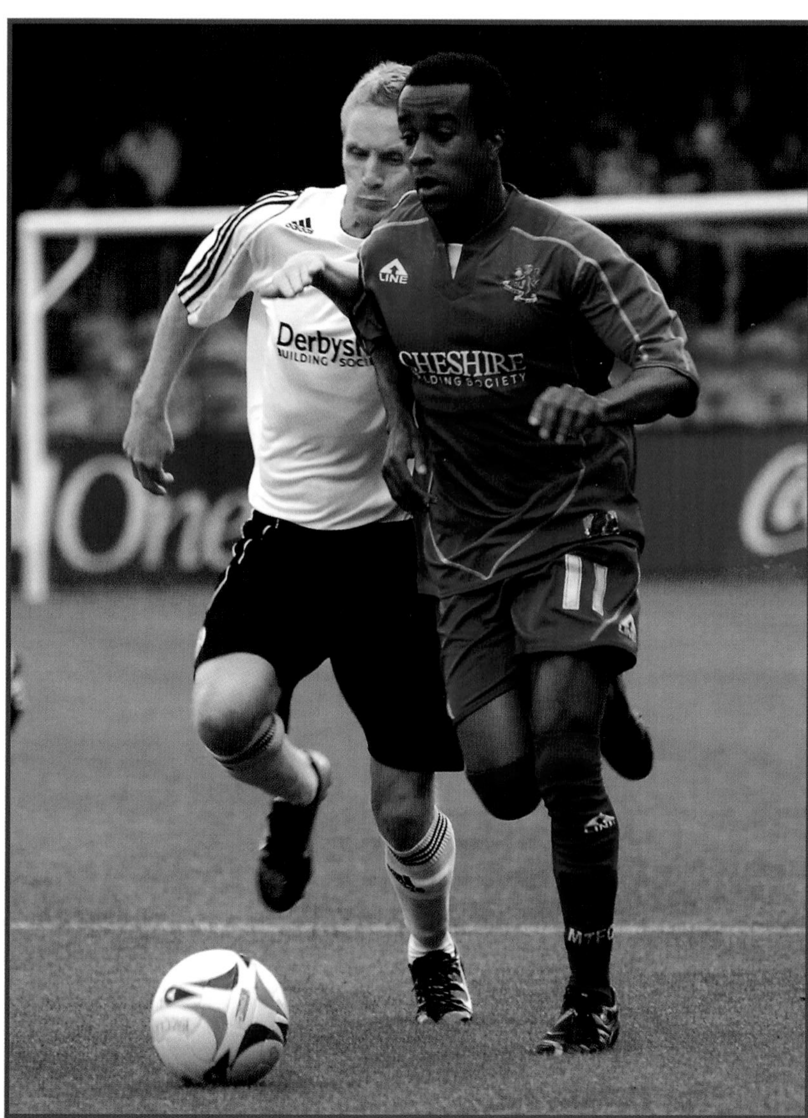

Danny Thomas scored the only goal in the pre-season victory against Derby County.

Overall there was better fortune in the matches at the Moss Rose. Stoke City were the first visitors with former Silkman Jon Parkin in the starting line up. The match was a pleasure to watch with the Silkmen playing with pace and passing the ball on the ground. They took the lead in the ninth minute when Green, Husbands and Thomas linked up well in a move which ended in Carl Regan side-footing the ball home from close range, but it was 'the Beast' Jon Parkin who equalised for the visitors before the break. Stoke had many chances after the interval but they were all squandered, the match finishing in a 1–1 draw.

Newly promoted to the Premier League, Derby County brought an under-strength side to the Moss Rose as they were involved in a match at Burton Albion on the same evening. Danny Thomas scored in the fifth minute with an excellent solo effort when he beat three Derby players and then beat the 'keeper with a low drive from 20 yards for the only goal of the match. Derby applied pressure throughout but they were denied by the Silkmen 'keepers, Tommy Lee and then Matt Baker, although to their credit there were times when Macclesfield looked dangerous on the break.

The final match against Oldham Athletic saw the Silkmen facing a physically superior and more experienced side who easily won the encounter with a goal in each half.

SEASON REVIEW

August

A first-ever visit to relegated Bradford City gave the Silkmen a difficult start to the season in front of a crowd of 13,401 with a referee in charge of his first Football League match. Francis Green soon silenced the Bradford supporters when he scored on his Macclesfield debut with a 15-yard shot in the ninth minute, but the home side equalised on the stroke of half-time after Tommy Lee had saved a hotly disputed Barry Conlon penalty-kick only for Guylain Ndumbu-Nsungu to slot home the rebound. The Silkmen withstood the Bradford pressure in the second half to earn a share of the points.

The first home match saw former manager Paul Ince bring his MK Dons side to the Moss Rose. The Macclesfield starting line up was:

Lee
Regan Dimech Edgehill McIntyre
Reid L Dunfield Murray Thomas
Husbands Green

The visitors took a first-half lead with a powerful 25-yard drive but Francis Green equalised 13 minutes later with an even better 25-yard drive. Martin Gritton replaced Michael Husbands up front and immediately cleared a Dons set piece and then, only three minutes into his debut, put Macclesfield into the lead, but even better was to come when Francis Green hit a second 25-yard strike to give the Silkmen what looked like 3–1 winning lead in the 63rd minute. But the home side could not hold out and the Dons pulled a goal back and then, deep into time added on, scored the equaliser to leave management and fans all with the feeling that this was a match which they had 'lost'.

Striker Franny Green on the score sheet against MK Dons.

A few days later, against the run of play, former Mariner Martin Gritton gave the Silkmen a second-half lead at Grimsby Town only for the home side to equalise 11 minutes later. The three points earned in the opening matches left Macclesfield in 16th place in the League table.

September

Darlington's visit to the Moss Rose ended goalless in an uninspiring match in which Kevin McIntyre missed his first penalty in 10. However, Ian Brightwell's first win as a manager came at high-flying Hereford United when current top scorer Francis Green's late goal secured all three points to take the Silkmen momentarily into the top half of the table.

On the same day as Macclesfield had recorded their first win of the season, central-defender Luke Dimech became only the third Macclesfield player after Nigerian George Abbey and Canadian Martin Nash to make an international appearance while registered as a Macclesfield player since the Silkmen were promoted to the Football League, when he represented Malta against Turkey.

Macclesfield dominated the first half when Wycombe Wanderers came to the Moss Rose. After the interval it was Wycombe who took the upper hand, scoring in the 65th and 90th minutes to win the match, although substitute Gareth Evans smashed home a consolation goal, his first senior goal, with only seconds left, leaving Macclesfield regretting a host of missed chances and unfortunately having two 'goals' by Franny Green disallowed.

There was a scrappy affair at Rochdale with the home side taking the lead when Jimmy McNulty put into his own net, but Kevin McIntyre was back on form scoring from the penalty spot to earn a share of the points, despite Rochdale's claim that they should have been awarded a second goal when the officials ruled that the ball had not crossed the line. When Chester City visited their former landlords, the Family Fun Day for children with face painting, balloons and a magician was not replicated on the pitch. The visitors took a two-goal first-half lead but Terry Dunfield pulled a goal back with a 20-yard free-kick into the top corner of the net in the second half. But it was Chester who held out to win the match 2–1, although Macclesfield were extremely unlucky when Adam Murray hit the post with almost the last kick of the match. Mediocre results saw the Silkmen slipping down the table, completing the month in 20th position.

October

Yet another draw transpired when the Moss Rose acted as hosts to Rotherham, but at least the Silkmen came from behind on this occasion with a Martin Gritton header to earn a 1–1 draw. A further draw came at Chesterfield when the home side took the lead in the fifth minute but Martin Gritton equalised before half-time. Within a minute of the restart the home side had taken the lead again in an entertaining match, but Francis Green celebrated his 300th career appearance when he collected a perfect through-ball from Simon Wiles to equalise with a fierce low shot.

A 12.30 kick-off due to an England international at 15.00 caught the Silkmen napping, allowing the visitors, Wrexham, to take a two-goal lead in the first 22 minutes, but Martin Gritton scored his 50th career League goal to reduce the deficit before the interval. The second half was stalemate with Wrexham looking as though they would win the encounter, but there was an unbelievable sequence of events in the final minutes of the match. Wrexham's

Smiles all round when Danny Thomas scores a very late winner against Wrexham.

Richard Garrett was dismissed in the 80th minute. Then, in the 85th minute central-defender Dave Morley left the defence to join the attack alongside Martin Gritton and substitute Gareth Evans, which paid dividends in the 90th minute when he met a pin-point cross from Kevin McIntyre to level the scores with a bullet header. But there was even more drama to come when, deep into time added on, a Danny Thomas cross-cum-shot sailed over the head of the Wrexham 'keeper Anthony Williams into the top corner of the net for Thomas' first League goal for the Silkmen. The Moss Rose erupted in celebration of an unlikely victory which was their first home win of the season.

After a routine first half at Accrington with neither side able to score, the game sparked into life after the interval. The home side took the lead with two goals in the space of three minutes, but, not to be outdone, Macclesfield then drew level with two goals in two minutes including a McIntyre penalty, but disappointingly the home side responded only a minute later to win the match 3–2.

The final match of the month saw the Silkmen take a first-half two-goal lead, but the visitors Bury stepped up a gear in the second half and pulled a goal back four minutes after the re-start and then equalised from the penalty spot, but at least the Silkmen had moved up to 17th position.

Towards the end of the month it was announced that central-defender Dave Morley's contract had been cancelled by mutual consent and shortly after he joined Blue Square North side Hyde United. Dave had lost his regular position in the starting line up as he had only recently returned to the side following close season surgery on an ankle, but he had signed off in fine style with his goal against Wrexham.

November

The month started in the worst possible way with a 5–0 defeat at Mansfield Town but the team redeemed themselves against visitors Brentford in the next

On-loan flying winger Simon Wiles (left) in good form.

match. A more disciplined side may well have taken the lead in the first half when they hit the cross-bar twice and Adam Murray headed wide from close range. Brentford started the second half in the ascendancy but the introduction of Simon Wiles for Richard Edgehill, who had broken a rib, changed the match. In the 76th minute, after a speedy run up the right wing, Simon Wiles made an excellent pass into the six yard box and caused mayhem in the Brentford defence, the ball rebounding off the Brentford 'keeper allowing Danny Thomas to strike home the winning goal.

In a move to strengthen the defence Ian Brightwell signed two central-defenders on loan. Firstly, Phil Doughty from Blackpool, who spent two months at the Moss Rose before signing for Accrington Stanley, and secondly Sean Hessey from Chester City, who remained with the Silkmen until the end of the season. His leadership qualities were recognised when he was made captain in the latter stages of the campaign. Moving in the opposite direction on loan was midfielder Jordan Hadfield, who became another player to link up with Paul Ince at MK Dons.

Despite having to replace Martin Gritton, Terry Dunfield and Sean Hessey through injury before the start of the second half at Notts County, Macclesfield went on to win the match when Francis Green scored the only goal, ending his six-week goal-drought. In their first-ever visit to the Moss Rose as a Football League side, Dagenham & Redbridge took an early lead which they held onto until the 90th minute when young Nick Blackman equalised, scoring his first senior goal to give the Silkmen a fortunate share of the points. A tally of seven points in the month lifted the Silkmen to 15th position.

Nick Blackman scored the 90th-minute equaliser against Dagenham & Redbridge.

December

With the side some nine points above the relegation zone and picking up points on a fairly regular basis, in comparison to the last two seasons there was every hope that a higher end-of-season League position would be achieved. However, the results in December came as a shock and provided a wake-up call. Certainly the supporters were in despair, worrying that they were about to witness a relegation battle for the third consecutive season.

For the first-ever visit to Shrewsbury's New Meadow Stadium, Tommy Lee was unavailable having undergone a minor hand operation and was replaced by Jonny Brain, who then went on to perform well enough to retain the 'keeper's position for the remainder of the season. Despite a good performance by Brain, Macclesfield could not stop Shrewsbury scoring a goal in each half to win the encounter. A trip to London to face Barnet came next. Playing conditions were poor, with standing water on parts of the pitch, but the Silkmen quickly adapted to the conditions and took a two-goal lead within seven minutes with goals from Jimmy McNulty and Levi Reid, but Barnet quickly pulled a goal back in the ninth minute. The score remained at 2–1 but Macclesfield could not withstand Barnet's late barrage and the home side equalised in the 90th minute.

In another frustrating match when Stockport were the visitors, Macclesfield dominated play but were continuously frustrated by the Hatters' 'keeper, who enjoyed a splendid match and made a string of saves. Two goals against the run of play gave Stockport a 2–0 victory. After this defeat manager Ian Brightwell was convinced that his current squad was more than capable of challenging at the upper reaches of the table. He told the *Macclesfield Express* 'We have good players and a good team spirit and we can still move up the table.'

Jimmy McNulty (number 21) scored the opening goal against Barnet.

There was still no joy at Adams Park, where the Silkmen took an early lead only to see the home side win 2–1 including a dubious penalty decision. Then on-loan Watford teenage striker Theo Robinson scored a second-half goal to give Hereford United victory on Boxing Day at the Moss Rose.

With heavy rain and a strong wind blowing throughout the match, the Silkmen adapted to the conditions quicker than visitors Rochdale and took a two-goal lead into the interval courtesy of goals from Levi Reid and Gareth Evans. But for the ninth time in the season the Silkmen failed to hold onto the lead and let the visitors pull a goal back in the second half and then equalise in the 90th minute. Having only taken three points out of the last 21 available they slipped down the table to 19th position, and to make matters worse, competent defender Jimmy McNulty turned down a new contract offer and opted instead to sign for Stockport County.

January

With both Martin Gritton and Francis Green out injured, Nick Blackman and Gareth Evans provided the strike force at Rotherham on New Year's Day. In this match the Silkmen held out until the 70th minute and then capitulated, the home side scoring three goals in the final 20 minutes to win 3–0.

The following week it was announced that Kevin McIntyre had moved to Shrewsbury Town for an initial fee of £30,000 with a further £20,000 payable depending on the performance of Shrewsbury Town. This was a blow as Kevin had been a key performer and was an expert set-piece player, although it has to be said that during the season he had appeared to be somewhat unsettled. Only the next day midfielder Adam Murray announced that his contract had been cancelled because he was unable to offer 100 per cent to the Macclesfield cause and that he did not want to continue playing at League Two level. Only days later he signed for Blue Square Premier side Oxford United.

Sammy McIlroy brought his Morecambe side to the Moss Rose for the first Football League meeting between the two sides, who had only met at non-League level in the past. Before the match, associate director Roy Higginbotham made a presentation on the pitch to Sammy McIlroy in gratitude for the work he did for the club while he was manager. Twenty-five minutes after kick-off a flowing movement down the left wing saw Gareth Evans pass the ball to Martin Gritton, who headed home from 10 yards to give the Silkmen the lead, but it was the same old story when Morecambe equalised only five minutes later. Having lost their ace penalty taker in Kevin McIntyre, Macclesfield gave the responsibility to Martin Gritton, leaving the side ruing his miss. In the second half, with Sammy McIlroy animatedly urging his side on and in direct contrast Macclesfield's Ian Brightwell standing motionless by his dugout, central-defender Luke Dimech sliced a clearance and gifted Morecambe their 86th-minute winner.

In an attempt to give his side some stability, Ian Brightwell made four loan signings. Midfielder James Ashmore and central-defender Ryan Cresswell both came from Sheffield United, left-back Neil Ashton, who was to prove a useful acquisition, moved from Shrewsbury Town and tall striker Michael Symes also moved from Shrewsbury Town.

Brightwell fielded a new-look side at Peterborough, which included all four of his new signings.

Brain
Regan Cresswell Hessey Ashton
Reid I Dunfield Ashmore Thomas
Evans Symes

An unlikely win against high-flying Peterborough saw Izak Reid score his first senior goal, the only strike of the match, when he found space before lifting his shot over 6ft 6in Peterborough 'keeper Joe Lewis, who was making his debut for the Posh after a £400,000 move from Norwich. In the 53rd minute Gareth Evans was dismissed for violent conduct after which it was a backs-to-the-wall performance by Macclesfield to give them their first win since the previous November.

Darlington were another high-flying team who took a home lead which they held onto until half-time. After the interval Martin Gritton and Ryan Cresswell put the Silkmen ahead, only for Ryan Cresswell to go from hero to villain when he headed into his own net, to turn what should have been another victory into Macclesfield's 12th draw of the campaign.

At the end of the month the Silkmen visited the plush Stadium *mk*, home of MK Dons, where striker Michael Symes volleyed home from 35 yards for his one and only Macclesfield goal. MK Dons' central-defender Sean O'Hanlon equalised in the second half, but the Silkmen held out for a share of the points, finishing the month in 19th position but with a cushion of seven points on the relegation zone.

On the last day of the January transfer window defender Carl Regan became yet another player who moved to join Paul Ince at MK Dons.

Terry Dunfield – popular midfielder.

February

In the home match against Bradford City it was a tale of two 'keepers. A monumental error by the Macclesfield 'keeper gifted Bradford the only goal of the match and salt was rubbed into the wound when Terry Dunfield's penalty was saved. Two late goals gave Lincoln City victory at the Moss Rose 2–1, the Silkman's goal scored in the 90th minute by the ever-improving young striker Gareth Evans.

Macclesfield gained their revenge for the defeat at the Moss Rose when they visited Christie Park. Francis Green won the match with his 87th-minute goal in a game which had been dominated by Morecambe who had been kept at bay by an excellent performance by Macclesfield 'keeper Jonny Brain.

When Grimsby Town came to the Moss Rose they took the lead in the fifth minute following a horrendous mix-up by Macclesfield's two central-defenders. Gareth Evans blasted home a 10-yard volley in the 79th minute to equalise but, as on so many occasions in the season, the Silkmen could not hold onto the lead and succumbed only three minutes later when Grimsby took a winning 2–1 lead.

An early lead at Lincoln through another Gareth Evans goal and domination of the first half turned into disaster as first 'keeper Jonny Brain was injured and then speedy midfielder Terry Dunfield also had to leave the field when he was injured. Yet again the Silkmen capitulated in the second half when the Imps scored three goals in the last 18 minutes. The last match of the month saw a reasonable first-half home performance against Peterborough which ended goalless, but the visitors scored 33 seconds after the break and went on to dominate the second half, scoring two more goals to push the Silkmen closer to the relegation zone.

By now Macclesfield had played more matches than any of the teams around them with the League Table showing the following position:

	Played	Goal Difference	Points
Notts County	33	-14	33
Bury	32	-12	32
Macclesfield Town	**34**	**-20**	**31**
Mansfield Town	31	-12	28
Wrexham	30	-21	25

With the team's precarious League position and the possibility of relegation, the directors took the decision to dismiss manager Ian Brightwell and his assistant Asa Hartford.

Keith Alexander, an experienced lower-league manager, was appointed with Gary Simpson as his assistant. Ian Brightwell had turned down the offer to become Keith Alexander's number two. On his appointment Keith Alexander told the official web site 'I have got to get to know the players pretty quickly and decide who is up for the task of turning the season around. Twelve games doesn't give us a lot of time but the positive thing is that our fate is still very

Keith Alexander (right), appointed manager in February, with his assistant Gary Simpson.

much in our own hands even though the sides around us do have games in hand. Saturday's encounter with Notts County is a big one and I will be expecting the side I put out there to give 110 per cent for the cause and show me they are up for the challenge of the next few months.'

March

There was certainly a buzz around the ground when the team was announced for the home encounter with fellow strugglers Notts County. Dropped altogether were Shaun Hessey, Danny Thomas and James Ashmore, with Levi Reid dropped to the bench. Promoted from the bench were Luke Dimech and Michael Symes, and with defender James Jennings recalled from his loan at Altrincham to take a midfield role for the first time in his career and youth-team defender Shaun Brisley handed his senior debut, the starting line up was:

Brain
Brisley Cresswell Dimech
Reid I Tolley Jennings Ashton
Evans Green Symes

Richard Edghill and Nick Blackman retained their position on the substitutes' bench but Tommy Lee was dropped altogether in line with Alexander's policy of not having a 'keeper on the bench other than for Cup ties. Youth-team member Christian Millar and newly-signed striker on non-contract forms Fola Onibuje, together with Levi Reid, completed the list of substitute players.

Macclesfield played more positively than they had in recent matches and took the lead in the first half when Izak Reid picked up a pass from Gareth Evans and slotted home from 10 yards.

They retained the lead but as in so many occasions in the season, the visitors equalised in the 72nd minute. In an attempt to secure a win Keith Alexander introduced the tall striker Fola Onibuje who came on to make his one and only appearance for the Silkmen, but they could not find that elusive winning goal. In fact, the visitors almost stole all three points but Paul Mayo fortunately only hit the side netting from 10 yards.

Izak Reid (left) celebrating his goal against Notts County with Franny Green.

On-loan full-back Neil Ashton, whose free-kick sneaked through a crowded Barnet defence.

The following week, forward Scott Spencer was signed on loan from Everton and tall, strong central-defender Richard Walker signed having been released by Port Vale.

At Brentford there was heartache when the home side secured victory with almost the last kick of the match with the only goal after a sterling performance by Jonny Brain, who again kept the Silkmen in the match at Dagenham & Redbridge with a string of saves including a penalty, but it was substitute Francis Green who secured all three points for the Silkmen with his second-half strike.

The first half against visitors Shrewsbury Town was a rather dull affair with far too many 'hit and hope' balls played by both sides, but it was the visitors who took the lead 20 minutes into the second half. Following three substitutions the home side found more drive and Jamie Tolley, a former Shrewsbury player, who was making his 200th career League appearance, celebrated by equalising eight minutes from time. Then Francis Green went one better, scoring the winning goal three minutes later with a curling left-footed shot from 25 yards. This match was followed by a blip in form when there was a 2–0 defeat against potential Play-off side Stockport County at Edgeley Park.

In the next match Barnet visited the Moss Rose for the Silkmen's 500th consecutive League match, a landmark which had only been achieved by two other former non-League clubs, Scarborough and Wycombe Wanderers, since automatic promotion to the Football League had been introduced. What a way to celebrate against a side which had scored five goals in their previous match. Danny Thomas was first on the score sheet with a header and then Neil Ashton's free-kick sneaked through a crowded defence to creep in at the far post, before Francis Green drilled the third home from 20 yards to give the Silkmen their eighth win of the season and move eight points clear of the relegation zone. In this match promising striker John Rooney, younger brother of England and Manchester United's Wayne, made his Football League debut with a cameo appearance.

The last match of the month belonged to trainee Shaun Brisley on a cold, wet and windy day. Taking the playing conditions into consideration the visitors, Accrington Stanley, gave the Silkmen the task of playing into the elements in the first half. The Silkmen adapted quickly and Shaun Brisley opened the scoring on 15 minutes when he hooked home a Danny Thomas cross. Stanley then equalised but only minutes later Brisley headed home from a Jamie Tolley corner for his second goal. The second half was an even affair but the Silkmen held out to earn all three points, finishing the month in 19th position.

Two-goal hero Shuan Brisley (number 34) won the match for the Silkmen against Accrington Stanley.

But the third consecutive win would just not come along. At Wrexham, Jamie Tolley gave the Silkmen a second-half lead only for bottom side Wrexham to equalise 11 minutes from time. This match was followed by a goalless draw at the Moss Rose against a Mansfield Town side who were fighting for their Football League life. To make matters worse, there then followed defeat by a single goal at Bury to leave the Silkmen still unsure of their Football League status for the following season.

Chesterfield came to the Moss Rose having just failed to make a Play-off position, when they missed a string of chances, but it was striker Gareth Evans's first-half goal, very much against the run of play, which gave the Silkmen victory and ensured that they would be playing in the Football League in the 2008–2009 season. The players justifiably celebrated at the end of the match and there was all-round relief on the terraces.

With neither side having anything to play for, Chester City and Macclesfield completed the season at the Saunders Honda Stadium with a goalless draw. The Silkmen finish in 19th position with 50 points with Mansfield Town and Wrexham relegated.

This had been another season where it had been necessary for the board of directors to take action by changing the manager to retain Football League status, and it had been a season of frustration for the supporters. The hardworking midfielder Terry Dunfield was voted Player of the Year and Francis Green was the top scorer with 11 goals.

Young striker Gareth Evans (right) in action.

Youth Team

Managed by John Askey, Macclesfield's youth team enjoyed a successful season, completing the season in fourth position in the Puma Youth Alliance North West Conference and reaching the fourth round of the FA Youth Cup for the first time ever.

Their very creditable performance in the League gave them a playing record of: Played 27, Won 15, Drew 5, Lost 7, Goals for 61, Goals against 52, Number of Points 50.

But it was in the FA Youth Cup competition where they excelled. In the first round at Bradford City they took an early third-minute lead when Danny Egan capitalised on the Bradford 'keeper's mistake. Tom Nadin fired the Silkmen further ahead in the 50th minute before Bradford then managed to pull a goal back, but the Silkmen held out to win 2–1.

A home tie against Rotherham in the second round saw the Silkmen take the lead 10 minutes into the second half. The visitors fought back to equalise with 20 minutes left but the home side were not to be denied as Kristian Dennis scored the winner five minutes from the end.

There was a visit to Blackpool for the third round when Macclesfield had to come from behind twice in the first half, with goals from Kristian Dennis and Nick Blackman. On the hour mark Kristian Dennis gave the Silkmen the lead which they held on to, progressing to the fourth round for the first time in their history.

Playing at the Stadium of Light against Sunderland supported by a small number of Silkmen fans, the team gave a very creditable performance. Unfortunately, the damage was done in the first half when the home side took a two-goal lead, the first goal coming from the penalty spot. However, Kristian Dennis managed to pull a goal back 10 minutes from time but Sunderland held out to win the tie 2–1 and progress to the fifth round.

Cup Competitions

Macclesfield were drawn against much troubled Leeds United for the first-round tie in the **Carling Cup** which the visitors won with a single second-half goal.

In the **Johnstone's Paint Trophy** the Silkmen travelled to Wrexham for the first round where a rather mediocre match was played, the highlight of which was Michael Husbands's successful conversion of a second-half penalty. The second round was also settled by a single goal when Stockport County visited the Moss Rose. Although Macclesfield put in a lot of effort, it was the visitors who bossed the match and secured victory with a second half goal.

The **FA Cup** brought no joy when non-League Rushden & Diamonds easily overcame the Silkmen 3–1 on their home territory. Martin Gritton scored the Silkmen's goal, converting a cross from the right wing by Simon Wiles. This was the first occasion that Macclesfield Town had been beaten in the FA Cup by a non-League side since their promotion to the Football League.

CHAPTER TWELVE: 2008–2009

FRUSTRATION AND INCONSISTENCY

Pre-season

Following the successful retention of Football League status over the final 12 games of the previous season, manager Keith Alexander was rewarded with a two-year contract.

Keith immediately released six players: Maltese international Luke Dimech, veteran defender Richard Edghill, midfielder Levi Reid and 'keeper Tommy Lee. Tommy had lost his place to Jonny Brain during the previous season, but he had played a vital role in Rochdale's progression to the League Two Play-off Final during his loan spell there. In addition, Keith Alexander, as a matter of principle at this time, did not include a 'keeper on the substitutes' bench for League matches, meaning that two first-team 'keepers were not required in the squad. Hardworking midfielder Jamie Tolley was originally released but after an unsuccessful trial at Luton Town, Jamie signed a six-month contract with the club just before the start of the season.

New signings included Ahmed Deen, a left-back from non-League St Albans, and former trainee at Peterborough United, midfielder Lee Bell from Mansfield Town, striker Neil Harvey from non-League Retford United, where he had been a prolific scorer, and veteran striker Simon Yeo from Chester City, who had played for Keith Alexander at Lincoln City. Defender Sean Hessey, who had spent much of the previous season on loan, made his move from Chester City permanent and was confirmed as team captain, Alexander believing that Sean would play his part well in the greater involvement of the team captain with the referee in the forthcoming season.

Defender Sean Hessey is appointed team captain.

In addition, defender Paul Morgan, another player who had worked with Keith Alexander at Lincoln City and Bury, signed a season-long loan from Bury having regained full fitness after being out of contention in the second half of the previous season due to injury.

It was decided to re-introduce a reserve side for the forthcoming season so that squad players who were not featuring regularly in the senior side and those returning from injury would have some match practice. In addition, the younger players would have the advantage of gaining experience in the reserve side prior to joining the senior side.

After two years of heavily discounted prices, the club increased the admission prices and the cost of season tickets. In most cases the number of 'free games' for season-ticket holders was increased and adult supporters, taking advantage of the early-bird purchase, obtained as many as five free games. Entry for children under 12 remained free and for the under 16s match admission remained at £5 with the cost of season tickets for them remaining at £50.

Arsenal's goalscorer Kelly Smith.

Led by members of the Silkmen Supporters' Trust, there was a clean-up of the Moss Rose Stadium on several successive weekends during the summer, including renovation work on the Blues Bar. All the advertising boards were renewed and Cheshire Building Society installed new advertising boards along the complete length of the perimeter fence facing the McAlpine Stand.

For the first time ever, a live open-air concert, called 'Blues at the Blues', was held at the Moss Rose in association with Ronnie's Bar of Duke's Court and promoted by the club chairman, Mike Rance. The concert was advertised throughout Cheshire and there was an advert on television's Channel M. Acts included Aynsley Lister, The Virginmarys, Jim Kirkpatrick's Heavy Weather, Sinnerboy and George Borowski and the Fabulous Wonderfuls, BlueFunk Rhythm and Blues' house band Cactus Moon. In addition, Duke's Court-based Ronnie's Bar moved its popular full cocktail and waitress service to the McIlroy Suite.

Thursday 7 August saw the Moss Rose hosting the 2008 FA Women's Community Shield match between Arsenal and Everton Ladies which was televised live by Setanta. The match itself was full of pace, good possession and excellent passing, with several England international players taking part. The ball was skilfully played out from the back along the ground and for much of the time both sides matched each other's performance.

There were several shots at goal, some of which were quite speculative from 20 and 30 yards, but it was Arsenal who broke the deadlock on 72 minutes. Having collected a long pass, Arsenal's Karen Carney raced clear, only for the Everton 'keeper to come well off her line to dispossess Carney with a sliding tackle, but the ball fell to England international Kelly Smith who coolly lobbed the ball into the centre of the empty net to win the match for the Gunners.

Friendly Matches

Manager Keith Alexander's pre-season philosophy is to play as many matches as possible to ensure that the players are match-fit for the start of the season, resulting in an unprecedented 16 matches being played between 9 July and 4 August. They can be broken down into three distinct groups – non-League sides, a mini tour of Northern Ireland and home matches.

Nine matches were played at non-League grounds resulting in three wins, four draws and two defeats. The defeats came at old FA Cup opponents Alfreton Town and when a young side played New Mills. There were drawn matches at Congleton Town, Buxton, Hednesford Town and Eastwood Town. At Hednesford, the players had fortunately left the pitch before the match because of the monsoon conditions when a bolt of lightning hit the centre spot; however, the elements cleared enabling the match to commence on time. The victories came at Bradford Park Avenue, Rainworth and at Steve Burr's Stalybridge Celtic.

For many years Keith Alexander has been taking his teams over to Northern Ireland on a short pre-season tour, and he continued the practice with the Silkmen. In the first match at Larne, the Silkmen were captained by Jordan Hadfield, and an own-goal together with one by Simon Yeo secured a 2–1 victory.

In the second match against Lisburn Distillery, a goal in each half by Danny Thomas gave the Silkmen their second victory with a final score of 2–1. In the third match, Colraine proved to be stiffer opposition and they ran out winners by a single goal scored from the penalty spot. As this match was played on a Saturday, it gave several Silkmen supporters the opportunity to travel over to Northern Ireland to support the team.

On home soil, Paul Ince's Blackburn Rovers came to the Moss Rose. A rather pedestrian first half saw Rovers taking the lead through a David Dunn goal but the visitors, having made wholesale changes at half-time, stepped up a gear and made the Silkmen work harder. Just seconds after the re-start Paul Gallagher scored Rovers' second goal, but minutes later the Silkmen pulled a goal back when Lee Bell's ball down the right wing was crossed by Izak Reid, allowing Martin Gritton to score from close range. Macclesfield had other chances including an ambitious attempt by young John Rooney, but the score remained 2–1 in favour of the visitors.

Bolton failed to live up to their pre-match promise to bring a strong team and fielded a second-string side. This was another match which did not take-off until the second half, on this occasion following several changes by the Silkmen. Sean Hessey won the match for the Silkmen with a speculative 20-yard drive which beat former international 'keeper Ian Walker.

The visit of Stockport County saw the return of former Silkmen Jimmy McNulty and Matty McNeill. The visitors cruised to a two-goal lead but Simon Yeo converted a cross on the stroke of half-time to pull a goal back. Again several substitutions were made at half-time, and yet again the Silkmen stepped up a gear in the second half with Shaun Brisley scrambling home the equaliser 11 minutes from time.

The last friendly match at the Moss Rose saw the Chinese side Chengdu Blades, in whom Sheffield United have a controlling stake, take on the Silkmen. Chengdu play in the Chinese Super League, and at the time of their visit were lying in ninth position. The city is the fifth largest in China and is located in the Sichuan Province in South-West

Chengdu Blades supporters at the Moss Rose.

China, the scene of a fairly recent horrific earthquake. In the match, the Silkmen were cruising along having taken a two-goal lead courtesy of Martin Gritton and Chris Hirst, only to see the visitors score two late goals in as many minutes to share the honours.

SEASON REVIEW

August

The first match of the season saw the Silkmen travel to Shrewsbury for their second visit to the new ground, now styled the Prostar Stadium. With only permit parking at the ground, most spectators had to travel from the centre of the town on public transport, and coaches were laid on from many of the surrounding towns and villages. One excellent aspect of this stadium is the facilities for disabled supporters who have their special area high up at the back of the stand, giving them one of the best views in the stadium rather than being at pitch level where their view of the action can be obscured by players. Under a reciprocal arrangement every away supporter received a free matchday programme on the basis that all Shrewsbury fans would receive a free Macclesfield programme when they visited the Moss Rose during the season.

The starting line-up included just two new faces – full-back Ahmed Deen and central-defender Paul Morgan, although new recruit, forward Simon Yeo, was also introduced in the second half. The team was: Brain, Deen, Hessey (Izak Reid 46), Walker (Yeo 76), Brisley, Morgan, Tolley, Dunfield, Thomas, Gritton, Green (Evans 63), with manager Keith Alexander retaining the defensive back-five line which had served the team so well in the final matches of the previous season.

In recent times before the start of all international and Premier League matches the players have formed a straight line, with the home players then walking down the away team line greeting each away player with a handshake. This 'welcome' was introduced for all League clubs at the start of the season as part of the Respect Campaign which resulted from a survey of football grassroots in 2007 to ensure a safe, positive environment for everyone enjoying football.

Pre-season, Shrewsbury Town were seen as one of the main contenders for the League title and had invested in their squad over the close season. Whatever early-season hopes the Silkmen fans had were soon dashed as Shrewsbury were faster, passed the ball well and retained possession better. After one or two scares their first goal came in the 31st minute. The second half introduction of Izak Reid gave the side more width and pace but three further goals, including a penalty, saw Shrewsbury run out easy winners 4–0, leaving the Silkmen fans extremely disappointed.

The first home match of the season was against strong opposition in Bradford City, who outplayed the Silkmen and won by two early first-half goals. In the next match two second-half goals in 10 minutes saw Accrington Stanley take all three points at the Fraser Eagle Stadium.

In the final League match of the month the team of Brain, Hessey, Brisley, McDonald (Gritton 46), Walker, Bell, Tolley (Dunfield 21), Green, Thomas, Evans and Deen faced Darlington at the Moss Rose. Unfortunately, Jamie Tolley was injured in the first half, although his injury had no impact on the final result. Darlington completely outclassed the Silkmen winning 6–0, the largest League defeat inflicted on the Silkmen since their promotion to the Football League.

To make matters worse, this was the first occasion when no points had been earned in the month of August, it was only the second time that no goals had been scored in the month and the total of 14 goals conceded was the worst League record for the month of August. In addition, in both League and Cup matches there had been four red cards issued, something of a concern when a suspended fine of £3,000 was hanging over the club following the disciplinary record the previous season. But with Luton deducted 30 points before the season commenced and both Rotherham and Bournemouth deducted 17 points, the Silkmen completed the month in 21st position as follows:

Position	Team	Points
20	Barnet	0
21	**Macclesfield T**	**0**
22	Rotherham	-7
23	Bournemouth	-15
24	Luton T	-23

After the Darlington match Keith Alexander told the *Macclesfield Express* 'I'll get it right, I'm big enough to take it on the chin. It's no good crying about it, I've tried to keep the lads upbeat, I take all the criticism and I'll be working as hard as I can to put things right.'

September

For the visit of Luton Town, Keith Alexander changed the make-up of the team with a reliance on youth coupled with a change of formation to 4-4-2. The back-five defensive line had served the side well at the end of the previous season but neither the tall, strong, central-defender Ryan Cresswell nor the every reliable and capable left-back Neil Ashton were still with the Silkmen, both of whom had been extremely influential. The change of personnel gave the following line-up: Brain, Flynn, Morgan, Brisley, Reid, Thomas, Dunfield, Bell, Jennings, Evans, Yeo.

And it worked. Veteran, and still highly capable, striker Simon Yeo picked up a long kick from 'keeper Jonny Brain which caught the Luton defence cold, allowing Simon to lob the 'keeper from 25 yards in the 12th minute. In the second half, from a short corner, James Jennings curled the ball towards goal allowing Paul Morgan to score with the faintest of touches; however, Luton pulled a goal back in the 90th minute but the Silkmen had earned their first points of the season.

Away at Bournemouth, Keith Alexander kept faith with the young side and Gareth Evans scored with just 65 seconds on the clock for Macclesfield's 600th League goal and what turned out to be the winning goal. Unfortunately, Gareth went from hero to zero in the space of 15 minutes when he was dismissed for elbowing an opponent, no less than 'Sicknote' himself, Darren Anderton. Nevertheless the Silkmen held out for their second win.

With defenders James Jennings, Matthew Flynn, Shaun Brisley and Paul Morgan playing well, central-defender Clayton McDonald returned to Manchester City at the end of his one-month loan at the club as there were no opportunities for him to claim a place in the senior side.

A third consecutive victory came at Port Vale when Terry Dunfield opened the scoring only for Vale to equalise a minute before half-time. Vale took the initiative early in the second half but two goals from Simon Yeo and one from Izak Reid in the space of 11 minutes saw the Silkmen run out easy winners 4–1.

Celebrating Simon Yeo's goal against Luton Town.

By now everyone thought that the side were on a roll and that another victory could be on the cards against recently promoted Exeter City, who were the next visitors to the Moss Rose. Exeter took the lead in the 47th second of the match and extended it in the 35th minute, but Simon Yeo pulled a goal back on the stroke of half-time.

The visitors took charge almost immediately after the re-start, extending their lead in the 48th minute, and went further ahead in the 85th minute to win 4–1, leaving the Silkmen faithful bemused, especially after such a good performance at Port Vale but, at least, the team had risen to 15th position. This match saw three players achieve personal milestones – Franny Green made his 300th League appearance, Martin Gritton his 300th career (ie all competitions) appearance with Danny Thomas making his 250th career appearance.

Midfielder Lee Bell in action against Exeter City.

October

The month started with a visit to in-form Brentford, who won by a single first-half goal despite a determined performance by the Silkmen.

Events in the first half of the first-ever League meeting between the Silkmen and Aldershot Town at the Moss Rose gave no indication that the second half would be so exciting and satisfying for the players and supporters alike. Five goals were scored in a period of 16 minutes, giving the Silkmen a 3–2 lead by the 64th minute, setting up the match for a thrilling finish. Macclesfield's goals had been scored by Gareth Evans and two by Danny Thomas, who enjoyed one of his best performances of the season. Francis Green replaced Simon Yeo in the 74th minute and nine minutes later he converted a Terry Dunfield cross with a powerful downward header to seal victory for the Silkmen 4–2.

At Notts County there was another goalless first half, but the home side took the lead early in the second half. Veteran striker Simon Yeo equalised after a Gareth Evans thunderbolt shot rebounded off the Notts County 'keeper Russell Holt, Yeo being the quickest to react. Unfortunately, shortly later Gareth Evans was dismissed for a tackle on County's Adam Tann, leaving Macclesfield to give a backs-to-the-wall performance to take a share of the points.

On a Tuesday evening at the Moss Rose, Macclesfield took an early lead courtesy of a Simon Yeo goal; however, despite playing positively two defensive lapses allowed the visitors, Lincoln City, initially to level the score on the stroke of half-time and then win the match in the second half.

For the second consecutive match, Macclesfield played well and enjoyed the majority of the possession but they did not make the most of their chances, unlike the visitors Rotherham United who won the match 2–1 having taken

Snowbound Wycombe Wanderers.

the lead in the fifth minute. The Silkmen had to be satisfied with Franny Green's 90th-minute scissor-kick goal.

The month ended in a most unusual way when the mid-week match at Wycombe Wanderers, attended by 64 hardy Macclesfield fans, was abandoned after 22 minutes due to a snowstorm with the score at 0–0. An impromptu snowball fight between the players and the Silkmen fans followed, and there was a very welcome gesture by the Macclesfield Town directors when they invited their fans into the bar for a drink before making their way home.

Despite playing some attractive football, with just four points earned during the month and taking into account the abandoned match, the side slipped to 20th position in the League Table.

November

On the first day of the month the Silkmen suffered their third consecutive League defeat when the visitors, Gillingham, won by a single first-half goal.

This match was designated 'Ladies Day' in recognition of the Macclesfield Town Ladies' Football Club, who have progressed to be the largest female football club in the county with eight teams from Under-10 to Open Age, four of the teams winning their respective leagues undefeated in 2008 and the Under-14s Silks tream winning the Knock-out Cup in 2009. The club is very

Members of the Ladies' Football Club enjoying their day at the Moss Rose.

Players' Guard of Honour on Ladies' Day.

well organised and hold regular social events to raise money for the running of their club in addition to which they have charity evenings, the most recent to raise money for breast cancer charities. There is an excellent and informative website providing news and match reports. Before the match, the ladies formed a guard of honour for the players and at half-time the more senior ladies took part in a penalty shoot-out, while the younger ones took part in mini-soccer matches.

The men's ship was steadied at Rochdale when, after a goalless first half, Rochdale took the lead midway through the second half. But Macclesfield responded well and Nat Brown, on loan from Wrexham, converted Izak Reid's cross to score his first goal for the Silkmen and level the scores.

Results continued to improve when a second away match, this time at Barnet, saw the Silkmen take an early lead with a Martin Gritton goal, his first for over three months. The second half saw Barnet applying pressure, resulting in them equalising with a fortunate goal which the Silkmen claimed had not crossed the line. However, late goals from Francis Green and Nat Brown sealed a 3–1 victory.

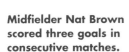

Midfielder Nat Brown scored three goals in consecutive matches.

There was even more good news when Nat Brown's third goal in as many matches gave the Silkmen victory in a dour match against Grimsby Town at the Moss Rose on a bitterly cold Tuesday evening with an attendance of only 1,182, the lowest League attendance since promotion, but this match clashed with televised Champions League matches including Manchester United's tie.

A much more satisfying month saw the side move up to 15th position with 20 points.

December

At the beginning of the month there was a 'gathering' of vehicles outside the Moss Rose far in excess of anything ever seen for a televised match, including two double-decker refreshment trailers and two cranes, one operating over the McAlpine Stand and one over the Silk FM Stand. Nike had selected the Moss Rose to shoot part of an advert as it was easier to lift some of the equipment over the stands. The major part of the advert was shot at Arsenal's Emirates Stadium.

The trip to Wycombe Wanderers for the re-arranged match, which had been abandoned due to snow at the end of October, saw the home side win 4–0 in fine style, bouncing straight back after a shock defeat in the FA Cup by non-League Eastwood Town the previous Saturday.

The following Saturday at the Moss Rose, the Silkmen earned a creditable draw against Bury when the only goals of the match came in the first eight minutes. Martin Gritton put the Silkmen ahead with a close-range effort followed by Bury's Stephen Dawson scoring the equaliser only two minutes later.

In poor conditions, it was raining and there was a swirling wind, Martin Gritton played one of his best games in his Silkmen career at Chesterfield, scoring two of the four goals with the opponents only achieving two strikes. Martin's first goal came when he collected a pass from Nat Brown, took on defender Robert Page and curled the ball to the right of the Chesterfield 'keeper. For his second goal, Martin converted Lee Bell's chip over the Chesterfield defence.

There then followed two disappointing defeats. The first against Dagenham & Redbridge at the Moss Rose, when the visitors were three goals to the good in the first 19 minutes and added a fourth early in the second half without any reply from the Silkmen. On Boxing Day at Morecambe, Izak Reid gave the Silkmen the ideal start with a well-taken goal in the third minute, but after that Macclesfield were outplayed by a very ordinary Morecambe side who went on to score four goals, the first two from set pieces, leaving the Silkmen fans voicing their disappointment at the end of the match.

Keith Alexander reacted to these defeats with five changes for the home encounter against Chester City. Out of the starting line-up went Flynn, Deen, Brisley, Gritton and Thomas. In came Hessey, Walker, Jennings, Dunfield and

Recalled to the side, central-defender Richard Walker (No. 5).

Yeo. The most interesting change was the inclusion of centre-back Richard Walker, who had been out of contention since incurring a training ground ankle injury in September. Richard was certainly the 'forgotten man' but, once he had settled in, he proved his worth as a strong defender and made good use of his aerial ability.

In addition, there was a change of formation to 5-3-2 as follows:

Brain
Walker Hessey Morgan
Reid Jennings
Dunfield Bell Brown
Yeo Evans

Macclesfield were the quickest out of the blocks when Nat Brown gave the home side the lead, but a scrappy first half could easily have seen Chester draw level. The visitors started the second half strongly and deservedly equalised, but a fortunate penalty was bravely converted by Gareth Evans, with substitute Martin Gritton consolidating the Silkmen's lead with five minutes to go. The 3–1 win saw a much more acceptable performance overall and sent the Silkmen fans home happy but perplexed over the team's inconsistent performance over the first half of the season. This victory left the side in 14th position with 27 points.

During the month it was good to see the club represented in the community. Captain Sean Hessey, with some of his team, visited the children's ward at Macclesfield Hospital to distribute presents purchased with funds he had raised during a charity run in the summer. They also visited Macclesfield High School to talk to pupils taking a citizenship course. Meanwhile, Keith Alexander gave an inspiring talk to King's School pupils emphasising the need to concentrate on education even if they had ambitions to be a professional footballer.

January

The weather played its part at the start of the month, firstly with the postponement of the re-arranged match at Exeter which originally had been scheduled for the day of the third round of the FA Cup, and secondly, the home match against Port Vale also fell foul of the freezing conditions.

The first League match of the year saw Macclesfield travel to Aldershot Town, who were enjoying an excellent first season back in the League. Gareth Evans gave the Silkmen a first-half lead, a goal which was described by Simon Carter on BBC Radio Manchester as a 'Thierry Henry finish'. It was good to hear the studio presenters acknowledging that players still have to be very capable even in League Two. Aldershot took control of the game in the second half with Jonny Brain regularly called into action, but just as six minutes' time added-on was announced, Kirk Hudson equalised for the Shots to leave the Macclesfield players and fans crestfallen.

Probably one of Macclesfield's best performances of the season to date saw them win 2–0 against second-in-the-table Brentford at the Moss Rose, with goals from on-loan Emile Sinclair and a penalty from Gareth Evans. Another fine performance at home saw the side battle hard against top-of-the-table Wycombe Wanderers to earn a goalless draw.

However, just as everyone thought the team were beginning to perform with more consistency having been unbeaten in the previous four League matches, the Jekyll and Hyde season reared its ugly head again against Rotherham who easily overcame the Silkmen 2–0, and there was worse to come as the Silkmen

On-loan striker Emile Sinclair, who scored on his home debut.

did not chalk up a victory for another five matches. Rotherham currently play at the Don Valley Athletics Stadium, which must be one of the worst venues for watching football. All spectators are housed in the single covered stand (the remainder is open seating, a similar design to Gateshead) with the action in the distance viewed over a ten-lane running track and a further wide space between the stand and the track. The away supporters are housed at one end of the stand with the direct line of sight behind the goal. Even at Brighton's Withdean Stadium supporters are closer to the action.

This result left the Silkmen in 15th position at the end of the month but with two games in hand.

In the week following the Rotherham match, central-defender Richard Walker was the subject of an FA charge of misconduct following an incident with Drewe Broughton seen by the referee's assessor sat in the main stand. This resulted in Richard receiving a three-match ban, bringing the total 'red card' suspensions for the club to 10 for the season to date.

Spencer Austin, the Gloryhunter.

In the latter part of the month 'the Gloryhunter' spent time with the Silkmen. Spencer Austin decided to follow League Two clubs, living in the town he was currently following, until they lost and then move onto the victor and support that team until they lost. His aim is to write a book about his experiences. Grimsby Town was randomly selected as the first team of the season and by the time he reached us he was supporting Brentford. Having beaten the Bees he supported (and filmed) the Silkmen at the Wycombe match and then at the Don Valley Stadium, but as we lost he then moved on to Rotherham.

The January transfer window saw changes in the squad. Nat Brown, who had performed well in the midfield, had his loan from Wrexham extended to the end of the season. Emile Sinclair, a 21-year-old striker from Nottingham Forest, was signed on a month's loan and made an immediate impact with his speed and scored on his home debut, and towards the end of the month Tom Elliott, a young centre-forward from Leeds United, was also signed on loan for a month. At the same time midfielder Jamie Tolley's contract was extended to the end of the season.

Leaving the club were Nick Blackman, who moved to Blackburn Rovers, where he had been training for much of the season and scored on his debut for the reserve side, Martin Gritton who ironically had one of his best performances of the season at Chesterfield and moved there when they offered him a two-and-a-half-year contract, and eventually, after much huffing and puffing, midfield dynamo Terry Dunfield moved to Shrewsbury Town. In addition, out-of-favour Jordan Hadfield moved on a month's loan to non-League Altrincham.

February

One of the coldest winters for many a year took charge of fixtures at the start of the month with the match at Lincoln and the home match against Notts County postponed. Postponement of matches has a two-sided impact on the cash flow of the club. Firstly, there are no receipts on the day of the postponement and playing the rearranged match on a midweek evening results in a lower attendance and, therefore, reduced income, in Macclesfield's case approximately £5,000 per match.

The first match to be played in the month was the doubly re-arranged match at Exeter. It had first been postponed due to the FA Cup match with Everton and the following week due to a frozen pitch. For the second time in the season Exeter City put four past the Silkmen in a disappointing performance when the visitors failed to score. For the 64 Macclesfield fans who attended this match they were further frustrated by long delays on the motorway for both journeys, some supporters arriving home at 4.15 in the morning.

In the first home match of the month, a controversial penalty decision gave the visitors, Rochdale, a 1–0 victory; although it has to be recorded that the Rochdale 'keeper, Frank Fielding, who was on loan from Blackburn Rovers, had a magnificent game.

For the home match against Notts County Keith Alexander started with a three-man forward line of Evans, on-loan Elloitt and Yeo, which initially worked with Simon Yeo giving the Silkmen a first-half lead. This was an unspectacular match with both teams playing the long-ball to little advantage. Failure by Jonny Brain to take a high ball coupled with an undefended back post presented the perfect opportunity for Notts County to equalise. Both teams hit the woodwork and also had an opportunity to win the match but both sides survived to share the points.

Midfielder Jordan Hadfield.

In the next match at Gillingham the home side were too strong for the Silkmen and won 3–1, a Gareth Evans penalty being Macclesfield's consolation goal. By now everyone was beginning to despair with the poor form being shown by the side.

With Manchester United playing in the Champions League on the Tuesday, the match against Port Vale at the Moss Rose was moved to the Wednesday, but there were still only 1,312 Macclesfield fans present, the total attendance bolstered by 955 Vale fans. There was little to cheer about in this match with both teams slogging it out. A speculative 40-yard shot by Port Vales' Adnan Ahmed hit Jonny Brain's arms and ended up in the net. An extremely well worked 90th-minute goal gave Vale a 2–0 victory. There were two consolations in this match. Firstly, the return of the ever entertaining midfielder Jordan Hadfield and a cameo appearance of the lighting fast on-loan Tottenham winger Kyle Fraser-Allen. In addition, this was manager Keith Alexander's 50th match in charge.

After this match striker Tom Elliott returned to Leeds United at the end of his one-month loan spell having failed to make any positive impact during his time at the Moss Rose.

The final match of the month saw Shrewsbury Town at the Moss Rose. They had put four past the Silkmen on the opening day of the season but had failed to register a victory in their previous 15 away matches. There were five changes to the starting line-up. Out went Reid (recovering from a knock), Deen (eye injury), Brown (on the substitutes' bench), Elliott (returned to Leeds) and Thomas. In came Flynn, Brisley, Yeo, Sinclair (who had just returned for a second loan spell) and Hessey, but the line-up still retained three recognised strikers. Macclesfield performed as a team and looked more solid in all departments, especially Jonny Brain who certainly deserved his Man of the Match award.

This match saw the return of the ever popular Terry Dunfield for Shrewsbury, but he was a shadow of his former self, and Shrewsbury were masters of their own downfall, with an own-goal in the first half and then a penalty conceded which Gareth Evans slotted home with ease. Substitute midfielder Nat Brown, playing in a striker's role, secured all three points when he rounded the 'keeper well into stoppage time for Macclesfield to register a well deserved 3–0 win to leave them in 16th position in the table with 36 points.

Goalkeeper Jonny Brain organising his defence.

For trivia quiz buffs this match threw up some interesting facts. Firstly, by the end of the match all three of Macclesfield's recognised strikers had been substituted leaving a forward line of two midfielders, Nat Brown and Danny Thomas. Secondly, both teams completed the match with a player named Richard Walker on the field. Thirdly, it was virtually three years since Macclesfield had profited from an own-goal, on that occasion against Wrexham, which was also a home fixture. Macclesfield scored three goals on that day as well, the own-goal was also the first goal to be scored and it came about in the first half.

March

March proved to be a difficult and trying month for both players and supporters alike. Defeat by a single goal at Bradford City was followed by the only success in the month when top-scorer Gareth Evans scored two goals, including his fifth consecutive penalty, to secure a 2–1 win against Darlington in their vast stadium, to give the Silkmen their first win on the road since December. Darlington had recently gone into administration but even after the 10 points deducted they remained in the upper half of the table.

The next match at the Moss Rose was named 'Credit Crunch Tuesday' when admission prices were reduced to £5 for adults for all areas of the stadium, with free entry for the under-16s, and season-ticket holders were given a free programme. This is one initiative of many which the club had embarked on over the years which was a success as the attendance was some 500 higher than a normal Tuesday evening match. Unfortunately, the success was not matched on the pitch when former Silkmen John Miles came back to haunt the Moss Rose, having a splendid match and acting as provider for Accrington's second goal to give the visitors a 2–0 victory. Half-time saw a wonderful sight on the pitch when some 90 youngsters from the club's Development Section displayed their footballing skills.

The following Thursday a fans' forum was held when several supporters took the opportunity to express their dissatisfaction at the style of play and the lack of entertainment being provided by the senior side. Keith Alexander was naturally defensive of the situation, emphasising that half the side included inexperienced youngsters, but neither he nor other members of the top table could satisfy the supporters who were present.

Before the next match against Bournemouth at the Moss Rose, Keith Alexander was taken to hospital for a scan having been unwell the previous day and before the match. Having suffered two aneurisms while manager at Lincoln, Keith's condition caused concern. Fortunately he was given the all clear and returned to work a few days later. In the match the Silkmen were undone by two goals from former Manchester City player Lee Bradbury, with the Silkmen failing to score yet again.

Worse was to come at Luton where the home side won by a single goal from the penalty spot. The infringement was observed by the assistant referee but subsequent television coverage clearly showed that the ball had gone out of play before being struck into the penalty area, where it merely brushed against the hand of Paul Morgan who did not move his hand at all.

Two new signings were made before the end of the month. Colin Daniel, a left-sided midfielder, came on loan from Crewe Alexander and Aaron Chalmers, a former Oldham Athletic trainee who plays in defence or midfield, signed non-contract forms.

Kyle Fraser-Allen returned to Tottenham after a month on loan. Tottenham had recorded that Kyle had been given the loan in recognition of his fine performances for their reserve side. It would be interesting to know Kyle's view on his 'reward' as he only made two cameo appearances from the substitutes' bench. Nevertheless, he made his full Football League debut against Luton Town in February and demonstrated his lightening speed down the right flank.

For the second time this season the Moss Rose was the venue for a prestige match when Macclesfield hosted the England versus Northern Ireland under-18 Schoolboys Carnegie Centenary International Shield match. The match was preceded by the parade of the UEFA Fair Play and Carnegie flags, presentation to visiting dignitaries together with the playing of the National Anthem. The attendance was just over 1,000, many of whom were youngsters who enthusiastically and nosily cheered on their team in a match which was full of pace and deservedly won 1–0 by Northern Ireland. It was pleasing to see former manager Sammy McIlroy return as one of the Guests of Honour at this match.

At Dagenham & Redbridge John Rooney scored his first senior goal on the same day that his brother Wayne scored two goals for England only 15 miles away, but the Silkmen were undone again, conceding two goals in the final 20 minutes leaving Paul Morgan nothing to celebrate on his 300th career appearance.

John Rooney scored his first senior goal at Dagenham & Redbridge.

The final match of the month saw the Silkmen slump to their fifth consecutive League defeat at Lincoln who won the match with a first-half goal to leave the side in 19th position with 39 points and only nine points above the relegation zone. Understandably there was concern from the supporters' point of view as to whether Football League status could be retained, but manager Keith Alexander continued to take an upbeat stance.

April

Although the team were almost at the end of the season they were still not safe from the possibility of relegation. Chesterfield were entertained on a bright but breezy day and, true to form, a former player came back to haunt the Silkmen when striker Martin Gritton gave the visitors the lead in the eighth minute, but the ever hardworking Gareth Evans struck back only seven minutes later to give the Silkmen a vital point. But it really should have been three points. A thunderbolt of a shot from John Rooney hit the underside of the crossbar and to many in stadium appeared to cross the line, but the 'goal' was not given. Subsequent viewing of video footage shows that the ball had actually crossed the line. This is more evidence that the introduction of goal-line technology needs urgent consideration.

Next it was off across Cheshire to play Chester City, who were battling against relegation. Lee Bell's free-kick rebounded off the wall to John Rooney,

Action at Chester City, with the Silkmen wearing their third strip.

who blasted the ball home from 20 yards. On-loan Colin Daniel then fed Gareth Evans, who smashed a right-footed drive in off the underside of the crossbar to give the Silkmen a 2–0 win and a further precious three points. For this match the players wore a green-and-yellow third strip as both the home and away strips clashed with Chester's colours.

Sammy McIlroy's Morecambe side had three goals disallowed at the Moss Rose before converting a corner in the 85th minute to win the match and set the Silkmen faithful on edge again with only a cushion of seven points to the relegation zone.

Anyone setting off for Bury with any hope of success must have forgotten that the Silkmen had never recorded a victory at Gigg Lane, and as Bury were flying high and Macclesfield were struggling at the other end of the table a 3–0 defeat, while disappointing, was not unexpected. However, there was a silver lining to the cloud when Chester City lost such that the seven-point difference between them and the Silkmen, with two matches to play, meant that Macclesfield had retained their Football League status for another season following the 44th League match. This was a marginal improvement on previous years when it had gone to the 45th and even 46th match before safety was reached.

Since Macclesfield moved to the former away designated dug-out, the home team have warmed up before the match at the Silkmen Terrace End with the visitors warming up towards the Star Lane End in front of the home supporters. Resulting from this arrangement more often than not the Silkmen attacked the Star Lane End in the first half, whereas it had always been policy to attack the home end in the second half which had brought a lot of success to the team in the past. For some reason, before the penultimate match of the season against Barnet, the Silkmen warmed up at the Star Lane End and attacked the away end in the first half – and it worked magically.

Nat Brown celebrated his 200th career League appearance in style with a well taken headed goal in the second minute, following which the Silkmen

Kristian Dennis (left) celebrates scoring his first senior goal.

dominating the first half. The second half was a different story, with Barnet taking the game to the Silkmen and pinning them into their half for much of the time, resulting in the inevitable equaliser being scored. But on came 19-year-old Kristian Dennis in the 72nd minute to score his first-ever senior goal some 10 minutes later, to give the Silkmen a 2–1 victory and a season double over Barnet. A tally of 46 points moved the Silkmen up to 18th place at the end of the month.

May

The result of the final match of the season at Grimsby was somewhat academic and finished in a goalless draw, but with teams adjacent in the League table winning their matches the Silkmen completed the season in 20th position. Two players made their Football League debut and debut for the Silkmen. Non-contract central-defender Patrece Liburd played for the full 90 minutes with first-year trainee Vinny Mukendi coming on for the final 14 minutes. It was good to see Vinny's performances in the youth team being recognised. He appeared on the score sheet regularly and scored a hat-trick against Bury youth in the Silkmen's 5–2 victory. Youngsters Christian Millar and Kristian Dennis were also given a run out late in the game.

Following a superb performance in the closing weeks of the 2007–08 season hopes were high at the beginning of this season for a stronger performance and for the team to complete the season, at least, in the top half of the League Table. A disastrous start dampened expectations, but veteran striker Simon Yeo kick-started the Silkmen's season, and even in December ambitions of a Play-off place were harboured. The inability to field a settled side had an impact on performance, especially in the first half of the season, though suspensions and then injuries took their toll, the younger members of the squad had to be rested, actual team selection saw many changes and then there was the loss of two key players in the January transfer window. An element of the supporters bemoaned the lack of entertainment on the field of play, but if the results had been more favourable would they have been happier despite the style of play? Winning is an essential part of the product offered and losing 25 matches (the same number as relegated Chester City) had not helped the cause. In the end the season just fizzled out.

Nevertheless, there were several positives to take from the season. The introduction of several younger members of the squad is evidence of the excellent work undertaken by youth development manager John Askey and his team. The club has reached out into the community again with the football in the community programme continuing to develop, the players have made visits to schools and the local hospital, and there were the ever-popular matchday visits of youngsters who fill the pitch at half-time showing off their football skills. The Ladies' Football club continued to go from strength to strength. Off the pitch, entertainment events had been organised and the finances of the club continued to be managed carefully.

But it is always better to look forward and a new season always brings a new dawn, anticipation, new players and new hope. Following a series of disappointing seasons there is no doubt that a heavy responsibility will rest on the shoulders of the manager and players to provide a much better product, far more victories, especially at home, and a much improved final League position. When the Silkmen play their first match of the 2009–10 season it will be their 553rd consecutive League match, second only to Wycombe Wanderers for continuous membership of the Football League since automatic promotion was introduced. Not a bad achievement for one of the smallest clubs in the Football League managing on one of the smallest budgets. It will also be Macclesfield's 13th season in the Football League, but Silkmen supporters are not superstitious – or are they?

Cup Competitions

Paul Morgan in action against Blackpool.

In the first round of the **Carling Cup**, a creditable 2–0 win, with goals from Shaun Brisley and Martin Gritton, was achieved against Championship side Blackpool at the Moss Rose, providing a second-round tie against Premier League side West Ham United at Upton Park.

428 Macclesfield fans made the journey south to watch an excellent performance by the Silkmen against, at that time, the out-of-form Premier League side. Gareth Evans headed home an Ahmed Deen corner in the fifth minute and it took until the 74th minute before Lee Bowyer scored the equaliser. With extra-time looming, the turning point of the match came when Izak Reid was dismissed for a second bookable offence. West Ham scored three further goals in extra-time, but the Silkmen held up their heads in pride with a performance which denied their current League form.

Crewe Alexandra won the first round of the **Johnstone's Paint Trophy** at Gresty Road, scoring all three of their goals in the first half, but the unfortunate dismissal of Martin Gritton in the 13th minute did not help the Silkmen's cause.

However, there was much better news in the **FA Cup** competition. In the first round draw Macclesfield's ball was the very last to be drawn, but the proverbial banana skin was avoided when two second-half goals by Shaun Brisley and Terry Dunfield gave the Silkmen an away victory against Ryman Premier League side Harlow Town. Yet again Macclesfield's ball was the last to be drawn in the second round (it is said that the odds for this happening were 3,200 to one) on this occasion setting up a tie at Port Vale. The match was brought forward to the Friday to avoid a clash with Stoke City's match the following day, and on a bitterly cold and foggy night Macclesfield outwitted Port Vale for the second time in the season to win 3–1 through two goals from Franny Green and one from Martin Gritton.

The third round gave the club a plum tie against Premier League side Everton at the Moss Rose. With hospitality places sold out the day after the draw, it was a certainty that there would be a full house for this match. However, in the week preceding the match there were concerns about the effect on the pitch of the freezing weather, resulting in a Herculean effort by volunteers, together with Event Solutions and help from other organisations. Initially the covers were put in place and on top the covers at the Star Lane End there was a second layer of protection with carpets provided by Mahood Marquees. The day before the match a tarpaulin was provided and hot air blowers were put in place to thaw the pitch. The task was made even more difficult when the tarpaulin only covered a third of the pitch at any one time time. Eight hardy volunteers remained at the Moss Rose overnight to ensure that the match could go ahead.

A crowd of 6,008 were treated to a fine encounter with Everton fielding a full-strength side with a starting line up of Howard, Lescott, Hibbert, Neville, Baines, Jagielka, Cahill, Osman, Arteta, Pienaar and Anichebe. Macclesfield lined up with Brain, Hessey, Walker, Brown, Morgan, Jennings, Dunfield, Bell, Reid, Gritton and Evans. The Silkmen could easily have taken an early lead but Nat Brown's header flew over the crossbar and it took a top-drawer strike two minutes before half-time by Leon Osman to win the tie for Everton. Substitute striker Simon Yeo almost snatched an equaliser for the Silkmen in time added-on but Tim Howard made a magnificent save to deny him.

This was a really enjoyable encounter to watch but still leaves Macclesfield striving to reach the fourth round of the Cup for the first time in their history.

Thawing out the ground overnight before the Everton Cup match.

Everton's Steven Pienaar challenges Izak Reid.

Qualification for the FA Cup competition requires each club to enter their respective County Cup competition, although it has been possible to obtain exemption by payment of a fine. The Cheshire County Football Association decided to introduce a new 'flagship' competition, the **Premier Challenge Cup**, solely for the Football League clubs who are members of the Cheshire FA, currently Chester City, Crewe Alexandra, Macclesfield Town, Stockport County and Tranmere Rovers, thereby taking them out of the Cheshire Senior Cup competition.

The inaugural Final of this competition was held at the Moss Rose on 6 May 2009 between Crewe Alexandra and Macclesfield Town. With only five teams involved, Crewe had reached the Final by beating Chester City and then Stockport County, but Macclesfield had only needed to play a single match which they won against Tranmere Rovers.

The match was witnessed by 381 supporters on a cold and windy evening. Macclesfield fielded a fairly young side against a much stronger Crewe team. Crewe opened the scoring in the seventh minute but Macclesfield's Gareth Evans, playing a Man of the Match role against his former employers, equalised in the 85th minute. During the 30 minutes of extra-time the Railwaymen converted a penalty and then secured their victory with a third goal in the 114th minute to become the first winners of this new competition.

EPILOGUE

The Silkmen's League story really started way back on the first Saturday in May 1993 at Wycombe Wanderers when Macclesfield Town could easily have slipped out of the GM Vauxhall Conference into oblivion. Everything was to play for, as a victory would keep the Silkmen in the Conference irrespective of other results. Roy Green's solo effort was the only goal of the match and gave the Silkmen a 1–0 victory over the already crowned GM Vauxhall Conference Champions. At the end of the match the Silkmen faithful, some of whom were in Kamikaze fancy dress, were still celebrating when manager Peter Wragg walked across the pitch, shook their hands and said 'thank you for your support, goodbye.'

Little did we know then that the match was the end of an era, but if anyone had predicted on that warm and sunny afternoon, or indeed, at the first match of the following season when the Silkmen lost 5–1 against Bath City at their Twerton Park ground, that Macclesfield Town would become members of the Football League only four years later and that they would enjoy 12 years at this level, they would have been ridiculed.

At that time it would have been hard to believe that the club would spend a season in the third tier of English football, play competitive matches at the Moss Rose against the likes of West Ham United, Watford, Middlesbrough, Bolton Wanderers, Burnley, Manchester City and many others, sometimes with television cameras present, and play at the likes of the Riverside Stadium, the Reebok Stadium, Turf Moor, the Madejski Stadium, Maine Road, Highfield Road and, of course, Stamford Bridge.

There have been many highs, and it has seemed that these have been more than compensated by lows leading to frustrating times; in addition, there have been times when it looked as though Macclesfield might drop out of the Football League, but the directors always acted incisively on these occasions. Whatever has happened, on and off the pitch, during the last 12 years, one thing is certain, both officials and supporters have witnessed history being made before their very eyes.

But none of this would have been possible without the grit, determination and wonderful team spirit of the 1997 Conference Championship-winning squad, ably supported by equally enthusiastic backroom staff but led and directed by one man – the last of the Busby Babes, Sammy McIlroy MBE.

APPENDIX ONE

STADIUM DEVELOPMENT

Over the years the directors of Macclesfield Town have looked at various options to upgrade the Moss Rose Stadium and have also considered other schemes to enhance the facilities of the club overall. At one time or another there were four potential large-scale projects under consideration.

- A new stadium.
- Soccer Complex on London Road.
- Development of the North End of the Moss Rose Stadium.
- A stand on the Estate Road side.

New Stadium

The club were working with Alfred McAlpine Construction to build a new stadium as part of a larger development on land between Congleton Road and London Road, known as the South Macclesfield Development Project, with the proposed stadium ready for use in 2001. In November 1999 McAlpine's plans were shortlisted by the borough council alongside four other bids. It was proposed that the stadium would have a capacity of between 6,000 and 10,000, with extensive corporate and community facilities and that the cost of the stadium would be self-funding; indeed, the club would have gained a sum of £1 million from the development.

Unfortunately, the council selected the proposed plan from Shepherds Construction, the consequence of which was that the directors then had to approach the company to discuss the viability of a new stadium. Eventually, it was announced that Shepherds had not included the provision of a new stadium in their proposed plans, which led to the then chairman of the club, Eddie Furlong, declaring that without a new stadium the facilities at the Moss Rose ground would have to be developed. In the end, the whole South Macclesfield project was never realised.

However, in 2009 the concept and feasibility of a new stadium being built only a mile from the Moss Rose, as part of an overall development, was under active consideration, with discussions taking place with the appropriate authorities.

Soccer Complex

In 2000 there was a proposed plan by the local council to re-locate the football facilities at Congleton Road to a site opposite Lyme Green Business Park covering an area from London Road to Bullocks Lane. The site would provide facilities for mini-soccer, junior football, women's and girls' football, with 10 senior pitches and three junior pitches. It was proposed that a football centre of excellence could be incorporated in partnership with Macclesfield Town Football Club and that the new playing fields could be the focus for training, reserve and youth-team matches and the Football in the Community Scheme. The development would have been completed in phases, initially with six pitches, changing rooms and car parking at a cost of £1.95 million with the total development cost £3.4 million. Financial assistance would have been forthcoming from the Lottery, the Football Association and the Foundation for Sports and Arts.

At a later date the above plan was developed further with a slightly different slant, the club and the borough council forming a partnership to develop a high-quality sports facility for the benefit of the community at a cost of £5 million. The club would obtain grants from the Football Foundation, the Sports Council, New Deal and National Lotteries Charities Board, and the council would receive a sum of £2.5 million from the South Macclesfield Development Project. Among the aims of the football club, through the partnership, would be the creation of hard-wearing pitches, a football academy and a base for the club's centre of excellence.

At the beginning of February 2001 there was an excellent exhibition in the former Fiesta Lounge at the club showing drawings of the proposed development. By this time the cost of the development had risen to £8 million with the developers, Shepherds, now contributing £2 million with the remainder to come from grants. However, it was made clear that this development relied heavily on the development of the South Macclesfield Development Project which, in the end, did not materialise, and so this project also fell by the wayside.

North End (Silkmen Terrace) Proposed Development

With schemes away from the Moss Rose failing, it was necessary to look at potential development of the existing stadium to provide improved matchday facilities, provide opportunities for the community and, at the same time, introduce additional non-football income streams.

There was an ambitious plan proposed to completely redevelop the Silkmen Terrace, the car park and the site of the former Silkmen Public House consisting of a two-level cantilever stand, with a four-storey block behind to include a sports shop, a health and fitness centre, offices, start-up business units, crèche, walk-in doctors' surgery, multi-use sports/concert hall, restaurant, lounge and meeting rooms.

A presentation was made in February 2002 outlining the plans but it was emphasised that the funding relied on grants being obtained. In April 2002 planning permission was granted for a £5.5 million development, the cost of which was to be funded by grants from sources including Sport England. The

The dream that never was.

borough council pledged a contribution of £100,000. In the 2003–04 season it was announced that further funding had been obtained but the cost had increased to £7 million.

In May 2004 it was announced that the project had been shelved as a government funder's budget had been placed on hold. This project did not go ahead as sufficient grant funding was never forthcoming.

The Alfred McAlpine Stand

Of the four projects, this is the only one which came to fruition – but not without its problems.

In the 1998–99 season, when the club were playing in the former Division Two, the structures on the Estate Road side were demolished and a modular stand with a seating capacity of 800 was erected to increase the total number of seats in the ground and, at the same time, increase income. However, with the rental costing the club £50,000 per year, a more permanent and cost effective solution had to be found.

At the beginning of the 2000–01 season construction of the stand covering almost the whole of the length of the Estate Road side was commenced, with the shell of the stand together with the seating accommodation funded by an 80 per cent grant from the Football Foundation. Incorporated into the seats were the logos for Adidas and Alfred McAlpine Construction Co. Ltd and the letters 'MTFC', and beneath the stand the concourse provided refreshment facilities, toilets, a first-aiders' room, 50-50 sellers' room and access to the Presidents' Bar. In this concourse are situated over 200 bricks which were sold to raise funds towards the cost of the stand on which the names of the purchasers are engraved.

The Estate Road side before the construction of the Alfred McAlpine Stand.

The Alfred McAlpine Stand.

The stand was first used on Sunday 11 March 2001 for the match against Barnet when Sammy McIlroy, a former manager, officially opened the stand before kick-off. Currently the total ground capacity is set at 6,141 as follows:

Area		Seating	Standing
Alfred McAlpine Stand	Home	1,050	-
	Away	413	-
Silk FM Stand	Home	576	-
London Road Terrace	Home		1,315
Star Lane End	Home	471	816
Silkmen Terrace	Away		1,500
Totals		2,510	3,631

The Presidents' Bar (which is today known as the Sports Bar) and the McIlroy Suite were still a shell as the cost of fitting out of these areas did not qualify for grant funding. However, as it was important that these facilities were available for use to add non-football income streams, they were developed over the summer of 2001 utilising the chairman's company, FBL (Builders) Limited, who were reimbursed out of the proceeds of the excellent FA Cup run in the 2001–02 season. These facilities were first used at the opening match of the 2001–02 season.

The specially designed carpet incorporating the Macclesfield Town Football Club logo provided a talking point, and the furnishings and décor together with the black-and-white photographs gave a luxurious feeling. The kitchen facilities are on a scale to fit the size of the facilities and while the Presidents' Bar is long and narrow, it is still impressive. There are bar facilities in each room.

The McIlroy Suite.

Both facilities were upgraded for the 2008–09 season with flat-screen televisions, new images on the wall, re-decoration and a matchday shop selling the new range of Adidas gear. In addition, the McAlpine logo on the stand seats was replaced with a second Adidas logo with the three horizontal Adidas lines incorporated on either side of the letters MTFC.

The corporate areas have been used for a number of events over the years including:

- On matchdays they act as a lounge for vice-presidents and the service of pre-match meals. The Sports Bar provides a facility for supporters to meet, enjoy pub food, have a drink and watch televised matches.
- The club has been able to host meetings such as those for the Third Division Chairmen and National Federation of Supporters' Northern Area.
- ITV Sport have broadcast from the McIlroy Suite, as have Radio 5 Live.
- Income has been gained from letting the premises for conferences, meetings and functions.
- The club now has a marriage licence for the McIlroy Suite.
- A Blood Transfusion Service.

The club has also been able to reach out into the community through the use of these facilities. There is no better example than the Laureus project, which helps to fight depression among young people. Sir Bobby Charlton explains the benefits of the project so well in his autobiography *My Manchester United Years:* 'Laureus have put some money into the Macclesfield project, which has helped them to employ a group of counsellors. Broken marriage and indebtedness are some of the causes of despair, and where else can a young person go for a quick chat beyond maybe 10 minutes with some overworked

GP. At Macclesfield Football Club that need is being supplied.' Since then the scheme has been transferred to Manchester United, where it continues to be successful. However, the 'It's a Goal' men's mental health project run by Pete Sayers remains an integral part of the community facilities at the Moss Rose.

Another area where there was outreach into the community came through the establishment of an Informational Technology Centre in an area adjacent to the McIlroy Suite which was financed through grants over a three-year period. Staffed, in the main, by volunteers, the centre ran courses not only relating to IT but also to other subjects such as do-it-yourself and gardening. It was a Learn Direct Centre and a National Skills for Life Centre. In 2003 the centre won the award 'UK Online Centre for the North West' and was named as third 'Best in Britain' centre. When the centre closed, the area was refurbished and now forms the administration offices for the club.

Football Association Investigation and Save Our Silkmen

Unfortunately, the financing of the McAlpine Stand became the subject of an investigation by the Football Association who, following a hearing at FA Headquarters on 19 December 2005, levied fines and repayments totalling £257,000 on the club with an amount of £195,000 initially to be repaid by 31 January 2006 representing repayment of grant monies from the Football Foundation. This deadline was eventually renegotiated, but the immediacy was the urgent need to raise funds and of the financial viability of the football club.

A supporters' meeting was held on 21 December 2005 which galvanised the fans into action. Amar and Bashar Alkadhi, directors, set the ball rolling with a donation of £30,000 to the newly set up 'Save Our Silkmen' fund. A Supporters' Trust was formed, initially to raise funds towards payment of the fine and repayment to the Football Foundation, but they have since developed into the supporters' representative organisation of the club.

Other fundraising events were organised including:

- Bucket collections at Premiership grounds.
- A fans' walk from Buxton to the Moss Rose.
- A Fan's United Day on Sunday 29 January 2006 when Carlisle were the visitors. The crowd of 4,140 included 2,193 Carlisle fans and there were fans from many other clubs including Wrexham, whose club were having their own problems at the time. Many signed shirts which had been donated from other clubs, were paraded at half-time after which they were sold for the SOS Fund.
- A Wheelchair Push.
- Local-born footballer Peter Crouch donated a signed shirt for auction.
- Sponsored Cycle Ride.
- Web Pixsale.
- Many donations.
- Macclesfield Town Legends against A-Line All Stars Football match.

The All Stars match was played on 7 February 2006 and was witnessed by over 4,000 spectators in pouring rain. There were several Chelsea supporters, with their flags on display, attending to support Gianfranco Zola as they had been unable to attend his farewell match at Stamford Bridge. In addition, there were well-known footballers in the crowd including Robbie Savage.

Phil Power and Sammy McIlroy.

The Macclesfield team was: Price, Edey, Ingram, Howarth, Tinson, Lyons, McIlroy, Bradshaw, Askey, Power, Barker, and the substitutes used were: Sodje, Lee, Smart, Miles, Townson, Briscoe and Edwards.

The All Stars team was: Hitchcock, Anderson, Festa, Gillespie, Tarrico, Karembeu, Robson, Poyet, Le Saux, Hughes, Zola, and subs used were: Connolly, Speedie, Spencer, Brown, and two Macclesfield youngsters, McDonald and Morgan.

It was an entertaining match with Sammy McIlroy pitched against Gianfranco Zola from time to time and the likes of Graham Le Saux running down the wing joking with the spectators that he was knackered after three

Efe Sodje and Ryan Price.

Gianfranco Zola.

minutes! Zola did not disappoint, scoring two goals, but it was the Macclesfield side who won the day with goals from Ingram, Poyet (own-goal), Power and two from Smart.

Christian Karembeu, Bryan Robson and Mark Hughes.

Later in February it was announced that contributions totalling £128,500 had been raised as follows:

Donations	£48,000
Collections	£9,500
Ebay Sales	£2,000
Silkmen Supporters' Trust (Share Purchase)	£20,000
All Stars Match	£29,000
Fans United Day	£20,000

In March 2006 it was agreed with the Football Association that the fine would be paid by monthly instalments to be completed by December 2008 and that the repayment to the Football Foundation would be settled with an immediate payment of £130,000 and the balance paid by October 2006.

As a consequence, the FA held Eddie Furlong, who was by this time no longer chairman of the club, responsible for the misdemeanours and subsequently banned him from holding office in any football club.

Thus ended one of the most difficult times in the history of Macclesfield Town Football Club, with a clear lesson that, like any other business, good financial planning and monitoring are essential.

Other Enhancements

The maintenance and continual improvement of any stadium is an ongoing exercise, and the football club is no exception. During the Football League years there have been many other improvements, including four new 80ft tall floodlights, a new control box and groundsman's garage, tea bars, new turnstiles and toilet facilities, replacement of seats in the Silk FM Stand and Star Lane End. In addition, in the 2003–04 season there were significant alterations under the Silk FM Stand when the two bars were closed and improved facilities were provided for the directors, manager, players, physiotherapist, kit-man and matchday officials.

With existing training facilities somewhat fragmented, it was announced in June 2009 that the club would be establishing their training base at Egerton Youth Club in Knutsford prior to the start of the 2009–10 season. This move will enable them to take advantage of a new full-size floodlit pitch, new changing rooms as well as a range of grass pitches, a sports hall, a well equipped gymnasium and a self-contained treatment area.

APPENDIX TWO

MACCLESFIELD TOWN FOOTBALL CLUB – PLAYERS

(This section provides a brief summary solely *relating to each player's time at Macclesfield who made at least one senior appearance from August 1997 to May 2009)*

George Abbey (1999–2000 to 2003–04)
The Nigerian-born attacking right-back was given his first taste of English football when he signed for Macclesfield Town in August 1999, using his natural style and flair to good effect. George made 10 international appearances for Nigeria while at Macclesfield, winning a third-place medal in the 2004 Cup of African Nations. He moved to Port Vale in the summer of 2004.

Danny Adams (2000–01 to 2003–04)
Played at left-back after moving from non-League Altrincham and soon became a fans favourite for his consistent performances, forceful play and no nonsense tackling, winning the Player of the Year award in 2002. Danny moved to Stockport County in March 2004.

Paul Aldridge (2002–03)
Son of former Liverpool star John, Paul only made one senior appearance due to injury.

James Ashmore (2007–08)
Signed on loan from Sheffield United, James made eight appearances as a central midfielder in the second half of the 2007–08 season.

Neil Ashton (2007–08)
Signed on loan from Shrewsbury in January 2008, Neil proved to be an excellent replacement for Kevin McIntyre at left-back, retaining the position to the end of the season.

John Askey (1984–85 to 2002–03)
John is a fans' favourite and affectionately known as 'Gentleman John'. He made over 650 appearances and scored more than 150 goals as a player on the right wing or as a striker. John won every non-League honour other than a winners' medal for the FA Trophy, played in the Silkmen's first League match at the age of 32 and scored on both his debut and his final matches for the club. He is currently overseeing the youth development at the club but has also held other positions including first-team coach, assistant manager and manager of the senior side, the reserves and the youth team.

Alan Bailey (1998–99)
Alan spent two months on loan from Manchester City, scoring his first League goal when Macclesfield won against Colchester.

Mark Bailey (2004-05 to 2005-06)

A useful, speedy right-back and an excellent crosser of the ball, Mark moved from Lincoln City but his time at the Moss Rose was blighted by injury and he left the club in April 2006.

Rikki Baines (2008-09)

A young defender signed on non-contract forms in the January 2009 transfer window as cover for the defence, Rikki only made two senior appearances.

Mike Bamber (1999-2000 to 2000-01)

A product of the Macclesfield youth set-up, his League debut lasted just 21 seconds but there were few opportunities for him in the right-back position, resulting in Mike only making a handful of appearances.

Dominic Barclay (1998-99)

Signed from Bristol City, striker Dominic only made a limited number of senior appearances, spending much of his time in the reserves where he was top-scorer. His one senior goal helped Macclesfield gain their first win in the former League Division Two at Oldham Athletic. After leaving the Silkmen he played for non-League clubs.

Richie Barker (1999-2000 to 2000-01)

Moving from Brighton & Hove Albion, Richie scored on his debut and soon became a firm favourite of the supporters, completing his initial season as the club's top-scorer. A strong and hardworking forward, Richie capped a fine first season when he was included in the PFA award-winning Third Division team. Richie moved to Rotherham in January 2001 for a total fee of £100,000. Richie has recently retired as a professional footballer.

Tony Barras (2004-05 to 2005-06)

A very experienced central-defender with good aerial ability, Tony moved from Notts County but throughout his time at the Moss Rose he was troubled by a number of injuries, including a recurring hip problem which led to his retirement from professional football in January 2006 after 17 years in the game.

Asmir Begovic (2006-07)

A young talented 'keeper who was signed on loan from Portsmouth, Asmir only managed four appearances before a knee injury forced him to return to his home club.

Lee Bell (2008-09 to date)

Signed from Mansfield Town in the summer of 2008, Lee had a slow start to his first season, but following the departure of fellow central-midfielder Terry Dunfield his performance improved and he was rewarded with a 12-month extension to his contract.

Ronayne Benjamin (2006-07)

A pacy left-winger who was signed as cover towards the end of the 2006-07 season, Ronayne only made three appearances from the substitutes' bench.

David Beresford (2003-04 and 2005-06)

A pacy, left-sided midfielder who always strove hard and had the ability to make telling crosses, David spent two spells at Macclesfield, the first on loan from Plymouth Argyle and the second when he signed from Tranmere Rovers. On leaving Macclesfield David retired from professional football.

Jon Beswetherick (2003-04)

Jon spent one month on loan from Sheffield Wednesday as cover for suspended players, featuring on the left flank.

Chris Bettney (2000-01)

Having enjoyed League experience with four different clubs, Chris signed non-contract forms but only made two appearances from the substitutes' bench as a winger.

Nick Blackman (2006-07 to 2008-09)

A tall young striker who came through the ranks at the club, with all but one of his appearances for the senior side coming from the substitutes' bench, Nick played an important part in the youth team's 2007–08 season and moved to Blackburn Rovers in January 2009.

Marc Boyd (2004-05)

Marc only made a handful of appearances when on loan from Gretna in the centre of midfield, where his steady approach and his good distribution served the team well.

Steven Brackenridge (2002-03 to 2003-04)

Progressing through the Centre of Excellence and the youth ranks, Steven was then a regular member of the reserve side playing in a wide midfield position; however, his senior appearances were limited but he made the most of them, netting twice, including the winner at Darlington in December 2003.

Jonny Brain (2006-07 to date)

Jonny joined the Silkmen from Port Vale and initially shared goalkeeping duties with Tommy Lee but, just as he was beginning to make an impression, he suffered a broken leg in November 2006 which sidelined for the remainder of the season. Having fully recovered, Jonny became the first-choice 'keeper and demonstrated his shot-stopping abilities on many occasions.

Ian Brightwell (2004-05 to 2007-08)

An experienced defender, Ian made his name at Manchester City and moved to the Moss Rose in the summer of 2004 where he was, at various times, reserve-team manager, first-team coach and manager. His player registration was retained, although he was usually only called upon when other defenders were unavailable.

Michael Briscoe (2004-05 to 2005-06)

Michael joined the Silkmen from Coventry City and made an immediate impact as an exciting, committed and enthusiastic player whether in the centre or right side of the defence. He was unlucky to lose out to more experienced players in both seasons and has since played for non-League clubs.

Shaun Brisley (2007-08 to date)

A local lad, Shaun has been involved with the club since he was 13 years of age. Even though he was still only a member of the youth side, Keith Alexander called him into the senior side when he made an excellent impression as a tall, strong central-defender. He was awarded his first professional contract in the summer of 2008 and featured regularly throughout the 2008–09 season.

Greg Brown (1997-98 to 1999-2000)
Another local lad, Greg joined the Silkmen from Chester City. A solid left-back, Greg was used as cover for absent players in the senior side; however, he was a stalwart defender in the reserve team. He moved to Morecambe in January 2000 and has since retired from professional football.

Nathaniel Brown (2008-09)
With no opportunities for him at Wrexham, Nat spent the majority of the 2008-09 season on loan. He brought height and strength to the midfield, making an immediate impact when he scored three goals in his first four appearances. Some of his best performances came towards the end of the season when he moved back to his more accustomed role of central-defender.

Steve Brown (1998-99)
An experienced striker, Steve signed from Lincoln City but he failed to make an impression in the senior side and, after only four games, found himself in the reserve side where he was a prolific scorer.

Martin Bullock (2005-06 to 2006-07)
An enthusiastic player who used his incisive runs to good effect, Martin moved from Blackpool and proved his versatility playing on both wings and as an occasional striker. During his time at the Moss Rose he made his 500th career appearance and in the summer of 2007 opted to move to Wycombe Wanderers.

Matthew Bullock (2001-02)
The right-winger spent a month on loan from Stoke City but only made three appearances before returning to the Britannia Stadium.

Tony Bullock (2000-01)
Having lost his place as 'keeper at Barnsley, Tony moved to the Moss Rose in the summer of 2000 where he proved to be an excellent shot-stopper with a huge kick and a long throw, but after suspension he lost his place to Lee Martin and moved to Lincoln City in March 2001.

Chris Byrne (1996-97, 1999-2000, 2001-02, 2002-03)
A valuable member of the 1997 Conference Championship side, Chris then moved to Sunderland and subsequently to Stockport County. He spent a month on loan at the Moss Rose before moving back permanently in the summer of 2001. Troubled by injury Chris, nevertheless, continued to display his ability as an attacking midfielder, scoring spectacular goals, many of which were winning strikes. While recovering from a medial knee ligament injury, Chris was shot in the leg in November 2002, an injury which unfortunately prematurely ended his professional football career.

Shaun Came (2000-01 to 2002-03)
Shaun showed good promise in the youth and reserve teams as a central-defender but could not break into the senior side on a regular basis only making 10 appearances. He moved to Northwich Victoria in October 2002.

Michael Carr (2002-03 to 2003-04)
Michael appeared regularly in both the youth and reserves sides as a strong central-defender and captained both teams. He performed equally well when selected for the senior side, especially when he deputised for George Abbey playing out of position at right-back. Michael was released in the summer of 2004.

Matthew Carragher (2003–04 to 2004–05)

A very experienced League player, Matthew used his versatility to good effect as a right-back, wide-right midfielder and, best of all, as sweeper. His time at the Moss Rose was blighted by injury and on leaving he retired from professional football.

Martin Carruthers (2003–04)

A vastly experienced striker, Martin partnered Matthew Tipton during his sole season with the club netting a total of 10 goals. On leaving Macclesfield Martin joined Boston United.

Leroy Chambers (1997–98)

Having been Boston's top-scorer in the 1996–97 season, Leroy joined the Silkmen halfway through the club's first season in the Football League. He made an immediate impact in his first few matches but then found it difficult to score goals and was replaced by other strikers.

Stephen Clark (2003–04)

Stephen spent a month on loan from Southend United, making four appearances as a striker.

Simon Collins (1999–2000 to 2000–01)

A powerful defender, who was not afraid to make telling tackles, Simon was good in the air and had the ability to go forward to score the occasional goal. In his second season he was troubled by injury which restricted the number of his appearances.

Darren Connell (2000–01)

Darren appeared regularly as a striker for the youth and reserve sides, making just one late substitute appearance for the senior side. He was released in the summer of 2001.

Mark Cooper (1997–98)

A vastly experienced central midfielder, Mark spent two months on loan from Hartlepool immediately fitting into the midfield where he created many opportunities for the strikers with long, pin-point crosses.

Ryan Cresswell (2007–08)

Signed on loan in January 2008 from Sheffield United, Ryan provided much needed height and stability in the centre of defence. He signed for Bury in the summer of 2008.

Colin Daniel (2008–09)

Colin was signed from Crewe Alexandra on a short-term loan at the end of March 2009, filling the wide left midfield role for the remainder of the season.

Peter Davenport (1996–97 to 1999–2000)

An experienced striker at the highest level of English Football, Peter joined the club in January 1997 and scored his 100th career League goal in the final match of the 1997–98 season. He was appointed first-team coach the following season, promoted to assistant manager in March 1999 and then manager in January 2000, relinquishing the position the following December.

Simon Davies (1998–99 to 1999–2000)

A former Manchester United player, Simon signed from Luton Town in December 1998 and played on the left wing, where he displayed skill and strength, but he never really fulfilled his potential. Simon left the club in the summer of 2000.

Tim Deasy (2005–06)

Tim progressed through the ranks at the club as a goalkeeper but only made three senior appearances. The first came against Chester City when he replaced the injured Alan Fettis and kept a clean sheet, and the second in the 5––4 victory at Wycombe Wanderers. Having been released by the club Tim joined Stockport County.

Ahmed Deen (2008–09)

A summer signing from Bishop's Stortford, Ahmed, a left-back, was in and out of the side throughout his one season at the Moss Rose. Ahmed represented Sierra Leone in the World Cup Qualifying matches in 2008.

Kristian Dennis (2007–08 to date)

Kristian featured regularly on the score sheet for the club's youth side and while still a trainee made his senior debut on New Year's Day 2008. He signed his first professional contract in the following summer. With opportunities limited for regular first-team football, he only made a few appearances in the 2008-09 season but scored his first senior goal in April 2009 in the home match against Barnet which secured victory for the Silkmen.

Luke Dimech (2007–08)

A no-nonsense Maltese central-defender, Luke signed for the club in the summer of 2007 for his second taste of English football and was a regular in the side until taller players were signed in January 2008. Nevertheless, he continued to represent Malta at international level including their record 7–1 win against Liechtenstein. Luke was released in the summer of 2008.

Nathan D'Laryea (2006–07)

A member of the Manchester City Reserve side which he had captained, Nathan spent a month on loan making just one appearance as a central-defender which was his Football League debut.

Phil Doughty (2007–08)

Phil spent six weeks on loan from Blackpool playing at centre-back but was recalled in January 2008 shortly after which he signed for Accrington Stanley.

Robbie Doyle (2006–07)

A former Blackburn Rovers trainee, Robbie signed in January 2007 but only made two substitute appearances, the first of which was his Football League debut. Robbie was released in the summer of 2007.

Terry Dunfield (2007–08 to 2008–09)

Having recovered from a serious injury, Terry successfully completed a trial with the club in the 2007 close season and was immediately given a two-year contract, quickly becoming a fans' favourite. A central midfield dynamo, Terry was a regular choice in the starting line up and was voted Player of the Year in his first season with the club. Although an improved contract had been tabled, Terry moved to Shrewsbury Town in January 2009.

Darren Dunning (2002–03)

A diminutive midfielder who spent three months on loan from Blackburn Rovers, Darren made an impression with his telling short-passing game and was combative when required.

Kieron Durkan (1997–98 to 2000–01)

Kieron usually played on the right flank, although there were times when he formed the strike force with Richie Barker. He was a good tackler, often beating defenders to provide pin-point crosses and was an expert set-piece player. He has now retired from professional football.

David Eaton (2002–03)

A tall forward with good pace, David scored with his first touch on his Football League debut and went on to score four further goals. With opportunities limited he was released in the summer of 2003.

Cec Edey (1995–96 to 1997–98)

A member of the 1997 Conference Championship-winning side, Cec remained on a part-time contract following promotion to the Football League. He made his League debut at the age of 32, when he still proved to be a versatile cover player, stepping into any position in the back four when other players were injured or suspended. Cec has now retired from professional football.

Richard Edghill (2007–08)

An extremely experienced defender, Richard spent just one season at the Moss Rose playing initially as a central defender and then in his usual position of right-back, but his season was cut short when he sustained a broken rib. Having recovered Richard usually featured as an unused substitute and was released in the summer of 2008.

Tom Elliott (2008–09)

The young Leeds United striker spent a month on loan at the Moss Rose but found it difficult to find his form at League Two level.

Gareth Evans (2007–08 to date)

A product of the Crewe Alexandra Academy, Gareth joined the Silkmen in the summer of 2007. Initially most of his appearances came from the substitutes' bench but, ever improving, he soon found himself in the starting line up on a regular basis as part of the strike force. He completed the 2008–09 season as top-scorer with 13 goals, including five penalties.

Richard Eyre (2001–02)

Richard moved from Port Vale signing a short-term contract. An enthusiastic left-sided midfielder, he found it difficult to maintain a consistent level of performance and was released in January 2002.

Jassim Fayadh (2004–05)

A regular in the Iraq international side, Jassim initially played for the reserve side and made his Football League debut in October 2004, becoming the first-ever Iraqi national to play at this level in England. Because of troubles in his native Iraq, he returned to Baghdad in November 2004 to be with his family.

Alan Fettis (2004–05 to 2005–06)

A vastly experienced 'keeper with 25 Northern Ireland international caps, Alan signed for the Silkmen in the summer of 2004. He rarely gave less than an assured performance, commanding his area well, distributing the ball thoughtfully and was good in the air. He started both seasons as first choice 'keeper but was sidelined by injury on more than one occasion resulting in Steve Wilson and then Tommy Lee taking his place.

David Flitcroft (2003–04)

On signing for the Silkmen David was immediately appointed captain, and while he was a committed central midfielder he never really settled at the club and left in January 2004.

Matthew Flynn (2007–08 to date)

Another graduate of the Macclesfield youth set-up, Matthew made his senior debut as a 90th-minute substitute in the first-round victory in the Johnstone's Paint Trophy at Wrexham in September 2007. A tall right-sided defender, Matthew appeared fairly regularly during the 2008–09 season.

Kyle Fraser-Allen (2008–09)

A young speedy attacking midfielder, Kyle spent a month on loan from Tottenham Hotspur making just two cameo appearances from the substitutes' bench, the first of which was his Football League debut in the home match against Port Vale.

Mark Gardiner (1995–96 to 1997–98)

Mark enjoyed success with the Silkmen, earning Semi-pro honours, was named in the Conference Team of the Year, gained a FA Trophy winners' medal and was a member of the 1997 Conference Championship-winning squad. A useful midfielder by trade, Mark also played at left-back during the club's first season in the Football League, but he sustained a number of niggling injuries which resulted in his decision to return to non-League football in December 1997.

Lee Glover (2000–01 to 2002–03)

Lee was Peter Davenport's first signing and completed his first two seasons as the Silkmen's top-scorer. As the designated penalty taker, it was appropriate that he scored the decider in the record-breaking penalty shoot-out in the FA Cup first-round replay at Forest Green Rovers in 2001. In his third year, Lee was unable to command a regular place and moved to Mansfield Town in September 2002.

Francis Green (2007–08 and 2008–09)

Franny was one of a number of players released by Boston in the summer of 2007 when he signed a two-year contract with the Silkmen, relishing the opportunity to play as an out-and-out striker. Always playing with pace and enthusiasm, his first season was his most successful when he went straight into the starting line up and finished as top-scorer with 11 goals. Injury kept him out of contention for much of the second half of the 2008–09 season, at the end of which he was released.

Peter Griffiths (1998–99)

An unassuming but pacy winger, Peter was brought to the Moss Rose principally to play in the newly-formed reserve team and only made a handful of appearances for the senior side. On leaving Macclesfield he signed for non-League Winsford United.

Martin Gritton (2007–08 to 2008–09)

Martin signed a two-year deal in the summer of 2007 on his transfer from Lincoln City. He appeared regularly, scoring on his debut against MK Dons, but a succession of injuries in the second half of the 2007–08 season restricted his appearances, nevertheless he completed the season as second-top scorer. Very much a target man he was equally proficient when defending set pieces. Martin moved to Chesterfield in the January 2009 transfer window.

Matt Haddrell (2002–03 and 2003–04)

Matt never really lived up to his £35,000 transfer fee tag as he failed to establish himself in the senior side, most of his appearances coming as a central-defender when other players were either injured or suspended, although he always made good use of his aerial ability. Having come from non-League Vauxhall Motors Matt decided to move back to the non-League scene in February 2004.

Jordan Hadfield (2005–06 to 2008–09)

His fine performances in the youth side were recognised when he was awarded his first professional contract in the summer of 2006. Jordan then featured regularly in the senior side playing with passion and determination in the centre of the midfield. However, having spent the majority of the 2007–08 season on loan at MK Dons, he became a bit-part player on his return in the summer of 2008 and was released at the end of the 2008–09 season.

Lee Hardy (2002–03)

A left-sided midfielder, Lee was unable to force his way into the senior side on a regular basis although when used he provided some useful pace. He was released in the summer of 2003 and subsequently played for non-League sides.

Paul Harsley (2003–04 to 2005–06)

Paul signed from Northampton Town in February 2004 and throughout his time at the Moss Rose featured regularly in the starting line up and was ever-present in the 2004–05 season. He usually played on the right side of midfield but could play in any of the midfield roles and occasionally filled in at right wing-back. A pacy player who never gave less that 100 per cent, Paul was voted Player of the Year in 2005 and moved to Port Vale in the summer of 2006.

Neil Harvey (2008–09)

Signed in the summer of 2008 from Retford United where he had been a prolific scorer, Neil spent just one season at the Moss Rose, but he found it difficult to force his way into the senior side on a regular basis. He even spent time back at Retford on loan, where he scored 11 goals in 13 appearances.

Colin Heath (2006–07)

Signed in the summer of 2006, Colin usually played in a wide right of midfield position but showed his versatility when used as a striker scoring four goals. A hardworking player, he rarely played for the full 90 minutes and fell out of contention for the final two months of the season when injured. He was released in the summer of 2007.

Sean Hessey (2007-08 to date)

Sean spent the majority of the 2007-08 season on loan at Macclesfield from Chester City as a central-defender. A hard-tackling player, he forged an excellent partnership with Ryan Cresswell on his arrival to give the back-line a more solid presence and in the latter part of the season he was given the responsibility of captain. Sean signed a permanent contract in the summer of 2008 but was sidelined with a groin injury for much of the second half of the 2008–09 season.

Steve Hitchen (1997-98 to 2003-04)

Steve was Sammy McIlroy's first League signing. Playing at right-back or right wing-back, Steve was a strong defender, tackled well, distributed the ball intelligently and was an effective attacking player. During his time at the Moss Rose he had his injury problems but when fully fit he was a valued member of the squad and won the Player of the Year award for the 1998–99 season. Steve has now retired from professional football and lives in France.

Ashan Holgate (2006-07)

Ashan spent the second half of the 2006–07 season on loan from Swindon Town. He was used mainly in the centre of midfield when Alan Navarro was unavailable and only made a handful of appearances.

Colin Holt (1998-99)

A left-footed striker, Colin spent a month on loan from Preston North End with his only goal coming on his debut in the home win against Reading.

Neil Howarth (1993-94 to 1998-99)

A stalwart of Macclesfield's central defence in their Conference days, Neil enjoyed success winning many honours including those at England semi-pro level and was a member of both Conference Championship sides. He was team captain and voted Player of the Year for the 1994–95 season. Unfortunately his time in the Football League was not as fulfilling when he was asked to play in the unfamiliar role of left-back and having spent most of the 1998-99 season on the bench Neil moved to Cheltenham Town in February 1999.

Michael Husbands (2007-08)

Michael was Ian Brightwells's first signing but was troubled by injury and only made a handful of appearances, including the first round Johnstone's Paint Trophy tie at Wrexham where his penalty strike was the winning goal. Michael left the club at the end of January 2008.

Paul Ince (2006-07)

After an illustrious playing career at the highest level, Paul was appointed to his first managerial role at a time when the Silkmen were well adrift at the foot of the League table, but under his leadership Football League status was retained. Paul made one appearance for the Silkmen, coming on in the 85th minute in the last match of the season in a central midfield role which turned out to be his last appearance as a player.

Rae Ingram (1997-98 to 2000-01)

Rae spent the end of the 1997–98 season on loan at the Moss Rose, signing permanently the following summer. Rae was a skilful player, filling both right-back and centre-back roles. During the 1998–99 season he suffered from a debilitating illness which left him unable to play, but after rest and a careful diet he returned the following season when he gave some of his best performances. Rae moved to Port Vale in the summer of 2001.

Richard Irving (1997-98)

Richard was a speedy striker who made intelligent runs and got into some good positions, but goals failed to materialise, resulting in him leaving the club in February 1998.

James Jennings (2006-07 to 2008-09)

James signed his first professional contract in the summer of 2006 and was a capable left-sided player, but he faced competition from other players restricting the number of his appearances. Nevertheless, he always proved himself to be a capable and useful member of the squad. He missed much of the second half of the 2008–09 season with a knee injury and was released at the end of the season.

Rob Jones (2003-04)

A tall powerful centre-back, Rob signed a three-month loan deal from Stockport County but after just one appearance he suffered a succession of training ground injuries and had to return to Edgeley Park.

Kevin Keen (2000-01 to 2001-02)

An experienced player, Kevin signed for the Silkmen in September 2000, forming an effective partnership with Chris Priest as a hard-working attacking midfielder. During the 2001–02 season he made his 600th career appearance and was acting manager for a month. Kevin returned to his first club, West Ham United, where he is now the first-team coach.

Richard Knight (1999-2000)

With no 'keepers available, Richard was signed on loan from Derby County the day before the match at Northampton and was only introduced to the team at the pre-match meal. He made three appearances after which Lee Martin returned from injury.

Rickie Lambert (2000-01 to 2001-02)

Rickie joined the Silkmen in December 2000, playing for the youth and reserve sides where he soon made his mark as a central midfielder. He was promoted to the senior side in the 2001–02 season where he was equally effective as a central midfielder or striker. He scored two spectacular free-kicks in his first-ever FA Cup match against Forest Green Rovers and the following week scored a hat-trick against Luton Town. Rickie moved to Stockport County in April 2002 for a club record fee of £300,000.

Richard Landon (1996-97 to 1998-99)

Richard was a member of the 1997 Conference Championship side while on loan from Stockport County and signed permanently in the summer of 1997. He scored Macclesfield's first away Football League goal and went on to complete the season as joint second-top scorer. In his third season he found himself out on loan for much of the time and was released in the summer of 1999.

Tommy Lee (2005–06 to 2007–08)
A successful loan spell from Manchester United saw Tommy signing permanently in the summer of 2006. He shared goalkeeping duties with Jonny Brain until Jonny broke a leg when he took over as first-choice 'keeper, a position which he retained until he, in turn, was injured in November 2007 when Jonny Brain returned. Tommy spent the final months of the 2007–08 campaign on loan at Rochdale and with Keith Alexander's policy of not including a reserve 'keeper on the bench for League matches, he was released in the summer of 2008.

Patrece Liburd (2008–09)
Patrece was team captain at Dorchester Town, but financial difficulties there saw him released in February 2009 after which he signed non-contract forms for Macclesfield. He has appeared at international level for St Kitts and Nevis and made just one appearance at centre-back for the Silkmen in the final match of the season.

Kyle Lightbourne (2001–02 to 2002–03)
Striker Kyle's first season with the Silkmen was blighted by injury but he enjoyed an injury-free second season, making a useful contribution showing more pace up front and good defensive work against set pieces, scoring 13 goals including his 100th career League goal. Kyle was released in the summer of 2003 when he returned to his native Bermuda to manage the national football team.

Colin Little (2002–03 to 2003–04)
Initially, Colin had two spells on loan from Crewe Alexandra, the first ending after just eight minutes with a reoccurrence of a hamstring injury and then signed permanently in the summer of 2003 when he was asked to play in a wide-left midfield position rather than his more accustomed striker's role. Nevertheless, he always made an impact with his sterling performances, especially when introduced as a substitute. He left the club in March 2004 when he signed for Halifax Town.

Mike Lomax (1998–99)
A key defender in the newly formed reserve side, Mike only made one appearance for the senior side.

Darren Lonergan (1998–99)
Darren was a big central-defender who took charge of the defence in the newly formed reserves but only made three substitute appearances for the senior side.

Steve Macauley (2001–02 to 2003–04)
Steve spent time on loan and then as a permanent member of the squad, but his time was littered with injuries. Nevertheless, when fit he used his experience as a central-defender to good effect including good aerial ability, telling tackles and effective marshalling of the players around him. Steve was released in April 2004.

Andy McAvoy (2001–02)
Andy spent most of his time in the reserve side but made a few appearances for the first team either as a striker or an attacking right-sided midfielder. He was released in the summer of 2002.

Clayton McDonald (2008-09)

A tall central-defender who spent a month on loan from Manchester City early in the season, Clayton made just two appearances, the first of which was his Football League debut against Accrington Stanley.

Martin McDonald (1993-94 to 1995-96 and 1997-98 to 1998-99)

A midfielder with a tremendous engine, Martin worked from box to box and helped the Silkmen win the 1995 Conference Championship and also won England semi-pro honours. He returned to Macclesfield on a £20,000 transfer from Doncaster Rovers in 1997 helping the Silkmen to an automatic promotion place but in the following season there were problems both on and off the pitch, resulting in a move to Altrincham in March 1999.

Marvin McDonald (2006-07)

A striker in both the youth and reserve sides, Marvin only made one substitute appearance for the senior side in the Football League Cup.

Kevin McIntyre (2004-05 to 2007-08)

In his time at the Moss Rose, Kevin was a key player as an accomplished left-sided player. As a dead ball expert he scored nine consecutive penalties and finished top-scorer in the 2006-07 season when he was voted Player of the Year. Kevin moved to Shrewsbury Town in January 2008.

Neil MacKenzie (2004-05 to 2005-06)

With previous League experience, Neil moved to the Moss Rose initially on loan and then permanently as an attacking midfielder. Unfortunately his appearances were restricted due to injury and he moved to Scunthorpe United in January 2006.

Matty McNeil (2005-06 to 2006-07)

Matty moved from Hyde United initially on loan and then permanently. In his striker's role he used his physical strength to good effect, could hold the ball up and was often involved in the build-up play and as provider for several goals; however, his 53 appearances only produced seven goals. In the 2007 close season he opted to move to Stockport County.

Jimmy McNulty (2006-07 to 2007-08)

Coming from Caernarfon Town, Jimmy featured regularly at left-back or left wing-back giving assured performances. Only a week after scoring the winning goal in the FA Cup replay at Walsall in November 2006 he broke a leg in training and was sidelined to April 2007. In the following season he was asked to play out of position at centre-back, but still performed admirably. On the expiration of his contract in December 2007 he opted to move to Stockport County.

Lee Martin (1999-2000 to 2002-03)

During his time at the Moss Rose, Lee often had to share goalkeeping duties with his fellow 'keepers but always quickly re-established himself when in the starting line up and was cool and calm even when under the most intense pressure. Lee also played an important role in helping the reserve side win the Avon Insurance League Championship in the 2001–02 season. Lee moved to Huddersfield Town in the summer of 2003 where he was, at that time, the club's physiotherapist.

Andy Mason (1997–98)

Andy joined the Silkmen in the summer of 1997 but goals did not materialise and he lost his place in October 1997, after which he found himself on loan at various clubs moving on permanently in the summer of 1998.

Pedro Matias (1998–99)

The former Spanish Under-21 striker moved to Macclesfield in December 1998 and was used as a speedy midfielder who easily turned the opposition and was provider for several goals. Due to budget constraints he left the club in the summer of 1999 to join Tranmere Rovers.

John Miles (2002–03 to 2006–07)

An end-of-season loan spell from Crewe Alexandra saw John score vital goals to assist the Silkmen retain their Football League status and then signed permanently in the summer of 2003, playing as a striker and later as a wide midfield player. There were many times when he was a bit-part player but he often came on as a substitute to positively change the direction of the game and maintained a strike rate of one goal every six matches. John moved to Accrington Stanley in the summer of 2007.

Christian Millar (2007–08 and 2008–09)

Christian, a young midfielder, was a member of the youth team when he made his senior debut at Morecambe in January 2008 and then signed his first professional contract in the summer of 2008. Having only made four substitute appearances he was released at the end of the 2008–09 season.

Neil Mitchell (1996–97 to 1997–98)

Neil played a useful part in the 1997 Conference Championship side but the midfielder could not break into the League side on a regular basis and moved to Morecambe in January 1998.

Neil Moore (1999–2000)

An experienced player, Neil moved to the Moss Rose in the summer of 1999, initially playing for the reserves and moving to the senior side in December 1999 having signed non-contract forms. A tall centre-back, he was good in the air and gave some solid performances but elected to accept a full-time contract with Telford United in March 2000.

Paul Morgan (2008–09)

Paul spent the whole of the 2008–09 season on loan from Bury where he played an important role at centre-back, often partnering less experienced colleagues. Paul took on the responsibility of team captain in the absence of Sean Hessey and was voted Player of the Year in recognition of his consistent performances.

Dave Morley (2005–06 to 2007–08)

A £15,000 move from Doncaster Rovers in January 2005 saw Dave link up with fellow centre-back Danny Swailes and the start of a run of eight consecutive matches without defeat. While at Macclesfield Dave was appointed team captain, gave some powerful performances, acted as emergency striker on occasions and played as the replacement 'keeper in the third round of the FA Cup at Chelsea. Having recovered from a close season ankle operation and returned to the side, Dave then decided to move to Hyde United in October 2007.

Karl Munroe (1999–2000 to 2003–04)

Karl moved from Swansea in October 1999, and having played for the reserves stepped up to the senior side in the 2000–01 season where he played in the centre of midfield and later as a central-defender in partnership with Michael Welch. Karl moved to Northwich Victoria in the summer of 2004.

Vinny Mukendi (2008–09)

Vinny is a first year trainee who appears regularly on the score sheet for the youth team. His fine performances were recognised when he made his Football League debut from the substitutes' bench in the final match of the season at Grimsby.

John Murphy (2006–07)

John was Paul Ince's first signing in October 2006. A regular in the starting line up, John formed a good partnership with Matty McNeil finishing the 2006-07 season as second-top scorer with nine goals, the best remembered will always be his strike at Chelsea in the third round of the FA Cup. John moved to Chester City in the summer of 2007.

Adam Murray (2006–07 to 2007–08)

Adam signed from Torquay United for a fee of £17,500 in January 2007 featuring in centre of midfield, latterly partnering Terry Dunfield. Adam joined Blue Sqaure Premier side Oxford United in January 2008.

Boaz Myhill (2003–04)

On loan from Aston Villa, Boaz was the first choice 'keeper at the start of the 2003–04 season when he quickly established himself in the side and produced a number of breathtaking saves, but injury forced an early return to Villa Park.

Martin Nash (2002–03)

The Canadian international was signed by David Moss from USA A-League side Rochester Rhinos in January 2003. Martin only made a handful of appearances as an attacking midfielder before being injured and returned to Canada in the summer of 2003.

Alan Navarro (2004–05 to 2006–07)

A two-month loan spell from Tranmere Rovers in December 2004 saw Alan make an excellent impression as a reliable, hard-working, defensive central midfielder. He returned on a permanent basis in October 2005 to feature regularly in the centre of midfield. Alan was given the opportunity to extend his contract in the summer of 2007 but decided to move to MK Dons.

James Olsen (2003–04)

Another player from Tranmere Rovers, James only made two substitute appearances for the senior side and a handful of appearances for the reserves as a pacy wide-left midfielder.

Paul O'Neill (1999–2000 to 2002–03)

Paul progressed through the ranks at the club making his senior debut at the age of 17 and signed his first professional contract in the summer of 2000. He was used as cover for injured or suspended players in the senior side in his accustomed centre-back role. However, much of his time was spent in the reserves where he worked resolutely and shared the captaincy of the 2001–02 Avon Insurance League Division Two Championship side. Paul was released in the summer of 2003.

Fola Onibuje (2007-08)

The 6ft 6in striker was Keith Alexander's first signing, but Fola only made one substitute appearance leaving the club in April 2008 having picked up an injury in training.

Jon Parkin (2003-04 to 2005-06)

A robust target striker, Jon moved from York City and completed the 2004–05 season as top-scorer with 26 goals in all competitions, a club league record which still stands. Jon was a favourite of the fans and was affectionately named 'the Beast', a nickname which he still retains. After recovering from injury in the 2005–06 season he attracted interest from a number of clubs, eventually moving to Hull City for an undisclosed fee. Jon now plays at Championship level.

Steve Payne (1994-95 to 1998-99 and 2003-04 to 2004-05)

Steve enjoyed success in Macclesfield's Conference days including England semi-professional honours. In the first two years in the Football League Steve was the backbone of the defence when he was captain for much of the time. In the summer of 1999 he moved to Chesterfield returning to the Moss Rose for the final few weeks of the 2003–04 season but sustained a knee injury in the 2004 close season which prevented him from playing in the 2004–05 season, resulting in his release in April 2005.

Nathan Peel (1996-97 to 1997-98)

Nathan made some appearances in the 1997 Conference Championship side and just a few in the Football League, but the big striker lost his place on the arrival of new faces and left the club in December 1998.

Tony Philliskirk (1997-98)

A vastly experienced striker, Tony spent the final few weeks of the 1997–98 season at the Moss Rose, mainly in a substitute's role

Graham Potter (2003-04 to 2004-05)

Coming from Boston United, Graham was a regular in the starting line up as an attacking left-back. Graham's performances were soon appreciated by the supporters who believed that he was one of the best left-sided defenders seen at the Moss Rose in recent times. His ability to press forward led to him scoring eight valuable goals but despite his consistent performances Graham was released in the summer of 2005 when he retired from professional football.

Phil Power (1993-94 to 1997-98)

Phil, affectionately known as the 'Maltese Falcon', is another player who enjoyed success in Macclesfield's Conference days earning many honours and was one of the team's leading scorers often striking home from opportunist positions. In the club's first year in the Football League Phil had to compete with other players and was unable to command a regular place in the starting line up and was released in the summer of 1998, after which he played for Altrincham.

Ryan Price (1995-96 to 1999-2000)

Ryan moved from Birmingham City for a fee of £15,000 in November 1995 to become the first choice 'keeper and was an important member of the 1997 Conference Championship side. He was a fearless 'keeper who, for a period of time, played with £20,000 worth of titanium plates and screws in his face following a collision with a fellow player. In the 1997–98 season he kept 19 clean sheets and was 'keeper in the Silkmen's sole season in the former Second Division. Ryan made his 100th League appearance in his last match with the Silkmen at the end of November 1999 before moving to Telford United.

Chris Priest (1999-2000 to 2003-04)

Moving from Chester City in the summer of 1999, Chris was a regular in the starting line up as an integral part of the midfield always using his experience to the full and worked tirelessly from box to box. Chris scored the very last goal in the 20th Century by any Football League player in the match against Carlisle United at the Moss Rose. Chris has now retired from professional football.

Isaiah Rankin (2006-07)

An experienced striker, Isaiah spent the final weeks of the 2006–07 season on loan from Grimsby Town only making a handful of appearances.

Carl Regan (2006-07 to 2007-08)

Carl joined the club from Chester City in the summer of 2006 and featured regularly in the starting line up as an attacking right-back or right wing-back. He moved to MK Dons in January 2008.

Izak Reid (2006-07 to date)

Izak progressed through the Macclesfield ranks and signed his first professional contract with the club in the summer of 2006. He is a versatile right-sided player equally effective in defence and midfield, always using his pace and strength to good effect.

Levi Reid (2007-08)

Coming to the club from non-League Stafford Rangers, Levi went straight into the starting line up and remained there until the appointment of manager Keith Alexander. A committed right-sided midfielder, there were several times when he and his brother covered the right flank together but he was released in the summer of 2008.

Marcus Richardson (2005-06)

An experienced striker who joined the club from Chester City for the final few weeks of the 2005–06 season when he scored three goals in the last two matches, including a late strike on the final day at Bristol Rovers which ensured retention of Football League status for the Silkmen. Marcus was released in the summer of 2006.

Dave Ridler (2001-02 to 2002-03)

Coming from Wrexham, Dave, a no-nonsense central-defender, was usually the first choice to partner Darren Tinson but lost his place to Steve Macauley in his second season and was released from his contract in March 2003.

Gregor Rioch (1999–2000 to 2000–01)
Son of Bruce Rioch, Gregor joined the club from Hull City in the summer of 1999 and proved to be a totally committed and extremely enthusiastic left-sided player who gave his all in every match. In his second season, appearances were limited due to injury and he moved to Shrewsbury Town in March 2001.

Marvin Robinson (2006–07)
Striker Marvin joined the club in the summer of 2006 but only made five appearance without any return before moving to Oxford United in August 2006.

Neil Robinson (2002–03 to 2003–04)
A young striker, Neil joined the Silkmen in the summer of 2002 for a fee of £12,000 from Prescot Cables where he had been a prolific scorer. Neil found it difficult to break into the senior side but appeared regularly for the reserves where he was often on the score sheet. After two loan spells at non-League Southport he moved there in March 2004.

John Rooney (2007–08 to date)
John is a promising young striker who was given his first professional contract in the summer 2008 after only one year as a trainee. Towards the end of the 2008–09 season he became a regular in the starting line up, often playing just behind the front two, and scored his first senior goal at Dagenham & Redbridge in March 2009. John is the younger brother of England and Manchester United's Wayne Rooney.

Tommy Rooney (2004–05)
With other strikers in good form, Tommy only managed two substitute appearances for the senior side but completed the 2004–05 season as top-scorer for the reserve side. He is a cousin of Wayne Rooney.

Colin Rose (1997–08)
Moving from Witton Albion, Colin played in the midfield in the early games of the club's first season in the Football League when he showed a good turn of pace, provided many pin-point crosses and proved to be a tough tackler. He lost his place on the return of Martin McDonald.

Neil Ross (2002–03 to 2004–05)
Signed in January 2003 for a fee of £30,000 with a view to supplementing the strike force, Neil found himself well down the pecking order and had to be content with his role in the reserve side, where he completed the 2003–04 season as the joint top-scorer. Neil moved to Northwich Victoria in November 2004

David Rouse (2006–07)
At a time when he was the club's goalkeeping coach, David made his Football League debut at the age of 30, in his one and only appearance, at Barnet in January 2007 when Tommy Lee was suspended and Jonny Brian was still recovering from a broken leg.

Alan Russell (2005–06)
The Scottish striker signed in the summer 2005 and featured in the opening games of the season, but having only managed two strikes lost his place on the arrival of Clyde Wijnhard in October 2005. Alan left the club for Mansfield Town when his contract expired in December 2005.

Kevin Sandwith (2005–06)

Kevin moved from Lincoln City in the summer of 2005 but had a rather indifferent start; however, after being rested, returned in November 2005 a much more determined player and was virtually ever-present for the remainder of the season at left-back or left wing-back often taking Macclesfield's set-pieces. Having been transfer listed during the season, he moved to Chester City in the summer of 2006.

Rob Scott (2006–07)

Rob joined the club in August 2006 and was a regular in the starting line up in the centre of the defence for the first three months but then was only called upon to deputise for unavailable members of the squad. However, he always used his height, strength and long throw-ins to good effect. Rob was released in the summer of 2007.

Ben Sedgemore (1997–98 to 2000–01)

A popular right-sided central midfielder, Ben was signed from Mansfield Town for a fee of £25,000 in March 1998. He always played with enthusiasm, had a good turn of pace, was adept at finding space and even took over in goal when Tony Bullock was dismissed at Southend. Ben scored some important goals, including one in the Worthington Cup victory over Bolton Wanderers. He moved to Lincoln City in February 2001.

Mike Sheron (2004–05)

Veteran striker Mike joined the club on a free transfer from Blackpool just before the start of the 2004–05 season and featured in a three-man attack until the manager reverted to a two-man attack consisting of in-form Matthew Tipton and Jon Parkin. On New Year's Day 2005 Mike scored his 150th career goal, but when opportunities for a regular position in the starting line up were limited he moved to Shrewsbury Town in March 2005.

Chris Shuker (2000–01)

Chris spent the final nine matches of the 2000–01 season on loan from Manchester City to gain first-team experience. During his short time at the club he proved to be a tricky and pacy left-winger.

Barry Shuttleworth (2001–02)

Barry was very much a fringe player for the senior side as a left-sided defender, nevertheless he made a useful contribution to the reserve side in their Avon Division Two Championship season. On leaving Macclesfield Barry signed for Altrincham.

Emile Sinclair (2008–09 to date)

A young Nottingham Forest striker who spent a total of three months on loan when he made good use of his pace, but only scored one goal, on his home debut, in the victory over Brentford.

Andrew Smart (2005–06 to 2006–07)

Having progressed through the ranks at the club, Andrew was given his first professional contract in the summer of 2005. He only made a dozen appearances for the senior side at left-back or emergency striker and found himself out on loan and then released in the summer of 2007.

David Smith (2001–02 to 2003–04)

David first came to the Moss Rose on loan from Stockport County in February 2002 as cover for the injured Kevin Keen when he impressed in the midfield with his precise passing. He linked up with the Silkmen in January 2001 but over the following 18 months his appearances were severely restricted due to injury and he was released in the summer of 2004 when he retired from professional football.

Jeff Smith (2001–02)

Jeff spent two months on loan from Bolton Wanderers to give him a taste of first-team football when he made good use of his pace and scored two goals.

Peter Smith (1998–99)

Peter spent three months on loan from Crewe Alexandra from September 1998 in a bid to boast the team's woeful strike rate, contributing three goals in 13 appearances.

Efe Sodje (1997–98 to 1998–99)

A tall, bandana-wearing central-defender, Efe signed from Stevenage Borough in the summer of 1997 for a tribunal agreed fee of £30,000. A great turn of pace and tenacious tackling served the Silkmen well and his desire to get forward for set pieces gave him the opportunity to score goals, including the Silkmen's first Football League goal. Efe was always a firm favourite of the fans, especially the youngsters, and since leaving Macclesfield in 1999 for Luton Town he has represented Nigeria on a number of occasions.

Steve Soley (1998–99)

Steve, an attacking midfielder, spent the last two months of the 1998–99 season on loan from Portsmouth to make up a depleted squad.

Neil Sorvel (1992–93 to 1998–99)

Signing from Crewe Alexandra in August 1992, Neil played an integral part in the centre of midfield in the Silkmen's Conference days, winning many non-League honours including the 1997 Conference Championship. He played an equally important part in the Silkmen's first two years in the Football League belying his unassuming nature off the field with strong performances on it. He made over 380 appearances and scored 55 goals for the Silkmen, re-joining Crewe Alexandra in the summer of 1999.

Scott Spencer (2007–08)

Scott spent a month on loan from Everton in March 2008 to give manager Keith Alexander an additional striking option.

Greg Strong (2004–05)

A month-long loan from Boston United in March 2004 saw Greg feature on the left side of a three-man central defence at a time when regular defenders were unavailable due to injury.

Danny Swailes (2004–05 to 2006–07)

A club record fee of £40,000 was paid to Bury for the transfer of Danny in January 2005 which enabled him to link up with fellow central-defender Dave Morley and the start of a run of eight consecutive matches without defeat. Danny was a tall, powerful and reliable player who put his skills to good use in both defence and attack. He moved to MK Dons in August 2007.

Michael Symes (2005-06 and 2007-08)

The 6ft 3in tall striker spent the second half of the 2007–08 season on loan from Shrewsbury Town scoring just one goal. This was Michael's second spell at the Moss Rose, his first was cut short before he had time to make an appearance.

Andrew Teague (2004-05 to 2007-08)

Another player who progressed through the ranks at the Moss Rose, Andrew was awarded his first professional contract in the summer of 2005. A useful defender on the right of a three-man central defence or at right-back, he always looked comfortable on the ball. Unfortunately, just as he had established himself in the senior side, he suffered a broken leg in November 2006 leaving him sidelined for 11 months, after which he spent time on loan and was released in the summer of 2008.

Andrejus Tereskinas (2000-01)

There were problems obtaining international clearance for the extremely experienced Lithuanian international left-back and coupled with injuries, resulted in him only making one substitute appearance in February 2001, and then out of position. He was released in the summer of 2001.

Danny Thomas (2007-08 and 2008-09)

The lively left-winger, who wanted to resurrect his career following limited opportunities at Hereford United, became one of Paul Ince's last signings in the summer of 2007. Danny featured regularly always using his pace to good effect, nevertheless, he was released at the end of the 2008–09 season.

Darren Tinson (1995-96 to 2002-03)

Darren moved from Colwyn Bay for a fee of £10,000 in February 1996 to become an important part of the Conference Championship squad. He slotted into League football with ease, initially at right-back and later at centre-back where he was a commanding figure and there were many times when his long throw-ins were used to good effect. In his time at the Moss Rose he was team captain, Player of the Year for the 2000–01 season, was the first ex-Conference player to achieve 100 League appearances and holds the club record for the most number of appearances since elevation to the Football League. He was released in the summer of 2003 when he signed for Shrewsbury Town.

Matthew Tipton (2001-02 to 2004-05 and 2006-07)

Matthew moved to the Moss Rose in February 2002 and soon started to notch up various achievements. In the 2002-03 season he was joint top-scorer with 14 goals, the following season after a health scare, he was the side's top-scorer with 19 goals, voted Player of the Year and in the 2004–05 season, when he notched up another 14 goals including a hat-trick and was appointed captain. He moved to Mansfield Town in the summer of 2005. He spent a second spell at the Moss Rose on loan from Bury for the majority of the 2006–07 season when he was used in a support role. Matthew holds the record for the highest total number of goals scored by a player for Macclesfield since promotion to the Football League.

Jamie Tolley (2006–07 to 2008–09)

Having been released by Shrewsbury, Jamie signed for the Silkmen in August 2006 and featured fairly regularly as a strong, hardworking midfielder; however, an injured shoulder in his first season and a serious wrist injury in the 2007 close season kept him out of contention for many matches. Even in the 2008–09 season he found it difficult to force his way into the side on a regular basis and was subsequently released at the end of the season.

Graeme Tomlinson (1998–99 to 1999–2000)

Graeme came to the Moss Rose from Manchester United in the summer of 1998, finishing his first season as top-scorer with eight goals including an 11-minute hat-trick in the second round of the FA Cup against Cambridge United. The following season he often found himself on the substitutes' bench and moved to Exeter City in the summer of 2000.

Kevin Townson (2004–05 to 2005–06)

Kevin initially came to the club on loan from Rochdale in March 2005, signing a permanent contract in the summer. Kevin was used to provide cover for other strikers, resulting in the majority of his appearances coming from the substitutes' bench. Having been released in the summer of 2005 he moved to Northwich Victoria.

Richard Tracey (2000–01 to 2001–02)

Richard signed from Rotherham United in January 2001 and featured on the left-side of midfield, where he displayed a good work rate and scored on his debut with his first touch. Only used in the opening weeks of the following season, Richard left the club in March 2002 when he signed for Scarborough.

Gary Twynham (2000–01)

After a successful trial, Gary signed in the summer of 2000; however, he only managed a handful of appearances in midfield as injury and illness kept him out of contention resulting in his contract being cancelled in February 2001.

Richard Walker (2007–08 and 2008–09)

Having been released by Port Vale, Richard spent the final two months of the 2007-08 season at the Moss Rose where he used his height and experience as a central-defender to good effect and helped to strengthen the defence as a whole. In the 2008–09 season he was used sparingly but his aerial ability proved a useful asset but was released at the end of the season.

Paul Ware (1999–2000)

Signing from non-League Hednesford Town, Paul provided a different option in the centre of the park but struggled to gain a regular place despite scoring a spectacular goal at Hull City. After a loan spell at Nuneaton and wanting regular first-team football, Paul moved to Rochdale in June 2000.

Simon Weaver (2004-05)

Simon spent two months on loan from Lincoln City as cover for unavailable players, usually on the right side of a three-man defence.

Spencer Weir-Daly (2006-07)

A young striker, Spencer spent two months on loan from Nottingham Forest when he provided plenty of pace and was always willing to find space and contributed two goals.

Michael Welch (2001-02 to 2004-05)

Michael progressed through the ranks at the Moss Rose and signed his first professional contract in August 2001. A tall central-defender, he made good use of his physical presence, made timely tackles and was renowned for his long clearances and spectacular goals. Michael moved to Accrington Stanley in the summer of 2005.

Andy Welsh (2002-03)

Andy spent six weeks on loan from Stockport County when he impressed on the right-wing with his pace, which caused problems for opposing defences.

Danny Whitaker (2001-02 to 2005-06)

A local lad, Danny progressed through the ranks at the Moss Rose to became a regular in the first team as a versatile midfielder. He was capable of filling any of the midfield positions but was best suited to an attacking role. His achievements included, scoring on his senior debut, a 16-minute hat-trick in the Worthington Cup match against Barnsley in 2002, being joint top-scorer in the 2002-03 season and Player of the Year in the 2005–06 season. Danny moved to Port Vale in the summer of 2006.

Damien Whitehead (1999-2000 to 2001-02)

Damien joined the Silkmen in the summer of 1999 from Warrington Town, where he had been a prolific scorer. He was a favourite with many supporters providing pace and an eye for goal; however, his unpredictability let him down and he gradually fell out of favour and having spent much of his final season out on loan, moved to Leigh RMI in the summer of 2002.

Stuart Whittaker (1998-99 to 1999-2000)

Signed from Bolton Wanderers for the Silkmen's first season in the Football League, Stuart played an important part as a tricky out-and-out winger with the ability to play on either flank and was provider for many of the side's goals. A groin injury kept him out of contention in his second season and was released in February 2000.

Tommy Widdrington (2003-04 to 2004-05)

A vastly experienced midfielder, Tommy joined the Silkmen in August 2003 when he became a regular in the side as a defensive central midfielder. Tommy was made captain at the beginning of the 2004–05 season but later younger players were preferred resulting in his departure in January 2005.

Clyde Wijnhard (2005–06)

An experienced striker, Clyde moved to the Moss Rose in October 2005 when he was ever present until sidelined by injury in March 2006. Nevertheless, Clyde was the season's top scorer with 12 goals in 26 appearances initially playing alongside Jon Parkin, but on Jon's departure he often operated as a loan striker. Clyde was released in the summer of 2006 and has since retired from professional football.

Simon Wiles (2006–07 to 2007–08)

Simon spent several spells on loan from Blackpool providing much needed pace on the right wing and was a very capable crosser of the ball. Most of his appearances came from the substitutes' bench when he had insufficient time to make a real impact, and in 2008 he opted to remain at Blackpool even though he had been offered a contract at the Moss Rose.

Anthony Williams (1998–99 and 1999–2000)

Anthony spent two separate loan spells from Blackburn Rovers as cover for injured first-choice 'keepers when he proved to be a very capable and popular 'keeper.

Steve Wilson (2000–01 to 2004–05)

Having spent 10 years at Hull City, Steve spent the last few weeks of the 2000–01 season on loan at the Moss Rose signing permanently in the summer of 2001. Steve was a competent 'keeper but it was his shot-stopping ability in making spectacular saves and penalty-kick saves, especially in FA Cup ties, for which he will be remembered most. He was voted Player of the Year for the 2002–03 season. On the arrival of Alan Fettis, Steve lost his place and moved to Tranmere Rovers in the summer of 2005.

Steve Wood (1993–94 to 2000–01)

Sammy McIlroy brought Steve from Ashton as his first signing in the summer of 1993 to become an influential player in Macclesfield's Conference days when he won many non-League honours as an attacking midfielder who regularly appeared on the score sheet. He made his Football League debut at the age of 34 when he was no less influential and continued to score some important goals. During his time at the Moss Rose he was top-scorer on two occasions and was voted Player of the Year twice. In January 2000 he stepped up to become joint first-team coach under Peter Davenport and continued to feature in the starting line up until the midfield partnership of Chris Priest and Kevin Keen was established relegating Steve to the reserve side which he often captained. Always a firm favourite with the fans, Steve moved to Stalybridge Celtic in the summer of 2001.

Matt Woolley (2001–02 to 2002–03)

Matt only made a few appearances for the senior side but he was a valued member of the reserve side as a speedy attacking midfielder with the ability to score sensational goals. In the 2001–02 season shared the reserve-team captaincy. He left the club in March 2003.

Andy Wright (1998–99)

Andy featured regularly on the score sheet for the newly formed reserve side but only made one appearance for the senior side in the Auto Windscreens Shield. On leaving Macclesfield in the summer of 1999 Andy moved to Merthyr Tydfil.

Simon Yeo (2008–09)

The veteran striker signed from Chester City in the summer of 2008 as back up for the strike force. Following a dearth of goals from the team in August, Simon was promoted to the starting line up and scored six goals in the next nine matches and continued to feature regularly for the remainder of the season. In the summer of 2009 Simon decided to retire as a professional footballer.

APPENDIX THREE

PLAYING SQUAD SEASON BY SEASON

1997–98

	Apps	Goals
John Askey	42	6
Greg Brown	2	0
Leroy Chambers	22	4
Mark Cooper	8	2
Peter Davenport	4	1
Kieron Durkan	4	0
Cec Edey	14	0
Mark Gardiner	8	2
Steve Hitchen	2	0
Neil Howarth	45	3
Rae Ingram	5	0
Richard Irving	11	0
Richard Landon	23	7
Martin McDonald	23	1
Andy Mason	15	1
Neil Mitchell	10	0
Steve Payne	44	0
Nathan Peel	16	3
Tony Philliskirk	10	1
Phil Power	43	7
Ryan Price	51	0
Colin Rose	23	0
Ben Sedgemore	5	0
Efe Sodje	46	3
Neil Sorvel	50	3
Darren Tinson	48	0
Stuart Whittaker	34	6
Steve Wood	47	15

1998–99

	Apps	Goals
John Askey	46	7
Alan Bailey	10	1
Dominic Barclay	13	1
Greg Brown	5	0
Steve Brown	4	0
Peter Davenport	2	0
Simon Davies	13	2
Kieron Durkan	32	3
Peter Griffiths	7	1
Steve Hitchen	41	0
Michael Holt	4	1
Neil Howarth	24	0
Rae Ingram	35	0
Richard Landon	14	2
Michael Lomax	1	0
Darren Lonergan	3	0
Martin McDonald	27	2
Pedro Matias	23	2
Steve Payne	46	0
Ryan Price	51	0
Ben Sedgemore	42	3
Peter Smith	13	3
Efe Sodje	50	4
Steve Soley	10	0
Neil Sorvel	47	4
Darren Tinson	44	0
Graeme Tomlinson	35	8
Stuart Whittaker	36	1
Anthony Williams	4	0
Steve Wood	51	5
Andy Wright	1	0

1999–2000

	Apps	Goals
George Abbey	21	0
John Askey	45	15
Mike Bamber	1	0
Richie Barker	40	17
Greg Brown	6	0
Chris Byrne	5	0
Simon Collins	43	3
Simon Davies	41	2
Kieron Durkan	46	6
Steve Hitchen	5	0
Rae Ingram	40	0
Richard Knight	3	0
Lee Martin	24	0
Neil Moore	16	2
Karl Munroe	5	0
Paul O'Neill	1	0
Ryan Price	14	0
Chris Priest	40	5
Gregor Rioch	47	5
Ben Sedgemore	40	1
Darren Tinson	51	1
Graeme Tomlinson	22	2
Paul Ware	19	2
Damien Whitehead	24	6
Stuart Whittaker	13	0
Anthony Williams	11	0
Steve Wood	40	1

2000–01

	Apps	*Goals*
George Abbey	23	0
Danny Adams	41	0
John Askey	43	3
Mike Bamber	7	0
Richie Barker	28	9
Chris Bettney	2	0
Tony Bullock	29	0
Shaun Came	8	0
Simon Collins	19	0
Darren Connell	1	0
Kieron Durkan	35	4
Lee Glover	40	10
Steve Hitchen	42	0
Rae Ingram	36	1
Kevin Keen	35	2
Rickie Lambert	9	0
Lee Martin	22	0
Karl Munroe	29	2
Paul O'Neill	14	0
Chris Priest	16	4
Gregor Rioch	18	1
Ben Sedgemore	32	5
Chris Shuker	9	1
Andrejus Tereskinas	1	0
Darren Tinson	51	3
Richard Tracey	13	3
Gary Twynham	11	0
Damien Whitehead	37	8
Steve Wilson	1	0
Steve Wood	34	1
Matt Woolley	3	0

2001–02

	Apps	*Goals*
George Abbey	19	0
Danny Adams	44	0
John Askey	19	1
Matthew Bullock	3	0
Chris Byrne	37	8
Shaun Came	1	0
Richard Eyre	16	0
Lee Glover	49	13
Steve Hitchen	35	1
Kevin Keen	36	1
Rickie Lambert	40	10
Kyle Lightbourne	30	4
Andy McAvoy	14	0
Steve Macauley	13	0
Lee Martin	10	0
Karl Munroe	31	0
Paul O'Neill	11	0
Chris Priest	38	1
Dave Ridler	45	0
Barry Shuttleworth	5	0
David Smith	8	0
Jeff Smith	8	2
Darren Tinson	52	1
Matthew Tipton	13	3
Richard Tracey	24	2
Michael Welch	6	0
Damien Whitehead	3	0
Danny Whitaker	16	2
Steve Wilson	43	0
Matt Woolley	4	0

2002–03

	Apps	*Goals*
George Abbey	24	1
Danny Adams	51	1
Paul Aldridge	1	0
John Askey	11	2
Steven Brackenridge	2	0
Chris Byrne	4	1
Shaun Came	1	0
Michael Carr	4	0
Darren Dunning	17	0
David Eaton	24	5
Lee Glover	5	1
Matt Haddrell	4	0
Lee Hardy	20	0
Steve Hitchen	39	0
Kyle Lightbourne	50	13
Colin Little	6	1
Steve Macauley	21	1
Lee Martin	2	0
John Miles	8	4
Karl Munroe	30	0
Martin Nash	5	0
Paul O'Neill	14	0
Chris Priest	41	2
Dave Ridler	20	0
Neil Robinson	11	0
Neil Ross	8	0
David Smith	3	0
Darren Tinson	51	0
Matthew Tipton	42	14
Michael Welch	44	3
Andy Welsh	6	2
Danny Whitaker	47	14
Steve Wilson	50	0

2003–04

	Apps	*Goals*
George Abbey	30	0
Danny Adams	33	1
David Beresford	6	0

2003–04 (Continued)

Jon Beswetherick	4	0
Steven Brackenridge	9	2
Michael Carr	8	0
Matthew Carragher	18	0
Martin Carruthers	45	10
Stephen Clark	4	0
David Flitcroft	16	0
Matt Haddrell	14	1
Paul Harsley	16	2
Steve Hitchen	11	0
Rob Jones	1	0
Colin Little	29	6
Steve Macauley	18	0
John Miles	33	7
Karl Munroe	41	0
Boaz Myhill	16	0
James Olsen	2	0
Jon Parkin	12	1
Steve Payne	13	0
Graham Potter	16	2
Chris Priest	34	2
Neil Robinson	1	0
Neil Ross	6	0
David Smith	11	0
Matthew Tipton	44	19
Michael Welch	42	0
Danny Whitaker	42	6
Tommy Widdrington	39	0
Steve Wilson	37	0

2004–05

	Apps	*Goals*
Mark Bailey	25	2
Tony Barras	31	2
Mark Boyd	5	0
Ian Brightwell	8	0
Michael Briscoe	19	0
Matthew Carragher	39	0
Jassim Fayadh	2	0
Alan Fettis	33	0
Paul Harsley	55	4
Neil MacKenzie	18	0
Kevin McIntyre	25	0
John Miles	37	3
Dave Morley	21	2
Alan Navarro	11	1
Jon Parkin	51	26
Graham Potter	48	6
Tommy Rooney	2	0
Mike Sheron	33	4
Greg Strong	4	0
Danny Swailes	19	0
Andrew Teague	5	0
Matthew Tipton	52	14
Kevin Townson	8	0
Simon Weaver	11	0
Michael Welch	36	2
Danny Whitaker	45	4
Tommy Widdrington	29	0
Steve Wilson	23	0

2005–06

	Apps	*Goals*
Mark Bailey	7	0
Tony Barras	9	0
David Beresford	22	1
Ian Brightwell	11	0
Michael Briscoe	17	1
Martin Bullock	48	8
Tim Deasy	3	0
Alan Fettis	42	0
Paul Harsley	55	7
Tommy Lee	12	0
Neil MacKenzie	7	2
Kevin McIntyre	53	5
Matty McNeil	13	2
John Miles	29	4
Dave Morley	55	1
Alan Navarro	33	0
Jon Parkin	15	9
Marcus Richardson	8	3
Allan Russell	14	2
Kevin Sandwith	42	5
Andrew Smart	12	1
Danny Swailes	49	2
Andrew Teague	29	2
Kevin Townson	22	4
Danny Whitaker	52	6
Clyde Wijnhard	26	12

2006–07

	Apps	*Goals*
Asmir Begovic	4	0
Ronayne Benjamin	3	0
Nick Blackman	1	0
Jonny Brain	13	0
Ian Brightwell	5	0
Martin Bullock	47	4
Nathan D'Laryea	1	0
Robbie Doyle	2	0
Jordan Hadfield	43	1
Colin Heath	31	4
Ashan Holgate	6	1
Paul Ince	1	0
James Jennings	11	0
Tommy Lee	35	0

Marvin McDonald	1	0
Kevin McIntyre	49	10
Matty McNeil	40	5
Jimmy McNulty	19	1
John Miles	32	4
Dave Morley	38	3
John Murphy	32	9
Adam Murray	11	0
Alan Navarro	38	2
Isaiah Rankin	4	0
Carl Regan	43	2
Izak Reid	8	0
Marvin Robinson	6	0
David Rouse	1	0
Rob Scott	29	2
Danny Swailes	44	3
Andrew Teague	16	1
Matty Tipton	33	4
Jamie Tolley	29	1
Spencer Weir-Daley	8	2
Simon Wiles	9	0

2007–08

	Apps	*Goals*
James Ashmore	8	0
Neil Ashton	19	1
Nick Blackman	11	1
Jonny Brain	31	0
Shaun Brisley	10	2
Ryan Cresswell	19	1
Kristian Dennis	1	0
Luke Dimech	29	0
Phil Doughty	6	0
Terry Dunfield	43	1
Richard Edgehill	16	0
Gareth Evans	46	7
Matthew Flynn	1	0
Francis Green	44	11
Martin Gritton	34	9
Jordan Hadfield	4	0
Shaun Hessey	26	0
Michael Husbands	4	1
James Jennings	13	0
Tommy Lee	20	0
Kevin McIntyre	26	2
Jimmy McNulty	22	1
Christian Millar	2	0
Dave Morley	6	1
Adam Murray	25	0
Fola Onibuje	1	0
Carl Regan	23	0
Izak Reid	27	2
Levi Reid	35	2
John Rooney	2	0
Scott Spencer	3	0
Michael Symes	14	1
Andrew Teague	1	0
Danny Thomas	46	4
Jamie Tolley	25	2
Richard Walker	10	0
Simon Wiles	21	0

2008–09

	Apps	*Goals*
Rikki Baines	2	0
Lee Bell	47	1
Jonny Brain	52	0
Shaun Brisley	43	2
Nat Brown	33	6
Colin Daniel	8	0
Ahmed Deen	32	0
Kristian Dennis	4	1
Terry Dunfield	25	2
Tom Elliott	6	0
Gareth Evans	44	13
Matthew Flynn	31	0
Kyle Fraser-Allen	2	0
Francis Green	28	5
Martin Gritton	26	7
Jordan Hadfield	18	0
Neil Harvey	6	0
Sean Hessey	38	0
James Jennings	20	0
Patrece Liburd	1	0
Clayton McDonald	2	0
Christian Millar	2	0
Paul Morgan	43	1
Vinny Mukendi	1	0
Izak Reid	43	2
John Rooney	16	2
Emile Sinclair	17	1
Danny Thomas	46	2
Jamie Tolley	18	0
Richard Walker	18	0
Simon Yeo	37	7

APPENDIX FOUR

MACCLESFIELD TOWN FOOTBALL CLUB MATCH RESULTS AUGUST 1997 TO MAY 2009

(Macclesfield Town score shown first)

Club	Date	H/A	Result		Competition	
Accrington Stanley	16 December 2006	H	3–3	D	CCL2	1
	28 April 2007	A	2–3	L	CCL2	2
	19 October 2007	A	2–3	L	CCL2	3
	29 March 2008	H	2–1	W	CCL2	4
	23 August 2008	A	0–2	L	CCL2	5
	10 March 2009	H	0–2	L	CCL2	6
Aldershot Town	11 October 2008	H	4–2	W	CCL2	1
	17 January 2009	A	1–1	D	CCL2	2
Alfreton Town	13 November 2004	A	1–1	D	FAC R1	1
	23 November 2004	H	2–0	W	FAC R1 Replay	2
Barnet	13 December 1997	A	1–3	L	NWL3	1
	13 April 1998	H	2–0	W	NWL3	2
	5 September 1999	A	1–2	L	NWL3	3
	12 February 2000	H	2–0	W	NWL3	4
	8 October 2000	A	2–0	W	NWL3	5
	11 March 2001	H	3–0	W	NWL3	6
	20 August 2005	A	0–1	L	CCL2	7
	17 December 2005	H	1–1	D	CCL2	8
	9 September 2006	H	2–3	L	CCL2	9
	13 January 2007	A	0–1	L	CCL2	10
	8 December 2007	A	2–2	D	CCL2	11
	24 March 2008	H	3–0	W	CCL2	12
	22 November 2008	A	3–1	W	CCL2	13
	25 April 2009	H	2–1	W	CCL2	14
Barnsley	11 September 2002	H	4–1	W aet	WC R1	1
Birmingham City	15 September 1998	H	0–3	L	WC R2 1st Leg	1
	22 September 1998	A	0–6	L	WC R2 2nd Leg	2
			Birmingham City won 0–9 on aggregate			
Blackpool	28 December 1998	H	0–1	L	NWL2	1
	30 January 1999	A	1–2	L	NWL2	2
	21 October 2000	A	1–2	L	NWL3	3
	24 March 2001	H	2–1	W	NWL3	4
Bolton Wanderers	22 August 2000	A	0–1	L	WC R1 1st Leg	1
	5 September 2000	H	3–1	W	WC R2 2nd Leg	2
			Macclesfield Town won 3–2 on aggregate			

Boston United	5 October 2002	H	2–0	W	NWL3	1
	26 April 2003	A	1–2	L	NWL3	2
	9 August 2003	H	0–0	D	NWL3	3
	8 November 2003	H	3–0	W	FAC R1	4
	10 January 2004	A	1–3	L	NWL3	5
	21 August 2004	A	1–1	D	CCL2	6
	28 March 2005	H	1–1	D	CCL2	7
	4 September 2005	H	2–2	D	CCL2	8
	7 January 2006	A	1–3	L	CCL2	9
	18 November 2006	H	2–3	L	CCL2	10
	9 April 2007	A	1–4	L	CCL2	11
AFC Bournemouth	10 October 1998	H	2–2	D	NWL2	1
	6 April 1999	A	0–1	L	NWL2	2
	31 August 2002	H	0–1	L	NWL3	3
	18 January 2003	A	2–2	D	NWL3	4
	13 September 2008	A	1–0	W	CCL2	5
	14 March 2009	H	0–2	L	CCL2	6
Bradford City	21 August 2001	H	1–2	L aet	WC R1	1
	11 August 2007	A	1–1	D	CCL2	2
	2 February 2008	H	0–1	L	CCL2	3
	16 August 2008	H	0–2	L	CCL2	4
	3 March 2009	A	0–1	L	CCL2	5
Brentford	6 November 2007	H	1–0	W	CCL2	1
	8 March 2008	A	0–1	L	CCL2	2
	4 October 2008	A	0–1	L	CCL2	3
	24 January 2009	H	2–0	W	CCL2	4
Brighton & Hove Albion	16 August 1998	A	1–1	D	NWL3	1
	27 January 1998	H	1–0	W	NWL3	2
	14 November 1999	H	1–1	D	NWL3	3
	21 March 2000	A	2–5	L	NWL3	4
	11 November 2000	H	0–0	D	NWL3	5
	28 April 2001	A	1–4	L	NWL3	6
Bristol Rovers	18 December 1998	A	0–0	D	NWL2	1
	8 May 1999	H	3–4	L	NWL2	2
	13 October 2001	A	2–0	W	NWL3	3
	16 February 2002	H	2–1	W	NWL3	4
	8 September 2002	H	2–1	W	NWL3	5
	22 February 2003	A	1–1	D	NWL3	6
	25 August 2003	A	2–2	D	NWL3	7
	13 January 2004	H	2–1	W	NWL3	8
	11 December 2004	A	0–0	D	CCL2	9
	26 February 2005	H	2–1	W	CCL2	10
	29 October 2005	H	2–1	W	CCL2	11
	6 May 2006	A	3–2	W	CCL2	12
	21 October 2006	A	0–0	D	CCL2	13
	24 April 2007	H	0–1	L	CCL2	14
Burnley	24 October 1998	H	2–1	W	NWL2	1
	28 March 1999	A	3–4	L	NWL2	2

Opponent	Date	Venue	Score	Result	Competition	No.
Bury	26 October 2002	A	1–2	L	NWL3	1
	15 March 2003	H	0–0	D	NWL3	2
	29 November 2003	H	1–0	W	NWL3	3
	8 May 2004	A	0–2	L	NWL3	4
	2 October 2004	A	1–2	L	CCL2	5
	29 January 2005	H	2–1	W	CCL2	6
	29 August 2005	H	1–0	W	CCL2	7
	4 April 2006	A	0–0	D	CCL2	8
	14 October 2006	H	2–3	L	CCL2	9
	17 March 2007	A	1–1	D	CCL2	10
	27 October 2007	H	2–2	D	CCL2	11
	19 April 2008	A	0–1	L	CCL2	12
	6 December 2008	H	1–1	D	CCL2	13
	18 April 2009	A	0–3	L	CCL2	14
Cambridge United	8 November 1997	H	3–1	W	NWL3	1
	3 March 1998	A	0–0	D	NWL3	2
	5 December 1998	H	4–1	W	FAC R2	3
	30 November 2002	A	1–3	L	NWL3	4
	5 April 2003	H	1–1	D	NWL3	5
	16 August 2003	A	1–3	L	NWL3	6
	6 December 2003	H	1–1	D	FAC R2	7
	16 December 2003	A	2–2	aet	FAC R2 Replay	8
		Macclesfield Town won 4–2 on penalties				
	17 January 2004	H	0–1	L	NWL3	9
	19 October 2004	H	1–1	D	CCL2	10
	12 February 2005	A	1–0	W	CCL2	11
	13 December 2005	H	4–2	W	LDV NQF	12
Cardiff City	20 December 1997	H	1–0	W	NWL3	1
	18 April 1998	A	2–1	W	NWL3	2
	23 December 2000	A	0–2	L	NWL3	3
	27 January 2001	H	2–5	L	NWL3	4
	20 September 2005	A	1–2	L	CC R2	5
Carlisle United	28 December 1999	H	2–1	W	NWL3	1
	15 April 2000	A	1–0	W	NWL3	2
	16 December 2000	H	1–0	W	NWL3	3
	31 March 2001	A	0–1	L	NWL3	4
	3 November 2001	H	1–1	D	NWL3	5
	1 April 2002	A	2–3	L	NWL3	6
	19 October 2002	H	2–2	D	NWL3	7
	18 March 2003	A	0–1	L	NWL3	8
	18 October 2003	A	1–0	W	NWL3	9
	21 February 2004	H	1–1	D	NWL3	10
	10 September 2005	A	0–2	L	CCL2	11
	29 January 2006	H	3–0	W	CCL2	12
	21 February 2006	A	1–2	L	LDV NAF1	13
	7 March 2006	H	3–2	W	LDV NAF2	14
	Aggregate 4–4. Carlisle United won on away goals rule					
Chelsea	6 January 2007	A	1–6	L	FAC R3	1
Cheltenham Town	11 December 1999	A	1–1	D	NWL3	1

Cheltenham Town (Continued)	8 January 2000	H	1–2	L	NWL3	2
	14 October 2000	H	2–1	W	NWL3	3
	6 March 2001	A	1–1	D	NWL3	4
	20 November 2001	A	1–4	L	NWL3	5
	6 April 2002	H	1–0	W	NWL3	6
	26 December 2003	A	2–3	L	NWL3	7
	7 February 2004	H	1–2	L	NWL3	8
	20 November 2004	H	0–2	L	CCL2	9
	30 April 2005	A	0–3	L	CCL2	10
	9 August 2005	H	2–2	D	CCL2	11
	10 December 2005	A	2–2	D	CCL2	12
Chester City	25 October 1997	A	1–1	D	NWL3	1
	25 April 1998	H	3–2	W	NWL3	2
	16 October 1999	A	2–1	W	NWL3	3
	22 April 2000	H	1–1	D	NWL3	4
	4 September 2004	A	0–1	L	CCL2	5
	1 January 2005	H	1–2	L	CCL2	6
	31 December 2005	H	1–0	W	CCL2	7
	1 April 2006	A	1–2	L	CCL2	8
	26 September 2006	H	1–1	D	CCL2	9
	26 December 2006	A	3–0	W	CCL2	10
	29 September 2007	H	1–2	L	CCL2	11
	3 May 2008	A	0–0	D	CCL2	12
	28 December 2008	H	3–1	W	CCL2	13
	11 April 2009	A	2–0	W	CCL2	14
Chesterfield	28 November 1998	A	0–2	L	NWL2	1
	13 April 1999	H	2–0	W	NWL2	2
	30 September 2000	A	1–4	L	NWL3	3
	9 January 2001	A	2–4	L	LDV R2	4
	3 March 2001	H	1–2	L	NWL3	5
	14 October 2003	A	1–2	L	LDV R1	6
	28 September 2004	H	2–1	W	LDV R1	7
	18 October 2005	H	2–0	W	LDV R1	8
	6 October 2007	A	2–2	D	CCL2	9
	26 April 2008	H	1–0	W	CCL2	10
	12 December 2008	A	4–2	W	CCL2	11
	4 April 2009	H	1–1	D	CCL2	12
Colchester United	4 November 1997	H	0–0	D	NWL3	1
	14 March 1998	A	1–5	L	NWL3	2
	6 November 1998	A	1–1	D	NWL2	3
	13 March 1999	H	2–0	W	NWL2	4
Coventry City	2 January 1999	A	0–7	L	FAC R3	1
Crewe Alexandra	2 September 2008	A	0–3	L	JPT R1	1
Dagenham & Redbridge	24 November 2007	H	1–1	D	CCL2	1
	11 March 2008	A	1–0	W	CCL2	2
	20 December 2008	H	0–4	L	CCL2	3
	28 March 2009	A	1–2	L	CCL2	4

Darlington	5 September 1997	H	2–1	W	NWL3	1
	26 December 1997	A	2–4	L	NWL3	2
	14 August 1999	A	0–3	L	NWL3	3
	15 January 2000	H	2–1	W	NWL3	4
	22 September 2000	H	1–1	D	NWL3	5
	24 February 2001	A	1–1	D	NWL3	6
	25 September 2001	H	1–1	D	NWL3	7
	16 October 2001	A	1–2	L	LDV R1	8
	5 March 2002	A	1–0	W	NWL3	9
	21 December 2002	A	0–0	D	NWL3	10
	19 April 2003	H	1–0	W	NWL3	11
	20 December 2003	A	1–0	W	NWL3	12
	6 March 2004	H	0–1	L	NWL3	13
	25 September 2004	H	1–0	W	CCL2	14
	3 January 2005	A	1–3	L	CCL2	15
	7 October 2005	A	0–1	L	CCL2	16
	19 November 2005	H	1–0	W	CCL2	17
	5 August 2006	A	0–4	L	CCL2	18
	3 February 2007	H	1–1	D	CCL2	19
	1 September 2007	H	0–0	D	CCL2	20
	26 January 2008	A	2–2	D	CCL2	21
	30 August 2008	H	0–6	L	CCL2	22
	7 March 2009	A	2–1	W	CCL2	23
Doncaster Rovers	23 August 1997	H	3–0	W	NWL3	1
	24 January 1998	A	3–0	W	NWL3	2
	11 October 2003	H	1–3	L	NWL3	3
	14 February 2004	A	0–1	L	NWL3	4
Everton	3 January 2009	H	0–1	L	FAC R3	1
Exeter City	21 October 1997	H	2–2	D	NWL3	1
	2 May 1998	A	3–1	W	NWL3	2
	25 September 1999	A	3–0	W	NWL3	3
	23 October 1999	H	1–0	W	NWL3	4
	9 September 2000	H	0–2	L	NWL3	5
	10 February 2001	A	0–0	D	NWL3	6
	29 September 2001	A	0–0	D	NWL3	7
	2 February 2002	H	1–2	L	NWL3	8
	28 December 2002	A	1–1	D	NWL3	9
	25 January 2003	H	1–1	D	NWL3	10
	27 September 2008	H	1–4	L	CCL2	11
	10 February 2009	A	0–4	L	CCL2	12
Forest Green Rovers	17 November 2001	H	2–2	D	FAC R1	1
	28 November 2001	A	1–1	aet	FAC R1 Replay	2
		Macclesfield Town won 11–10 on penalties				
Fulham	8 August 1998	H	0–1	L	NWL2	1
	9 January 1999	A	0–1	L	NWL2	2
Gillingham	3 October 1998	A	2–2	D	NWL2	1
	9 March 1999	H	1–0	W	NWL2	2
	1 November 2008	H	0–1	L	CCL2	3

Gillingham (Continued)	21 February 2009	A	1–3	L	CCL2	4
Grimsby Town	11 September 2004	H	3–1	W	CCL2	1
	26 December 2004	A	0–0	D	CCL2	2
	11 November 2005	A	1–3	L	CCL2	3
	29 April 2006	H	1–1	D	CCL2	4
	1 September 2006	A	1–1	D	CCL2	5
	24 February 2007	H	2–1	W	CCL2	6
	25 August 2007	A	1–1	D	CCL2	7
	12 February 2008	H	1–2	L	CCL2	8
	25 November 2008	H	1–0	W	CCL2	9
	2 May 2009	A	0–0	D	CCL2	10
Halifax Town	9 October 1999	H	0–2	L	NWL3	1
	6 May 2000	A	1–0	W	NWL3	2
	28 October 2000	H	0–0	D	NWL3	3
	16 April 2001	A	0–3	L	NWL3	4
	9 August 2001	A	0–0	D	NWL3	5
	26 December 2001	H	1–1	D	NWL3	6
Hartlepool United	30 August 1997	A	0–0	D	NWL3	1
	15 November 1997	A	4–2	W	FAC R1	2
	17 January 1998	H	2–1	W	NWL3	3
	27 November 1999	H	3–3	D	NWL3	4
	19 February 2000	A	4–1	W	NWL3	5
	16 September 2000	A	2–2	D	NWL3	6
	17 February 2001	H	0–1	L	NWL3	7
	23 October 2001	H	0–1	L	NWL3	8
	22 March 2002	A	2–1	W	NWL3	9
	17 August 2002	A	2–0	W	NWL3	10
	21 January 2003	H	0–1	L	NWL3	11
	24 August 2004	A	1–2	L	CC R1	12
	8 August 2006	H	0–0	D	CCL2	13
	2 December 2006	H	2–1	W	FAC R2	14
	20 February 2007	A	2–3	L	CCL2	15
Hereford United	24 January 2006	H	2–0	W	LDV NSF	1
	30 September 2006	A	0–1	L	CCL2	2
	20 January 2007	H	3–0	W	CCL2	3
	8 September 2007	A	1–0	W	CCL2	4
	26 December 2007	H	0–1	L	CCL2	5
Huddersfield Town	13 December 2003	H	4–0	W	NWL3	1
	13 March 2004	A	0–4	L	NWL3	2
Hull City	12 August 1997	H	0–0	D	C-C Cup R1 1L	1
	26 August 1997	A	1–2	L	C-C Cup R1 2L	2
			Hull City won 1–2 on aggregate			
	22 November 1997	H	2–0	W	NWL3	3
	28 March 1998	A	0–0	D	NWL3	4
	28 August 1999	A	3–2	W	NWL3	5
	30 October 1999	H	0–0	D	FAC R1	6
	9 November 1999	A	0–4	L	FAC R1 Replay	7
	29 January 2000	H	0–2	L	NWL3	8

Opponent	Date	Venue	Score	Result	Competition	No.
Hull City (Continued)	26 August 2000	H	0–0	D	NWL3	9
	6 January 2001	A	0–0	D	NWL3	10
	15 September 2001	H	0–0	D	NWL3	11
	22 February 2002	A	1–0	W	NWL3	12
	17 September 2002	A	3–1	W	NWL3	13
	16 November 2002	A	3–0	W	FAC R1	14
	4 March 2003	H	0–1	L	NWL3	15
	1 November 2003	A	2–2	D	NWL3	16
	17 April 2004	H	1–1	D	NWL3	17
	4 December 2004	A	0–4	L	FAC R2	18
Kidderminster Harriers	2 December 2000	A	1–2	L	NWL3	1
	7 April 2001	H	1–0	W	NWL3	2
	7 October 2001	H	0–1	L	NWL3	3
	19 February 2002	A	1–0	W	NWL3	4
	12 October 2002	A	2–0	W	NWL3	5
	29 March 2003	H	2–0	W	NWL3	6
	13 September 2003	H	1–1	D	NWL3	7
	20 March 2004	A	4–1	W	NWL3	8
	18 September 2004	A	0–1	L	CCL2	9
	15 January 2005	H	2–0	W	CCL2	10
Leeds United	14 August 2007	H	0–1	L	CC R1	1
Leicester City	22 August 2006	A	0–2	L	CC 1R	1
Leyton Orient	4 October 1997	A	1–1	D	NWL3	1
	14 February 1998	H	1–0	W	NWL3	2
	18 December 1999	H	1–0	W	NWL3	3
	1 April 2000	A	0–0	D	NWL3	4
	25 November 2000	A	1–2	L	NWL3	5
	5 May 2001	H	0–2	L	NWL3	6
	15 December 2001	H	2–1	W	NWL3	7
	9 March 2002	A	0–2	L	NWL3	8
	13 August 2002	A	2–3	L	NWL3	9
	11 March 2003	H	3–1	W	NWL3	10
	4 October 2003	A	0–2	L	NWL3	11
	10 April 2004	H	1–0	W	NWL3	12
	7 August 2004	A	3–1	W	CCL2	13
	19 March 2005	H	3–1	W	CCL2	14
	6 August 2005	A	1–2	L	CCL2	15
	26 November 2005	H	0–0	D	CCL2	16
Lincoln City	29 November 1997	A	1–1	D	NWL3	1
	4 April 1998	H	1–0	W	NWL3	2
	22 August 1998	H	0–0	D	NWL2	3
	26 December 1998	A	0–1	L	NWL2	4
	18 September 1999	A	1–1	D	NWL3	5
	26 February 2000	H	1–1	D	NWL3	6
	12 September 2000	H	2–0	W	NWL3	7
	20 February 2001	A	2–1	W	NWL3	8
	20 October 2001	H	0–1	L	NWL3	9
	9 February 2002	A	0–1	L	NWL3	10
	26 August 2002	A	0–3	L	NWL3	11

Opponent	Date	Venue	Score	Result	Competition	No.
Lincoln City (Continued)	26 December 2002	H	0–1	L	NWL3	12
	21 October 2003	A	2–3	L	NWL3	13
	30 March 2004	H	0–0	D	NWL3	14
	7 December 2004	H	2–1	W	CCL2	15
	16 April 2005	A	0–2	L	CCL2	16
	14 May 2005	A	0–1	L	PO SF 1st Leg	17
	21 May 2005	H	1–1	D	PO SF 2nd Leg	18
			Lincoln City won 1–2 on aggregate			
	3 December 2005	A	2–2	D	CCL2	19
	18 February 2006	H	1–1	D	CCL2	20
	12 September 2006	A	1–2	L	CCL2	21
	1 January 2007	H	2–1	W	CCL2	22
	5 February 2008	H	1–2	L	CCL2	23
	16 February 2008	A	1–3	L	CCL2	24
	21 October 2008	H	1–2	L	CCL2	25
	31 March 2009	A	0–1	L	CCL2	26
Luton Town	12 December 1998	H	2–2	D	NWL2	1
	1 May 1999	A	2–1	W	NWL2	2
	24 November 2001	H	4–1	W	NWL3	3
	13 April 2002	A	0–0	D	NWL3	4
	6 September 2008	H	2–1	W	CCL2	5
	21 March 2009	A	0–1	L	CCL2	6
MK Dons	12 August 2006	H	1–2	L	CCL2	1
	13 March 2007	A	0–3	L	CCL2	2
	18 August 2007	H	3–3	D	CCL2	3
	29 January 2008	A	1–1	D	CCL2	4
Manchester City	12 September 1998	H	0–1	L	NWL2	1
	20 February 1999	A	0–2	L	NWL2	2
Mansfield Town	18 October 1997	H	1–0	W	NWL3	1
	24 February 1998	A	0–1	L	NWL3	2
	2 November 1999	H	5–2	W	NWL3	3
	11 March 2000	A	0–1	L	NWL3	4
	28 August 2000	A	4–4	D	NWL3	5
	14 January 2001	H	0–1	L	NWL3	6
	27 August 2001	A	0–4	L	NWL3	7
	29 December 2001	H	0–1	L	NWL3	8
	6 September 2003	A	2–3	L	NWL3	9
	28 December 2003	H	1–1	D	NWL3	10
	2 November 2004	H	4–0	W	LDV R2	11
	6 November 2004	A	1–0	W	CCL2	12
	23 April 2005	H	3–1	W	CCL2	13
	27 September 2005	H	1–1	D	CCL2	14
	4 February 2006	A	1–1	D	CCL2	15
	28 October 2006	H	2–3	L	CCL2	16
	23 March 2007	A	2–1	W	CCL2	17
	3 November 2007	A	0–5	L	CCL2	18
	12 April 2008	H	0–0	D	CCL2	19
Middlesbrough	19 September 2000	A	1–2	L	WC 2R 1st Leg	1
	26 September 2000	H	1–3	L	WC 2R 2nd Leg	2
			Middlesbrough won 2–5 on aggregate			

Millwall	29 August 1998	A	0–0	D	NWL2	1
	26 January 1999	H	0–2	L	NWL2	2
Morecambe	5 January 2008	H	1–2	L	CCL2	1
	9 February 2008	A	1–0	W	CCL2	2
	26 December 2008	A	1–4	L	CCL2	3
	13 April 2009	H	0–1	L	CCL2	4
Northampton Town	31 October 1998	H	0–1	L	NWL2	1
	20 March 1999	A	2–0	W	NWL2	2
	7 August 1999	H	1–0	W	NWL3	3
	4 December 1999	A	0–2	L	NWL3	4
	20 September 2003	A	0–0	D	NWL3	5
	27 March 2004	H	0–4	L	NWL3	6
	18 December 2004	H	1–3	L	CCL2	7
	5 March 2005	A	0–1	L	CCL2	8
	17 September 2005	H	1–4	L	CCL2	9
	21 January 2006	A	0–5	L	CCL2	10
Nottingham Forest	23 August 2005	A	3–2	W	CC R1	1
Notts County	11 October 1997	A	1–1	D	NWL3	1
	28 February 1998	H	2–0	W	NWL3	2
	31 August 1998	H	0–1	L	NWL2	3
	4 May 1999	A	1–1	D	NWL2	4
	10 October 2004	H	1–2	L	CCL2	5
	25 January 2005	A	5–0	W	CCL2	6
	1 October 2005	H	0–0	D	CCL2	7
	15 April 2006	A	1–1	D	CCL2	8
	9 December 2006	A	2–1	W	CCL2	9
	5 May 2007	H	1–1	D	CCL2	10
	17 November 2007	A	1–0	W	CCL2	11
	1 March 2008	H	1–1	D	CCL2	12
	18 October 2008	A	1–1	D	CCL2	13
	17 February 2009	H	1–1	D	CCL2	14
Oldham Athletic	8 September 1998	A	2–1	W	NWL2	1
	13 February 1999	H	1–0	W	NWL2	2
Oxford United	18 November 2000	H	0–1	L	FAC R1	1
	18 September 2001	A	2–0	W	NWL3	2
	26 February 2002	H	0–1	L	NWL3	3
	29 October 2002	H	2–1	W	NWL3	4
	22 March 2003	A	1–0	W	NWL3	5
	22 November 2003	A	1–3	L	NWL3	6
	1 May 2004	H	2–1	W	NWL3	7
	23 October 2004	H	1–0	W	CCL2	8
	6 April 2005	A	1–1	D	CCL2	9
	14 January 2006	H	1–1	D	CCL2	10
	15 February 2006	A	1–1	D	CCL2	11
Peterborough United	27 September 1997	H	1–1	D	NWL3	1
	21 February 1998	A	1–0	W	NWL3	2
	20 November 1999	A	2–2	D	NWL3	3

Peterborough United (Continued)	18 March 2000	H	1–1	D	NWL3	4
	15 October 2005	H	0–4	L	CCL2	5
	22 April 2006	A	2–3	L	CCL2	6
	19 August 2006	A	1–3	L	CCL2	7
	17 February 2007	H	2–1	W	CCL2	8
	12 January 2008	A	1–0	W	CCL2	9
	23 February 2008	H	0–3	L	CCL2	10
Plymouth Argyle	3 January 2000	A	2–3	L	NWL3	1
	8 April 2000	H	4–1	W	NWL3	2
	2 September 2000	A	1–0	W	NWL3	3
	3 February 2001	H	3–1	W	NWL3	4
	22 September 2001	A	0–2	L	NWL3	5
	2 March 2002	H	1–1	D	NWL3	6
Port Vale	20 September 2008	A	4–1	W	CCL2	1
	29 November 2008	A	3–1	W	FAC R2	2
	25 February 2009	H	0–2	L	CCL2	3
Preston North End	13 January 1998	H	0–1	L	AWS R2	1
	20 October 1998	A	2–2	D	NWL2	2
	10 April 1999	H	3–2	W	NWL2	3
	1 October 2002	H	1–2	L	WC R2	4
Reading	26 September 1998	H	2–1	W	NWL2	1
	6 March 1999	A	0–1	L	NWL2	2
Rochdale	2 September 1997	A	0–2	L	NWL3	1
	28 December 1997	H	1–0	W	NWL3	2
	19 October 1999	A	1–0	W	NWL3	3
	11 January 2000	A	2–3	L	AWS R2	4
		Rochdale won on the Golden Goal rule				
	29 April 2000	H	1–2	L	NWL3	5
	24 October 2000	A	2–2	D	NWL3	6
	14 April 2001	H	0–0	D	NWL3	7
	18 August 2001	A	1–1	D	NWL3	8
	12 January 2002	H	0–1	L	NWL3	9
	28 September 2002	A	1–3	L	NWL3	10
	3 May 2003	H	3–2	W	NWL3	11
	30 September 2003	H	2–1	W	NWL3	12
	12 April 2004	A	2–1	W	NWL3	13
	30 October 2004	A	0–3	L	CCL2	14
	19 February 2005	H	3–0	W	CCL2	15
	27 August 2005	A	1–3	L	CCL2	16
	11 March 2006	H	1–3	L	CCL2	17
	5 December 2006	H	1–0	W	CCL2	18
	21 April 2007	A	0–5	L	CCL2	19
	22 September 2007	A	1–1	D	CCL2	20
	29 December 2007	H	2–2	D	CCL2	21
	15 November 2008	A	1–1	D	CCL2	23
	14 February 2009	H	0–1	L	CCL2	23
Rotherham United	1 November 1997	A	0–1	L	NWL3	1
	7 March 1998	H	0–0	D	NWL3	2

Opponent	Date	Venue	Score	Result	Competition	No.
Rotherham United (Continued)	30 August 1999	H	1–1	D	NWL3	3
	5 February 2000	A	1–2	L	NWL3	4
	22 November 2005	A	2–1	W	LDV R2	5
	2 October 2007	H	1–1	D	CCL2	6
	1 January 2007	A	0–3	L	CCL2	7
	25 October 2008	H	1–2	L	CCL2	8
	31 January 2009	A	0–2	L	CCL2	9
Rushden & Diamonds	25 August 2001	H	0–0	D	NWL3	1
	29 January 2002	A	0–2	L	NWL3	2
	14 December 2002	H	0–1	L	NWL3	3
	21 April 2003	A	0–3	L	NWL3	4
	27 November 2004	A	2–0	W	CCL2	5
	7 May 2005	H	1–0	W	CCL2	6
	13 September 2005	H	3–1	W	CCL2	7
	25 February 2006	A	0–1	L	CCL2	8
	10 November 2007	A	1–3	L	FAC R1	9
Scarborough	20 September 1997	A	1–2	L	NWL3	1
	7 February 1998	H	3–1	W	NWL3	2
Scunthorpe United	20 January 1998	H	2–0	W	NWL3	1
	11 April 1998	A	0–1	L	NWL3	2
	12 August 2000	H	0–1	L	NWL3	3
	1 January 2001	A	2–2	D	NWL3	4
	1 September 2001	H	4–3	W	NWL3	5
	12 February 2002	A	1–1	D	NWL3	6
	21 September 2002	H	2–3	L	NWL3	7
	8 March 2003	A	1–1	D	NWL3	8
	15 November 2003	H	2–2	D	NWL3	9
	24 April 2004	A	0–1	L	NWL3	10
	28 August 2004	H	2–2	D	CCL2	11
	2 April 2005	A	0–0	D	CCL2	12
Sheffield United	12 August 2003	H	1–2	L	CC R1	1
Shrewsbury Town	18 November 1997	A	3–4	L	NWL3	1
	21 March 1998	H	2–1	W	NWL3	2
	26 December 1999	A	1–0	W	NWL3	3
	25 March 2000	H	4–2	W	NWL3	4
	19 August 2000	A	2–2	D	NWL3	5
	13 February 2001	H	2–1	W	NWL3	6
	21 December 2001	A	1–1	D	NWL3	7
	22 January 2002	H	2–1	W	NWL3	8
	2 November 2002	H	1–2	L	NWL3	9
	15 April 2003	A	3–2	W	NWL3	10
	10 August 2004	H	2–1	W	CCL2	11
	12 March 2005	A	1–0	W	CCL2	12
	31 January 2006	A	1–1	D	CCL2	13
	25 March 2006	H	2–0	W	CCL2	14
	6 October 2006	A	1–2	L	CCL2	15
	10 March 2007	H	2–2	D	CCL2	16
	1 December 2007	A	0–2	L	CCL2	17
	15 March 2008	H	2–1	W	CCL2	18

Shrewsbury Town (Continued)	9 August 2008	A	0–4	L	CCL2	19
	28 February 2009	H	3–0	W	CCL2	20
Slough Town	14 November 1998	H	2–2	D	FAC R1	1
	24 November 1998	A	1–1	aet	FAC R1 replay	2
		Macclesfield Town won 9–8 on penalties				
Southend United	11 September 1999	H	1–2	L	NWL3	1
	3 March 2000	A	0–1	L	NWL3	2
	4 November 2000	A	1–3	L	NWL3	3
	21 April 2001	H	1–0	W	NWL3	4
	9 November 2001	A	0–3	L	NWL3	5
	20 April 2002	H	0–0	D	NWL3	6
	14 September 2002	A	0–1	L	NWL3	7
	1 March 2003	H	2–1	W	NWL3	8
	25 October 2003	H	1–2	L	NWL3	9
	28 February 2004	A	0–1	L	NWL3	10
	30 August 2004	A	1–2	L	CCL2	11
	19 April 2005	H	1–2	L	CCL2	12
Stockport County	26 December 2005	H	6–0	W	CCL2	1
	18 March 2006	A	0–2	L	CCL2	2
	17 October 2006	H	0–1	L	JPT R1	3
	25 November 2006	A	1–1	D	CCL2	4
	14 April 2007	H	2–0	W	CCL2	5
	9 October 2007	H	0–1	L	JPT R2	6
	15 December 2007	H	0–2	L	CCL 2	7
	21 March 2008	A	0–2	L	CCL 2	8
Stoke City	11 August 1998	H	3–1	W	WC R1 1st Leg	1
	15 August 1998	A	0–2	L	NWL2	2
	19 August 1998	A	0–1	L	WC R1 2nd Leg	3
		Macclesfield Town won 3–2 on aggregate				
	27 April 1999	H	1–2	L	NWL2	4
	10 August 1999	H	1–1	D	WC R1 1st Leg	5
	25 August 1999	A	0–3	L	WC R1 2nd Leg	6
		Stoke City won 1–4 on aggregate				
Swansea City	13 September 1997	H	3–0	W	NWL3	1
	31 January 1998	A	1–1	D	NWL3	2
	21 August 1999	H	1–2	L	NWL3	3
	22 January 2000	A	0–1	L	NWL3	4
	11 August 2001	H	1–3	L	NWL3	5
	8 December 2001	H	4–1	W	FAC R2	6
	19 January 2002	A	1–0	W	NWL3	7
	9 November 2002	A	0–1	L	NWL3	8
	8 February 2003	H	1–3	L	NWL3	9
	16 September 2003	A	0–3	L	NWL3	10
	3 January 2004	A	1–2	L	FAC R3	11
	16 March 2004	H	2–1	W	NWL3	12
	14 August 2004	H	1–0	W	CCL2	13
	25 March 2005	A	0–2	L	CCL2	14

Opponent	Date	H/A	Score	Result	Competition	No.
Swindon Town	23 December 2006	H	2–1	W	CCL2	1
	27 January 2007	A	0–2	L	CCL2	2
Torquay United	9 August 1997	H	2–1	W	NWL3	1
	10 January 1998	A	0–2	L	NWL3	2
	2 October 1999	H	1–2	L	NWL3	3
	24 April 2000	A	2–3	L	NWL3	4
	17 October 2000	H	2–1	W	NWL3	5
	10 April 2001	A	0–2	L	NWL3	6
	1 December 2001	A	2–1	W	NWL3	7
	16 March 2002	H	0–2	L	NWL3	8
	23 November 2002	H	3–3	D	NWL3	9
	12 April 2003	A	2–2	D	NWL3	10
	23 August 2003	H	1–1	D	NWL3	11
	24 January 2004	A	1–4	L	NWL3	12
	22 October 2005	A	1–1	D	CCL2	13
	17 April 2006	H	0–2	L	CCL2	14
	23 September 2006	H	3–3	D	CCL2	15
	30 December 2006	A	1–0	W	CCL2	16
Tranmere Rovers	12 November 2002	H	1–2	L	LDV R2	1
	Tranmere Rovers won on the Golden Goal rule					
	30 November 2004	H	0–1	L	LDV R3	2
Vauxhall Motors	7 December 2002	H	2–0	W	FAC R2	1
Walsall	6 December 1997	H	0–7	L	FAC R2	1
	21 November 1998	H	1–1	D	NWL2	2
	17 April 1999	A	0–2	L	NWL2	3
	16 September 2006	A	0–2	L	CCL2	4
	13 November 2006	H	0–0	D	FAC R1	5
	21 November 2006	A	1–0	W	FAC R1 Replay	6
	30 January 2007	H	0–2	L	CCL2	7
Watford	4 January 2003	H	0–2	L	FAC R3	1
West Ham United	6 January 2002	H	0–3	L	FAC R3	1
	27 August 2008	A	1–4	L aet	CC R2	2
Wigan Athletic	19 September 1998	A	0–2	L	NWL2	1
	27 February 1999	H	0–1	L	NWL2	2
Wrexham	5 September 1998	A	1–2	L	NWL2	1
	8 December 1998	H	0–1	L	AWS R1	2
	6 February 1999	H	0–2	L	NWL2	3
	24 August 2002	H	0–1	L	NWL3	4
	1 January 2003	A	3–1	W	NWL3	5
	24 September 2005	A	1–1	D	CCL2	6
	14 March 2006	H	3–2	W	CCL2	7
	4 November 2006	A	0–0	D	CCL2	8
	7 April 2007	H	2–0	W	CCL2	9
	18 September 2007	A	1–0	W	JPT R1	10
	13 October 2007	H	3–2	W	CCL2	11
	5 April 2008	A	1–1	D	CCL2	12

Wycombe Wanderers	17 October 1998	A	0–3	L	NWL2	1
	3 April 1999	H	1–3	L	NWL2	2
	28 December 2004	H	2–1	W	CCL2	3
	22 January 2005	A	1–1	D	CCL2	4
	2 January 2006	A	5–4	W	CCL2	5
	8 April 2006	H	2–1	W	CCL2	6
	26 August 2006	H	0–2	L	CCL2	7
	3 March 2007	A	0–3	L	CCL2	8
	15 September 2007	H	1–2	L	CCL2	9
	22 December 2007	A	1–2	L	CCL2	10
	2 December 2008	A	0–4	L	CCL2	11
	27 January 2009	H	0–0	D	CCL2	12
Yeovil Town	30 August 2003	H	4–1	W	NWL3	1
	31 January 2004	A	2–2	D	NWL3	2
	16 October 2004	A	2–1	W	CCL2	3
	5 February 2005	H	3–1	W	CCL2	4
	5 November 2005	H	1–1	D	FAC R1	5
	15 November 2005	A	0–4	L	FAC R1 Replay	6
York City	10 November 1998	A	2–0	W	NWL2	1
	24 April 1999	H	1–2	L	NWL2	2
	6 November 1999	A	2–0	W	NWL3	3
	7 March 2000	H	1–1	D	NWL3	4
	26 December 2000	H	0–1	L	NWL3	5
	20 January 2001	A	3–1	W	NWL3	6
	27 October 2001	A	0–1	L	NWL3	7
	30 March 2002	H	2–1	W	NWL3	8
	10 August 2002	H	1–1	D	NWL3	9
	2 February 2003	A	1–2	L	NWL3	10
	27 September 2003	H	0–0	D	NWL3	11
	4 April 2004	A	2–0	W	NWL3	12

KEY

aet	After extra-time
AWS	Auto Windsreens Shield
CC	Carling Cup
C-C	Coca-Cola Cup
CCL2	Coca-Cola League 2
JPT	Johnstone's Paint Trophy
LDV	LDV Vans Trophy
NQF	Northern Area quarter-final
NSF	Northern Area semi-final
NAF	Northern Area Final
NWL2	Nationwide League 2
NWL3	Nationwide League 3
POSF	Play-off semi-final
WC	Worthington Cup

ROLL OF HONOUR

A copy of this book has been presented to all Vice-Presidents together with Adult and Concession Season Ticket holders in recognition of their loyalty and commitment to Macclesfield Town Football Club for the 2009-10 season.

Vice-Presidents
Bank Fashion
Ann Boothby
Alan Boothby
Carl Bradshaw
Eddie Furlong
Arthur Grace
Ray Howlett
Tina Howlett
Chris Hulme
Christopher Hulme
Mr B.W. Jones
Josolyne & Co
Tim Lomas
Paula Lowe
Bill Milligan
Margaret Milligan
Linda O'Brien
Roger O'Brien
Richard Pattrick
Mike Rance
Steve Roxborough
Andy Scott
Geoffrey Scott
Jessie Scott
Robin Siggins
Mr J.D. Simpson
Mr K.J. Stafford
Ann Turner
Christopher Turner
Jeremy Turner
Peter Turner
Mrs P.R. Venables
Andrew Venables
Mr M. Walker
Paul Whaley

Adult & Concession Season Tickets

Mr J.A. Abbott
Christopher Abbott
Don Ainsworth
Mr A. Aked
Royce Alexander
Alternative Futures
Martin Arrowsmith
Edward Aspinall
Mr G.R. Astle
David Bailey
David Bailey
Victor Banks
Bill Barclay
Mr M. Barden
Mr G.J. Barlow
Mr G. Barnes
Graham Barrow
Jonathan Barton
Mr J. Bates
Julie Bayman
Paul Bayman
Steven Bayman
Harold Beard
Paul Beech
Beryl Bell
Michael Bell
Robert Bemment
Mrs C. Betteridge
Mr M. Betteridge
Mr R. Biggar
Patrick Birch
David Blakeley
Sarina Bloor
Jon Bowers
Christopher Bowyer
Mrs I. Bradley
Mr P.K. Bradley
Mr R.P. Bradley
Julian Bramhall
Michael Brammer
Mr A.W. Brant
Stephen Briers
Philip Brocklehurst
Andrew Brown
David Brown
Peter Bryant
Mr W.J. Buchanan
Jonathan Buckley
Ian Buckley
Michael Bull
Edwin Burgess
Nicole Byram
David Campbell
Ian Carroll
Michael Carty
Alan Cawley
Keith Chapman
Mr R. Chapman
Peter Cheer
Simon Justin Churchman
Mrs C.M. Clark
John Clark
Michael Clark
Paul Clark
Robert Clark
Andrew Clarke
Natalie Clarke
Trevor Clowes
John Colclough
Wendy Colclough
Gary Collins
Edward Connor
Mr M. Connor
John Cooper
Mr R. Cooper
Mr P. Cotterill
Mr P. Cotterill
Mr B. Cox
Susan Crowe
David Cunningham
Mr N. Cunningham
Isobel Cuthbert
Murray Cuthbert
Heather Dale
Philip Davies
Simon Davies
Paula Davies
John Dines
Mr P. Dobson
Frank Dossor
Peter Drabble
Ian Duncan
David Eardley
Leon Eardley
Robert Edge
Ian Edy
Richard Eisenberg
David English
Michael Faricy
Steven Farmer
Nicolas Fellows
John Finan
Mark Findlow
Cyril Flood
Rachel Flower
Mr P.E. Flynn
Steve Forshaw
Gary Paul Foster
John Franklin
Geoff Frith

Glyn Genders
John Gibson
Mr T. Giles
Michael Gill
Trevor Goodey
Dennis Goodwin
Mr N. Gosling
Stuart Gosling
Wayne Grant
Don Greaves
Joan Greaves
Brian Griffiths
David Griffiths
Mr D.A. Griffiths
Mary Griffiths
Steve Griffiths
Jeffrey Grimes
Alison Hacking
Michael Hacking
Steven Hadfield
Rose Halford
John Hall
Garrod Halliwell
Nicholas Hammond
Mr P. Hampson
Mr T. Hampson
Vicki Hampson
Ray Hardman
Alan Hare
Stephen Hare
Brian Harradine
David Harrison
Mr P. Harrop
David Hassall
Paul Heaven
Melvyn Henson
Gavin Hewson
Mr P. Higginbotham
Joan Higginbotham
Roy Higginbotham
Mr F. Hill
Keith Hill
Terry Hill
Mike Hinde
David Hockenhull
Bryan Hodgson
Kate Hogan
Anthony Holmes
Jim Holohan
Stephen Holt
Mr R. Hooley
Derek Hopper
Jeffrey Brian Horsfall
Mr A.M. Hough
Miss J. Hudson
Kevin Hudson
Les Hughes
Mrs S. Hughes
Cherrill Hunter
Glenn Hunter
Terence Hunter
Mr D.T. Hyde
Mr P. Jackson
Peter Johns
Mr P. Johnson
Mr B.M. Jones
David Jones
Martin Jones
Peter William Jones
Mr W.M. Jones
Ben Jordan
Jim Kelly
Mr P.H. Kent
Dennis Keogh
Haydn Anthony King
Ronald Kirk
Lisa Kirkup
Mr J.R. Knight
Geoff Knights
Shirley Knights
Iain Laird
Brian Laird
Christina Lawrence
Michael Leigh
Jeffrey Leigh
Brenda Lingard
Margaret Littler
Miss Z. Lloyd
Mr R.A. Lloyd
Andy Lloyd
Harry Lowery
Malcolm MacBean
Colin Marlow
Anthony Marsh
Doreen Mason
Paul Mason
Steven Mason
John Matheson
Mr D. McCoy
Mr A. McMillan
Mr R. McMillan
Rodger McMillan
Brian Melling
Andrew Melling
Lisa Middlehurst
Peter Miles
Sarah Miles
Mr J. Miller
Brian Mitchell
Edward Mitchell
James Mitchell
Joseph Mitchell
Julia Ann Mitchell
Pamela Mitchell
Steven Mitchell
Geoff Molyneux
Michael John Moores
Adrian Morris
David Nigel Morris
Philip Morton
Robert Moruzzi
Andy Moss
Mr D. Moss
John David Moss
Andrew David Mothershaw
Mark Paul Mothershaw
Steve Mundy
Peter Carl Munsch
David Murray
Wilf Myers
John Narraway
Chris Nelson
Richard Nelson
Simon David Nelson
Colin David Newboult
Eric Newboult
Lorraine Debra Newboult
Kenneth Newsome
Mr J.H. Nixon
Christine Noden
Fred Noden
Alison Norman
Mr G.W. Nottage
Mr P. Oates
Mr B. Offiler
Andrew Oldfield
Kenneth Oliver
Mr T. O'Regan
Mr P. O'Regan
William Osbaldiston
Matthew Palmer
Robert Palmer
Mr M.R. Parker
Stuart Parks
Tony Parry
Peter Parsonage
Alistair Pattrick
Alan Pearson
Mr Alan J. Pearson
Mr J. Pemberton
Ian Percival
John Perkin
Mr E.T. Perry
Jonathan Perry
Kevin Phillips
David Pointon
Diane Porter
David Porter
Michael Potts
David Poynton
Steve Poynton
Edward Priest
Thomas Rance

Frank Rathbone
John Rayner
Mark Reddiough
Bernard Reece
William Renard
John Revill
Peter Richards
Mr C.T. Riley
Mrs D.M. Riley
Leslie Riley
Donald Riseley
Bernard Robinson
Margaret Robinson
Mr S.L. Robinson
Allan Rogerson
Ronald Rogerson
Christopher Rose
Alan Rousham
Maureen Routley
Mr M. Russell
Mrs A. Rutland
Mr C.T. Rutland
Jennifer Saxon
John Saxon
John Brian Shatwell
Richard Shaw
Terry Shaw
Thomas Shaw
William Shaw
Ronald Short
Philip Siddons
Jeanette Silvester
Mr P. Silvester
Alan Sime
Michael Singleton
Patrick Slattery
John Smart
Alan Smith
David Smith
Derek Smith
Mr G. Smith
Mr P. Smith
Paul James Smith
Mr R. Smith
Steven Smith
Susan Smith
Vickey Smith
Steve Snowball
Michael Sparkes
Graham Sparkes
Mr G. Stevens
Christine Stewart
Ian Stott
Mr L. Stubbs
Graham Stubbs
Mr D.F. Styles
Richard Swallow
Eric Swindells
Mark Swindells
Ryan Joseph Swindells
Michael Taylor
Christopher Taylor
Steven Taylor
Jeffrey Teasdale
Michael Thomason
Chrissie Thompson
Mr D.R. Tipper
Andrew Todd
Arthur Tomlinson
Robert Trafford
Mrs M.M. Tragheim
Gavin Trevena
David Turner
Gerald Turner
Graham Turner
William Turner
Michael Tute
Mike Twigg
James Philip Tyler
Philip Tyler
Michael Ventris
John Thomas Vermeulen
Mr C. Vernon
Thomas Virtue
Steven Wainwright
Mr J. Walker
Matthew Wallis
Stephen Ward
Mrs B.E. Wardle
Glyn Warhurst
Lee Warhurst
Sean Waring
Mr B. Watson
Mr C. Weaver
Michael Webb
Steve Webb
Dave Westbury
Mrs S. Whalley
Miss V. Whalley
Stephen Whitehurst
Steven Whiting
Geoffrey Whittaker
Suzanna Whittaker
Jean Wilkinson
Peter Wilkinson
George Williams
Richard Williams
Barry Williamson
Margaret Wills
Robert Wilson
Mr M. Wood
Anthony Wood
Brain John Woodhall
Michael Woodward
David Wooliscroft
Hilary Wooliscroft
Sean Andrew Worth
Clive John Wright
John Yates

The Club is grateful to the following who placed a pre-publication order for the book

Mike Bolshaw
Andrew Vincent Bradley
Patrick Howard Bradley
Julie Briggs
Andrew Brinkhurst
Colin Brooks
David Bury
Hedley Cooper
Jakob Ebrey
Chris Edge
Gareth, Penny & Rhys Evans
Paul James Furse
Phil Gibbons
Dr Brian Green
Neil Hayes
Daniel Hayman
Nicholas Hayman
Chris Higgins
John Hughes
Matthew Jones
John T. Kearns
Derek Leonard
Joyce Mann
Peter Moody
Roger Morrow
Alex Oxford
Tony Oxford
Lars Erik Pedersen
James Percival
Neal & Jennifer Riley
John Robinson
Jonathan Tate
Nicolai Thorning
Bjorn Thorsdalen
Rune Thorsdalen
Terje Thorsdalen
David Richard Stewart
Trevor Surtees
Kate Whiston
Paul Whiston
Stephen Wood
Nick Wright